Where Iron Runs Like Water!

A New History of
Carron Iron Works
1759–1982

BRIAN WATTERS

JOHN DONALD PUBLISHERS LTD
EDINBURGH

ISBN 0 85976 505 9
British Library Cataloguing in Production Data
A catalogue record of this book is available from the
British Library.

Printed & bound in Great Britain by Bell & Bain Ltd., Glasgow.

Preface

The story of Carron Company has been of great interest to me from a very early age. The publication of *The Story of Carron Company* in the bicentenary year, 1959, fuelled this interest, by providing a fuller account of the Company's history and the development of the Works, than had hitherto been seen. In 1961, RH Campbell's *Carron Company* took the story a stage further and, in particular, admirably examined the economic and financial history of the firm from the earliest period. My approach has been slightly different, driven by the desire to find out even more about what Carron Company did in this district where I have lived for many years. The many fascinating characters who frequent the story, some of whom might have stepped from the pages of a novel, have been examined in greater detail, as has the technical development of the Works at each period, and the effects the Company's growth has had on the surrounding area. Though the story has been written in chronological order, there are many interrelated topics, which, because of their importance, warranted more attention; subjects as diverse as the local landed gentry, the Carron Branch Railway, the Shipping Line and the village of West Carron, have been dealt with separately from the main narrative. The emphasis in this account is therefore on people, places and the more important events that have unfolded in the Company's past under different regimes.

To many generations of employees, Carron Company was more than a commercial concern; it was a way of life, always expected to be there providing a livelihood for those workers and their descendants. With the collapse of the Company in 1982 after 223 years, that assurance was lost forever but the name and the memories still exercise a powerful influence on the minds of Falkirk people. There is undoubtedly much more to the story than can be contained within the confines of a book such as this and some will find that their particular memory has not been recorded here, for which I apologise.

Carron 1998.   B.W.

Acknowledgements.

I owe a debt of gratitude to many people who have assisted me in many ways, leading to the publication of this book. The librarians and keepers of archives who offered advice and help are high on that list, but too numerous to mention individually. It was Ian Scott of the Falkirk Local History Society who first suggested that I should write this book and who arranged for its publication by John Donald of Edinburgh. He then took charge of the layout, a considerable task. Geoff Bailey, Keeper of Archaeology and Local History at Falkirk Museums, never failed in his support and was always ready to offer advice or additional material, and to listen to my many 'theories' as they arose during the research. There were others, whom I never met, but who were kind enough to correspond with me; Ruth Brown of the Royal Armouries offered valuable advice on Carron ordnance, and Dr Roger Bartlett of the University of London, assisted me with his paper on Charles Gascoigne's activities in Russia. Mrs Elizabeth Paley of Carron was most helpful and I am also very grateful for the interest shown and financial help given, by Roger Clark and Carron Phoenix Limited. Lastly, but most importantly, my wife Janey who has been living with my Carron obsession for more years than either of us care to remember! Without her patience and support this book would not have seen the light of day.

Carron 1998   B.W.

*The author and publisher are delighted to
acknowledge the generous financial support of
Carron Phoenix Limited
in the production of this book*

Contents

Most of the maps, drawings and photographs in this book are from contemporary sources or have been specially drawn by the author for this publication. The Scottish Record Office kindly gave permission for two photographs and one drawing from their collection to be included here. It has not been possible to trace the copyright holders of all the photographs included and the author apologises to anyone whose work has been used without acknowledgement.

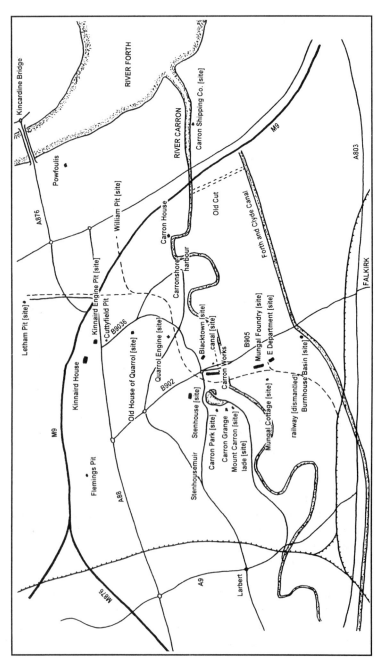

Location Map of the Falkirk/Carron/Larbert area

CHAPTER 1

The Early Days and the Building of the Works

At a spot on the River Carron on the Stenhouse Estate, two miles north of the town of Falkirk, Sir Michael Bruce, 6th Baronet of Stenhouse was supervising some workmen who were repairing the mill damhead. The stones used, brought from another part of his estate, had once been part of a building thought to have had Roman origins, called "Templi Termini" or, more commonly, "Arthur's O'on or Oven". His act of destroying this structure, soon brought upon him the wrath of antiquarians far and wide; some even said that it led to a curse on his family. This damhead fed water into a lade and drove the waterwheel of the Stenhouse Mill, a meal mill of many years standing used by people living within the barony. This was in the year of 1743.

In that same year, at the University of Leyden in Holland, a young man aged twenty-five had just obtained his MD. John Roebuck was born in Sheffield in 1718, the son of a master cutler and his early education took place at the academy of one Philip Dodridge at Northampton where he quickly established himself as an enthusiastic and enquiring pupil. John's family were known dissenters, that is those who opposed the views of the established Church, and this had precluded him from entrance to Oxford or Cambridge Universities, going instead to Edinburgh in 1738. He studied medicine and chemistry and soon: "distinguished himself among his fellow pupils in their literary societies and conversations".[1] It was after completing his Edinburgh qualification that he graduated from Leyden, on the 21st of February 1743.

Dr. Roebuck returned to Birmingham where he practised medicine; but he devoted a great deal of his time to the study of the application of chemistry to industry. According to an account given years later by his daughter, Mrs. Stewart, his sensitivity of nature was such that the death of any of his friends became a severe trial, and latterly he could no longer bear to witness the inevitable scenes of suffering which passed before him in his daily work.[2] Chiefly for this reason, he threw up his practice and turned to chemistry, which had always been to him a congenial study. Whilst experimenting with an improved method of refining gold and silver, he made the acquaintance of Samuel Garbett, a man often described as a ring-maker, die-maker or merchant. They became friends and business associates, setting up a laboratory at Steelhouse Lane to capitalise on Roebuck's experiments. A part of their activities at this refinery may have included the removing of silver from old silver-plated copper goods, a process that involved the use of sulphuric acid as a "stripping liquor".[3] Their next venture was, in 1746, the manufacture of this sulphuric acid, known then as Oil of Vitriol, which was also used extensively as a metal cleaning agent.

At the time this acid was costly to produce, due to the fact that it was made in small quantities in fragile glass retorts that were subject to frequent breakage. Dr Roebuck came up with the idea of using large lead containers - acid does not corrode lead - which were sturdier than the retorts and allowed larger amounts of this acid to be made, gradually bringing down the price to one quarter of what it had been. These works, known as the Birmingham Vitriol Manufactory, soon attracted the attention of one Dr Joshua Ward who held the patent for the basic process and it is thought that it was partly to avoid legal action by Ward in England, that the partners decided to move production to Scotland. Another reason may have been due to the fact that the Board of Trustees for Fisheries, Manufactures, and Improvements in Scotland had been subsidising the laying down of bleach-fields. Perhaps Roebuck and Garbett wanted to take advantage of this trade, as it is generally believed that it was Roebuck who had suggested the substitution of acid for the soured milk then used by the bleachers.[4]

They re-established themselves at Prestonpans near Edinburgh in 1749 just four years after the battle there had brought a first victory to the Jacobite army of Bonnie Prince Charlie. In order to protect the new factory, situated at the 'Cuttle', and the process, a stockade was built around it and armed men employed to guard it; hence the Prestonpans Vitriol Works became known locally as the "secret factory".[5] They imported sulphur from Leghorn in Italy and bought salt-petre from the East India Company and in 1750, were exporting sulphuric acid to Holland. Dr Ward soon took action against Roebuck but found that his patent did not hold in Scotland; a similar disappointment awaited Roebuck when a "dishonest workman" betrayed his process to others.[6] By 1784, the Prestonpans Vitriol Works was the largest in Britain.

At nearby Cockenzie House, there lived a wealthy merchant and ship owner by the name of William Cadell and he soon became a friend of the two Englishmen; it may have been his ships that Roebuck and Garbett used to export their goods. In 1750, Cadell, in partnership with Samuel Garbett, set up a pottery at Prestonpans for the production of 'creamware'.[7] One of the many products he imported was iron from Norway and Sweden and, realising the increasing importance of iron and the huge rise in price brought

Samuel Garbett   William Cadell Senior

about after by the outbreak of the 'Seven Years War' in 1756, he had tried unsuccessfully to make his own. At that time, iron was being manufactured in Scotland, but in fairly small quantities and in out of the way places such as at Bonawe and Invergarry, near to the forests that were the source of the charcoal used in the smelting process. These early ironworks were English owned and their produce, pig iron, was in the most part sent back to England. William Cadell, who was in his fiftieth year at the time and ten years senior to his two friends, is described as having been a patriotic Scot who desperately wanted to improve the industrial capability of his country, which he knew was far behind that of her southern neighbour. It may be that in his fertile mind that the idea for a new Scottish ironworks came about.

In the first half of the 18th century, iron founders had awakened to the fact that iron could be manufactured commercially using coke instead of charcoal, a process sometimes attributed to Dud Dudley in the 17th century and perfected by Abraham Darby at Coalbrookdale in Shropshire around 1708. Some said that Darby's method had been a closely guarded secret, others that it was well known and used by many. Roebuck and Garbett knew about it and are said to have carried out some experiments in this field, at the instigation of Cadell and with the intention of setting up a small establishment near to the works at Prestonpans.[8] Encouraged by the prospect of success arising from these experiments, the three men, John Roebuck, Samuel Garbett and William Cadell, agreed in principle that together they would embark on the making of iron using the 'Darby process'. The whole business appears to have been thought out step by step, to utilise the Darby method and the relatively untapped mineral resources of central Scotland. To a trained chemist such as Roebuck, the experiment of making iron in this new fashion may only have been a natural extension of his existing talents; the realization of the planned works was an even greater achievement. However, one small difference arose between William Cadell and his two friends, that is, the scale of the impending works. Roebuck from the outset wanted it to be a large affair and in hindsight was proved correct. But if he had gone Cadell's way with perhaps a slightly less ambitious scheme, at least to begin with, the ensuing difficulties that would later cause significant burdens on all concerned, may just have been avoided. It has been said that Garbett had also been wary of such a large project at first, because of the very limited funds available to them,[9] but Roebuck had his way, believing that it would be wrong to forfeit such an opportunity.

Dr Roebuck's three brothers, Thomas, Ebenezer and Benjamin along with Cadell's son, William junior, joined the original three and a company was agreed upon, to be known as "Roebucks, Garbett and Cadells", their remit: to "project a very extensive manufactory of iron". To begin with, there was to be an exploration of the mineral resources of the Forth valley, the geology of which was known to Cadell, who also knew who possessed most of the land. The location of the new works was entirely dependant on its close proximity to a suitable supply of coal and ironstone and to a river with a good fall of water, to be harnessed to drive the works machinery. When these were established, the proper people to build and then to operate the works and the construction materials, would all have to be found, but not in Scotland.

It was either in late 1758 or early 1759, that samples of ore were taken at locations along the banks of the river Forth and these were promptly dispatched to Roebuck in Birmingham. After assaying, it was determined that the best of these iron ores had come from around Bo'ness. Later, Dr. Roebuck returned to Scotland bringing with him a man called Thomas Lewis who was known as a "burner of coal" and both gentlemen toured the area by coach with Lewis carrying out tests on the local deposits of coal.[10] Various river sites were looked at, with the flow of water being measured by a man called Michael Muckle[11]; the Cadells favoured one near to Cockenzie, but were told by Samuel Garbett that he had often seen people use their own property for no reason other than convenience, only to find out later that somewhere more suitable should have been chosen in the first place.

Eventually the place that met all of the main requirements was found, on the Stenhouse Estate by the banks of the River Carron. Larbert Parish at that time was thinly populated, consisting of a few country people who grazed cattle and ploughed a small portion of the land.[12] In other words, it was a poor district, ill-cultivated, with farming in a rude state and the roads were appalling. Trade, inward and outward, was conducted from the small port of Quarroleshore, which had risen to some prominence with the decline of the harbour at Airth. The Carron site was discovered by Garbett who wrote to Roebuck of his find: "the advantages of the Carron location are numerous, nearby deposits of limestone, ironstone and coal, and goods can be transported by river to the sea and by land carriage to Glasgow and beyond"[13]. Another attraction here may well have been the many mills close by, suitable for conversion from agricultural use to the needs of a heavier industry. Even with this site found, the Cadells were still favouring others such as Spinnelford Mill in East Lothian, but at that particular place, there was no room for expansion.[14] Thus, Garbett wrote to William Cadell in June 1759: "We shall however cheerfully join you in beginning a furnace in your own neighbourhood, but we shall not be willing to leave the Water of Carron open for others to engage in, but shall probably soon make a beginning there". The Cadells of course fell in with the Carron decision. It may be that Garbett's discovery of the site in May 1759 had not just been pure chance, as it will be seen later that his son-in-law was a descendant of a family of nobility who had once lived nearby and he may have known about this area. Garbett had only a verbal agreement with Sir Michael Bruce for the use of his land along with the Stenhouse Mill Lade and its damhead on the river, but it is doubtful if Bruce realised then the enormity of the changes that were about to take place in the sylvan surroundings of his estate.

For two men new to this industry, Roebuck and Garbett seem to have had an uncanny knowledge of the workings of the major ironfounders of the English Midlands; when it came to recruiting workers, that knowledge also stood them in good stead. Two workmen were found whose task it would be to construct the works, one a carpenter, millwright and bellows-maker called William Downing and the other, a mason and bricklayer by the name of Thomas Bourne. These men were well respected in their trades, by the owners of the established ironworks in the Midlands; but they were told to bring only two of their usual workers with them, the remainder to be recruited locally. "It was always the intention of the company", wrote Garbett, "that we should train Scottish labour for future use"[15]. Downing's nephew was put in charge of the millwrights. The Cadells were not happy with the importing of English craftsmen, preferring the venture to be a wholly Scottish one, so Garbett had to explain that he only wanted the best: "It would be egregious folly to venture any other way...........but I hope when these men have built us one furnace, that we shall be able to build another without them as we will employ some Scotsmen as masons and bricklayers"[16]. [Whilst this sentiment was admirable in principle, in practice Thomas Bourne was involved with the building of blast furnaces at Carron until the late 1770s.]

At that time around the town of Falkirk, there existed many who were unemployed and also those who lived out a frugal existence working on the land, an untrained workforce waiting to be harnessed. This 'workforce' would also come cheap. Garbett at the same time warned against letting the English workers know of their intention to replace them with local labour. These craftsmen and the foundrymen who would follow, were brought to Scotland, which was thought of as an uncivilised country, at a high cost, but they were also expected to teach the Scots their trades, which they did. The works for many years was therefore known as "the English foundry" and some difficulties were experienced early on, because of this English connection. Various disagreements have been recorded between the indigenous population and the imported workforce, including a skirmish between "some countrymen" who were mending the roads and "a parcel of English workmen belonging to the ironworks"[17]. This particular incident occurred after the Englishmen had taunted the road-menders about their country and her inhabitants; it took place in June 1762. Although the arrival of the Company, according to Samuel Garbett in 1765, was a "blessing to the neighbourhood"[18], the partners could still not command the respect of, or influence over, the local inhabitants; a privilege reserved for the established landed gentry. On more than one occasion, applications had to be made for soldiers, "to protect us in the execution of the laws."[19]. A parallel can be drawn here, to the similar way in which it took years for the Forbes family at Callendar Estate to be accepted by the people of Falkirk, who still felt that the rightful 'superiors' were the descendants of the Livingstons of Callendar. Perhaps the people of the district then had a fear of strangers in general, immaterial of their place of origin.

William Cadell junior, at the age of twenty-two, was appointed works manager, or residing partner, and given the responsibility of overseeing the building work; his salary was £100 and to be closer to the works he took up residence at Dorrator House. For the recruitment of foundrymen, Garbett and Roebuck again looked south and at Coalbrookdale in June 1759, "a clever furnaceman who was used to working with pit coals as well as wood fuels", was found, his salary to be £50. This man was probably the "Mr Smith" referred to in Cadell's Memoranda Book[20] in connection with air furnaces; he was also required to perform another service: "when he hath Leisure, to Ride into the Country to Promote the Sales". He was also not expected to remain long with the company. Thomas Cranage was engaged and would be given the charge of the first blast furnace; he came from a long line of Coalbrookdale men but would eventually be dismissed from the company's service in 1761. His name appears again at Coalbrookdale in 1766, where, along with his brother George, he found a method of making bar iron using pit coal. Another two employees, who would be given the charge of air furnaces, were George Munro and John Onions; both had "eloped" from the Madleywood Furnace near Coalbrookdale.[21] More were to follow, recruited by Garbett or Roebuck. It is obvious that the best men were being enticed north with the promise of high wages; these men, according to 'the Doctor', had a "high character" in Shropshire. The specialised material for the building of the works, the hearthstones for the furnace, the boards and leathers for the bellows and the waterwheel parts, all had to be obtained in England; these had been ordered in July 1759, to be shipped from Bristol in late August:-

Garbett to Messrs. W Cadell & Sons.   14th July 1759

I don't see that I have anything more to say till you see the Doctor, except that I did on Thursday last order the Hearth Stones, two sets, and a Shaft for the wheel, and the Bellows Board and Leather, and the necessary Iron plates for a Furnace, all to be at Bristol, if possible, by the 31st of August.[22]

A large enough tree for the water-wheel axle could not be found, so a smaller one had to be procured, leading to a delay. The ship it is said, finally sailed in October 1759.

On the 19th of November 1759, an agreement was reached with the Earl of Elgin for ironstone from his Fife estate, at 4d for every cartload "betwixt 50 and 60 Dutch stone weight"[23] and more was to be brought from Redhousedean. Limestone also came from Fife and would continue to do so for many a long year. A deal was made on the 21st with a local laird, Thomas Dundas of Quarrole, to supply coal, 80 tons weekly at 4/6d a ton. A fire engine (steam powered water pump) existed at Quarrole Pit then, as well as an engine for raising coal which was a horse gin, and from a note included in the company letterbook of the time, it is apparent that the operation at the neighbouring Kinnaird Pit was also being scrutinised: - "Peter Smith engineer at Dysart would be willing to assist in the erection of the fire engine at Kinnaird! Apply to Adam Smith Quarrole"[24]. The month of December was to prove the busiest for the partners; the Dunipace Mill was leased from Robert McKell on the 5th [McKell had sublet it from Spottiswood of Dunipace in 1758]; that same day an order for bricks was placed with John Marr and over the 4th, 12th and 14th, contracts were signed with Alexander

Stenhouse - the home of Sir Michael Bruce

Hodge, James Heugh, Alexander Brown senior (Feuars of Broomidge) and Archibald Lamont (portioner of Larbert), for "lands for watercourse and wagonways"[25]. These people were tenants of Robert Chalmers of Larbert, and around seventeen separate feues had to be obtained in order to secure the run of the lade![26] More bricks were ordered on the 14th of December, from one William Barker.

However, the most important business was conducted on the 13th of December at Falkirk, when the necessary document was signed by Dr Roebuck and Samuel Garbett for the Company and Sir Michael Bruce of Stenhouse, agreeing to the feuing of 14 acres of the Stenhouse Estate. Roebuck and Cadell had to grant a bond of £1000 payable to Sir Michael on Whitsunday 1761 and to pay a feu duty of 25/- per acre. The first feu included ground for a blast furnace, a wagon road to the nearby coalfield and a waterlead (furnace lade). The road to Airth, and later to Stenhousemuir, which stretched towards Stenhouse, formed the northern boundary of the works site. There was a problem with a tenant on the site of the new works, who was a farmer by the name of John Melvin; he had to be compensated for surrendering his lease. Tradition has it that when Roebuck was negotiating with Melvin, he, that is Dr. Roebuck, had confused pounds Scots with pounds

Sterling and inadvertently paid twelve times the amount asked for.[27] Melvin may have kept this slip in mind, for future use. He had also been the miller at Stenhouse Mill and has been described as "a muichurer and merchant of some wealth" who had lived in the Stenhouse area all his life.[28] Other farmers, through whose land the lade would run, had to be recompensed also, but not to the same extent as John Melvin. They were Michael Ronald, John Rae and William Lamond. All of these arrangements are shown on the feu plan of 1761 drawn by John Scott.[29]

James Boyd, Earl of Errol, leased to the Company part of Callendar estate for wood on the 18th December and on the following day he leased the Mills of Larbert, with the water from a damhead on the river Carron below Larbert.[30] This would be the source of the water for driving the furnace bellows at the works, although it seems that it had been planned to commence the furnace lade at the Dunipace Mill. Difficulties were experienced with the superior of that mill, Spottiswood of Dunipace, who became awkward over the alterations there and as Cadell wrote in February 1760: "I do not think we have any great reason to purchase the continuation of his [Spottiswood's] lease at a very high price"[31]. Roebuck mentioned the difficult Laird again in a letter of March 1760[32] and future dealings with him were suspended until the early 1770s. Everyone, it is evident, wished to take advantage of this new business, and at the highest possible price.

As we have seen, the iron to be produced at the Carron works was to be based on the principle of smelting with coke [or coked pit coals], but great importance was still placed on the acquisition of wood for charcoal. This was still necessary to feed the 'fineries' or forges, where pig iron was cleansed of its impurities for the production of bar, or malleable, iron. In this respect, more woods were leased, this time from Mrs Elizabeth Buchanan of Leny, on the 19th and 25th December.[33]

On the 21st December at a public roup (auction) at the St Johns Coffee House in Parliament Close Edinburgh, Dr Roebuck bought the slitting mill at Cramond for £1010.[34] The mills of Cockle and Fairyfare would provide Roebucks, Garbett and Cadells with their first production facility and would be used until eclipsed by the works at Carron. Thus, as 1759 drew to a close, the new Company was in possession of the works site and with many of the preliminary arrangements in place. Dr Roebuck was able to say with confidence: "Now as we have a much better coal and also much more skilful workmen..........I have not the least doubt of our making good Mettle and Mr Downing is of the same opinion".[35] However, their plans for the blast furnace and peripheral plant came to an abrupt halt; the ship with its precious cargo from Bristol, was lost at sea[36], but the cargo had been insured.

Over the years, a story has been told of a demonstration in front of invited guests, of the first production of iron at Carron Works. This momentous event is purported to have taken place on the 1st January 1760 and the story was originally published in a company booklet in 1900 called *The Story of Industrial Enterprise* and in another in 1909 called *A Century and a Half*; it was repeated later by Henry M Cadell and Thomas J Salmon in their respective books. It began: "at the close of 1759, operations were begun with an air furnace". The demonstration was then described in great detail and the outcome was that nails were made from the iron produced and these were then given to the assembled guests. Whilst there is no contemporary documentary evidence of that day and the first proper air furnace was not ready until late March 1760, the event itself was still entirely feasible. Imported pig iron, or scrap iron, could easily have been converted into bar-iron in a hastily erected forge or a prototype air furnace. According to some of the early correspondence, it is evident that Roebuck and Garbett were keen to have the "clever founder" commence work, even to the extent of erecting an air furnace on the site of the new blast furnace:-

Garbett to Messrs. W Cadell & Sons.   15th September 1759

our present plan is for the workman we have engaged to bring another two with him and immediately set to work at an air furnace if we can get metal.[37]

Roebuck to Messrs. W Cadell & Sons. September 1759

If we had not hired the founder at present we could not hereafter have had an opportunity. However we must immediately endeavour to find some employment for him which must be by erecting an Air Furnace instantly in the place where we purpose to build the Bellows Furnace [blast furnace]. And that no time may be lost in carrying into execution this part of the plan, we must desire you to get 10 or 12 thousand of White Bricks, and also to purchase if possible, upon easy terms, 50 or 100 tons of old Cast Mettal. You need not regard the size of the pieces of Cast Mettal whether the pieces are 2 or 3 tons or only 1/4 lb. weight each or less.[38]

Whatever the truth of the account of the first iron production at Carron, we can be sure that by the end of 1759 the dream of the founders was close to realisation, though they probably had little idea of the problems awaiting them during the first difficult years of operation.

CHAPTER 2

The Troublesome First Decade

The Articles of Co-partnery which established the business of Roebucks, Garbett and Cadells, were drawn up on the 19th January and on the 9th February 1760, but it was stated then: "that the said Co-partnery did begin and commence on the 11th day of November 1759"[1]. This document also ratified the appointment of William Cadell junior as works manager. The capital was £12,000 and the shares were in 24 parts as follows:

John Roebuck	6	twenty-fourths	£3,000
Samuel Garbett	6	twenty-fourths	£3,000
William Cadell snr	3	twenty-fourths	£1,500
William Cadell jnr	3	twenty-fourths	£1,500
Benjamin Roebuck	2	twenty-fourths	£1,000
Thomas Roebuck	2	twenty-fourths	£1,000
Ebenezer Roebuck	2	twenty-fourths	£1,000
Total	24	twenty-fourths	Total £12,000

They agreed to engage in the

art and business of smelting iron ore and ironstone, and casting the same into pig, cylinders for fire engines, pump barrels, cannons, mortars, or other engines and utensils, civil and military; converting pig iron into barr iron, and slitting and rolling of barr-iron into rods, and plate iron, and for making and hammering of iron into shovels, spades and other tools whatsoever.

The original outline for the works is shown in William Cadell junior's 'memoranda book' as:

4 Blast Furnaces and assisting Air Furnaces when wanted.
4 Air Furnaces to be constantly employed.
1 Boring Mill to be used occasionally for Sad Irons.
1 Double Forge
1 Forge for drawing salt pans.
1 Forge for drawing out Melted Scraps from Holland.
1 Slitt or Rolling Mill.

These came under the heading: "The General Plan at Carron & General Remarks"[2], and included detailed observations on the operations to be carried out at the coal pits, at the various woods and also on the need for many reservoirs to be made. A closer inspection of this book suggests that it is in actual fact the 'Minutes' of discussions held by the founders, on the progress and intentions of the various concerns necessary in setting up the works. Most of the instructions are from 'the Doctor', with the exception of those made by a Mr Gibbons, who was advising on all mining operations. This projected plan for the works would be completed within the period of Cadell's management; the basic layout remained relatively unchanged for over 100 years. All of the leases, contracts and agreements are detailed in the Co-partnery and also shown are the "Obligations for the Mills of Craigforth and for the fulling mill on the river Avon" (these were never taken). From the beginning, Roebuck had based the design and model of the new works on the one in Shropshire called 'The Coalbrookdale Company' - in early 1760, he was already referring to Roebucks, Garbett and Cadells as 'The Carron Company', the analogy now obvious. It was generally or commonly acknowledged as such, as will be seen, until 1771, when it became official. As the weeks passed, more foundrymen were hired, among them those who would be in charge of the moulding and casting floors[3]:

John Dodd	caster and potter	10/- per week
Thomas Ingle	blacksmith	10/- per week
Peter Price	labourer	8/- per week

Peter Price was hired as a labourer and later became foreman of the boring shop. He eventually returned south helping to start the Perran Foundry in 1792, and later, the Neath Abbey Company of Glamorgan[4]. Garbett and Roebuck were back in England at the end of January 1760, their correspondence in the form of letters of explanation or instruction, could take weeks to arrive at Cockenzie or Dorrator House. Cadell junior at Carron worked on in solitude. He was by then drafting letters to business associates and merchants such as James Dunlop, the 'tobacco baron' of Glasgow, to whom he offered on the 10th of January to send cast metal samples and enquired as to the availability of: "old cannons, not exceeding £3 10/- a ton", most likely for melting down[5]. This early contact with the merchants of Glasgow, especially the most influential such as John Glassford, paved the way for the export of much of the Carron goods to the colonies. Many of these people had long standing business dealings with the Cadells. It is fascinating to note from these early letters just how quickly acquaintances were being made both locally and elsewhere; it is assumed that the early letters from Cadell junior were written at Dorrator House, as it is unlikely that accommodation then existed at the works site. He frequently advised correspondents that there was nowhere available to even store some of the materials under a roof and that suitable storage space would have to be obtained elsewhere. It was not long however before Cadell junior had problems, one came in the form of John Melvin, possibly remembering Roebuck's earlier misunderstanding and taking advantage of his absence. He had "the impudence to ask a years Advance Rent of his land besides 30 guineas as agreed for immediate possession"[6]. Young Cadell would not comply with this request, finding no mention of it in his contract. Melvin had "pretended" that he had a private promise from Dr Roebuck, but neither Sir Michael Bruce nor John McGowan, the Company's law agent, knew anything about it. McGowan advised Cadell not to pay Melvin a farthing of rent as "we hold the land of the proprietor not the tenant".

Back in Bristol, a large cargo of hearthstones, 20 tons of pig iron and 10 tons of Stourbridge clay, had still not been dispatched. Samuel Garbett had also hoped to add 20 thousand Stourbridge bricks to this and he explained in a letter to W. Cadell and Sons, the reason for the delay: -

Birmingham Jan 31st 1760

The Trow or Boatmaster at Bewdley whose name is Glover is a substantial honest man, he says we have been badly imposed upon by our correspondent Lavender at Bristol and Captain Hay who I find is a drunken fellow, as well as a mean scoundrell. He actually hid himself three days in order to gain three days more demurrage. I shall be glad to hear that the ship is safe with you. And if you can take advantage of Mr. Hay pray do for he hath been picking our pockets in company with Mr. Lavender.[7]

This ship had still not left Bristol by March. Roebuck, in a letter to Cadell junior dated 11th March[8], informed him that the ship was to sail on the 15th of March. He also mentioned that he had sent a "person" from Derbyshire into Yorkshire to purchase bellows boards, to replace "the ones we have lost". The last statement alludes to the ship of the previous October, lost at sea off the coast of Ireland. A delay in the sailing of the replacement ship, has sometimes been put down to a severe drought at the time, which had lowered the level of the river. The vessel that Garbett saw at Bristol under Captain Hay, was called the 'Providence' and it would eventually arrive in the Firth of Forth, but under a different man.

Back at Carron, the manager was fretting over the implications of the enormous weight of the ship's cargo; the hearthstones alone were each of around 5 tons. Robert McKell at Dunipace was asked for an estimate for: "one or two small but stout cranes for the use of the iron works, to be made as soon as possible as we daily expect a vessel with some large stones for hearthing, of 5 tons weight"[9]. Another letter was dispatched to Alex Fiddes the harbourmaster and merchant at Quarroleshore, explaining about the ship with the heavy cargo; and a carpenter was to build a "flatt", which was a barge or lighter, for use on the River Carron. Fiddes was also asked for his advice on the danger to such a ship coming into the River Carron. A letter of less concern was sent to Thomas Cranage, furnace keeper designate, at Coalbrookdale, in which he was advised of the large ship's departure from Bristol and, as there was more room on it than was required, anything else for the works that he or the rest [his colleagues were always referred to in this way] wanted, was to be noted: *"and they shall be got"*. Another man, who would be a key worker, was recruited, he had come highly recommended: -

> If Robert Hawkins answers the descriptions given of him by Thos. Lewis he will be a useful person.[10]

Robert Hawkins was also from Coalbrookdale and was the son of Richard Hawkins of the Bersham Furnace and a nephew of Abraham Darby the second[11]. He had been trained at the 'Dale' and at the Bersham works, where he was the outside superintendent at the time. His salary was to be £100, the same as the manager's, and he was to teach Scotsmen "the art of boring cylinders and grinding sad irons".

Cadell resumed his enquiries as to a suitable course for the ship and was told that a vessel of 300 tons could, with safety, come within the River Carron to a place called Greenbraes, but only during spring tides and if it did not draw above 15 feet of water. He arranged with Mr Fiddes to send a "sufficient pilot" to bring the ship up the Firth into Carron. There was no "key" at Greenbraes [situated to the south-east of present day Skinflats], so unless the hearthstones were removed from the ship using its masts and a triangle erected on deck, the alternative was to unload at Bo'ness. The River Carron was obviously more convenient, because the "stones" could be placed on the lighter [flatt] that was being built and from there brought up to the furnace site[12]. By the 1st March, arrangements had been made regarding a start to the construction of the "waggon road" [tramway] to the coalfield; Mr William Davidson at Quarrole was told to advise Thomas Dundas to settle with his tenants: "in order that the making of the road may not be hampered"[13].

According to the very first plans[14], a tramway or 'waggonway' left the works in a north-easterly direction. In those days, the rails were made of wood and they only acted as guides for the wheels of the 'wagons', which ran on another wooden base or track. These wagons were pulled by horses. The locals began to use the tracks as walkways, in preference to the roads, which were appalling. This wagonway appears to have met another one which connected the Quarrole Pit with the coalshore and which later extended to another pit known as Flemings on the north side of Bellsdyke near to the old road called the Crosshillmuirhead Road. Not long after its construction, it traversed the Quarrole section on its route to Kinnaird and another part was put down, this time from Kinnaird to the harbour. A branch also left the main run near to the Skaithmuir Mill and swung over to the harbour. Some detail can be seen from early plans such as the harbour lease of 1763[15], made to record the activities of Carron Company when it leased the property from Thomas Dundas of Quarrole. But, as with all plans of that time, they do not have the accuracy of their successors. The wooden rails from the works to Kinnaird were replaced in 1767 by rails, "wholly cast of iron from Coalbrookdale"[16]. Carron Company often claimed that these rails had been laid directly from the works to Kinnaird, but the wooden rails of the Quarrole section were still to be seen in the late 1770s, if one story is to be believed. Eventually all of the wooden rails were replaced with iron ones. Part of the old tramway bed can still be seen in the field behind Cuttyfield farm; the section that led to the Kinnaird Engine, which once existed on the north side of the present day Bellsdyke Road beside the stone boundary wall of Kinnaird House. In the early 1780s when the Company gave up operations at Quarrole and Kinnaird, some of these waggonways were dismantled but were later restored when mining was resumed.

All of the activity at Carron must have been a novelty for onlookers, as there were then around 60 men employed about the furnace and the water lead. A request had been sent to Bo'ness for 30 soldiers who were to be used to dig out the foundations for the furnace, but only 20 came. The lade or water lead was to be on average, four and a half to five feet deep, allowing for the unevenness of the ground and the breadth at the top fourteen feet, sloping to ten feet at the bottom. The "Bromige Portioners", especially "old Brown", were troublesome over its construction and McGowan, the law agent, was asked by Cadell for a copy of the agreement made with the tenants of Robert Chalmers of Larbert. Alexander Brown wanted more money for the ground: "than was taken up by the lade, he is for having us pay for all the Riggs that are broke and I know not what"[17]. These lands through which the lade was to run, had been leased to the tenants on the runrig system and they had only just realised that while the lade only took up a small part of their property, it would effectively cut their fields in half. Carron Company built, and maintained for many years, small bridges over the lade which allowed the tenants to cross from one part of their ground to the other. An aqueduct had to be built, to carry the lade over the Broomage Burn; eighteen years later it collapsed, causing the reservoirs to empty. McGowan was also asked for the agreements for the Mills of Larbert: "in order that we may regulate the present tenants of Lord Errol and McKell's mills to continue in them till we have occasion for the water".[18] The Wester mill was to be taken down soon after Whitsunday 1760 for carrying on the water lead, but the tenants at the Easter mill were to be allowed to continue, as long as the water could be spared.

Dr Roebuck, again in England, sent the following request to young Cadell: "Pray send by the first ship for London five tons of hoops such as are proper for the specific market. If you have not five tons ready send what you have to T. Roebuck & Co. that they may lose no time in trying how they can succeed in the sale of them".[19] This was probably the Company's first order and these hoops would most likely have come from the ironmill at Cramond. There was also an enquiry about the making of cannonballs: "let me know how many can be cast at one Air Furnace and whether you have workmen enough to employ at three furnaces"; this request is dated 11th March 1760.[20]

The 'Providence', under a Captain Leishman, arrived off the mouth of the River Carron by the 23rd of April; but the Captain was against risking the safety of his ship by taking her into the river, resulting in an angry letter from William Cadell junior on the 26th:

> It will be inconvenient of the ship to go to Bo'ness especially when I am informed that she can come with as much safety within Carron.........We can get the attestations of all the Shipmasters belonging to Carron that your ship can be brought to a place where she can lay safe .[21]

Seven of the soldiers who had been brought to the works were put on board, assisting with the task of unloading the smaller articles such as bricks. However, on the 28th, the Captain took his ship along to Bo'ness, which further angered Cadell who accused Leishman of having moved his ship without permission or orders "which will occasion a considerable additional expense". Eventually the "stones" were taken to the furnace site at Carron by using the 'flatt'; some of the materials were unloaded at Melvin's Green and the rest at a point near to the Stenhouse Mill Damhead. Much to the relief of the manager, Bourne and Downing's "hands" eventually got to work and as promised earlier by Samuel Garbett, it was reported that Scots masons were also at work. These hearthstones were mentioned by John Gibson years later in his book, *The Lands and Lairds of Dunipace and Larbert*; apparently no longer required, as they had been part of the original two furnaces replaced in 1776 and 1777, they lay for many years on vacant ground outside the works.

The activities at Carron during that first year amply demonstrate the abilities of William Cadell junior, left there for the most part on his own and to his own devices. He was at times critical of the ways of some of the English workers, but was always warned by Dr. Roebuck not to reprimand them but to leave that task to him. Cadell, in a letter to Roebuck and Garbett wrote "We shall make it our duty to Oblige the Englishmen all we can, they seem all well pleased. I hope they never will have reason to be otherways." He had also made one observation on the English and this too was included: "I find they will never do to be under Subjection of one Another".[22]

In August 1760, the company, probably now wise to the limited operation at Quarrole, took over the lease of the pit from Thomas Dundas. Dundas had acquired it when he bought the estate of Quarrole in 1749 and it was probably quite a relief to him when Carron Company decided to continue operations themselves, as by all accounts, he had not been much of a businessman.[23] By September, the lade was nearing completion but one of Bruce's tenant farmers was threatening to stop it. Michael Ronald alleged that Sir Michael "never spoke to him about it", Sir Michael was told on no uncertain terms, "please therefore settle it with him, that there may be no stop or interruptions to the works". On the 12th November, the Company began its own coal mining operation at Kinnaird when it secured the lease from James Bruce. Bruce would later cause no end of trouble to the Company, complaining about such mundane occurrences as people "splitting coal" on his land or more seriously, of wagons leaving his pit under weight and the lack of air in the No 2 pit. He also prospered by this arrangement, which freed him to go off on his journeys of exploration.

The first blast furnace at Carron was 'blown in' on the 26th December 1760 and it was followed by a second on the 4th September 1761. In the same year, on the lands of Quarrole, a method of coal extraction new to Scotland was first used. New pits were sunk and Garbett brought in miners from Shropshire, who were paid "Shropshire" wages; with these men came the introduction of the 'longwall' system of mining, but the Scots miners

The lintel still preserved at Carron and said to be from the first blast furnace

were kept at their own pits with their traditional methods. The English, it was said, had "better" working and living conditions, the difference or excuse made that they were not under bond like the Scots. This bonding, which was in fact a form of slavery, meant that the miners and their families could be transferred to new owners with the sale or lease of the pit, as was the case with the miners of Quarrole and Kinnaird. It would be many years before this practice finally disappeared. Understandably, it added to the friction between the two nationalities.

A pumping engine had to be installed at Kinnaird when the Company took control there - its location would later be criticised by James Bruce and lead to legal action. Many smaller pits were worked by Carron in the vicinity of Kinnaird and Quarrole and included: 'Flemings', 'Dogger', 'Crank Gin', 'Proof', 'Tinkertoun', 'Cuttyfield', 'Skaithmuir', 'Adams', 'Polloks', 'Dam', 'Mill' and 'Lady Janet'[24]; each time a new pit was opened, a new arrangement had to be entered into with the owners. The persons in charge of these pits were known as 'Bailleys'. The Quarrole and Kinnaird Pits were overseen by James Fish. The company's first mining consultant was a Mr Gibbons, followed by James Landers and then John Beaumont He was apparently used as a contractor and given responsibility for coal extraction. From the correspondence of William Cadell junior, it can be seen that operations were scrutinised down to the last detail, even to the cost of a humble sharpening tool. For instance, with regard to the pumping engine at Kinnaird, it had a cylinder of seventy-two inches in diameter and a pumping cylinder of thirteen and a half inches in diameter, the Engine Pit being 44 fathoms deep.[25] It was calculated that it cost 10/3d to raise 100 tons of water! Detailed reports from the mining engineers showed the location and projection of coal in certain fields and the estimated cost, down to the last farthing, including wages, leases, royalties etc., of obtaining that coal. The lease of the Quarrole Pit also included the use of the harbour at "Quarroleshoar", free from all duties. When the Company took over the lease of the harbour in 1763, Samuel Garbett is said to have changed the name to Carronshore, a trait of the founders to alter ugly local names, as they had done in 1761 when the land around the steading at Hungry Hill was "to be called Carronhill".

The works of the early 1760s was something of a giant experiment. with attempts being made to manufacture pig iron with different types of coal, mixtures of coal and coke and even on one occasion with peat. All of this had already been tried by some of their more experienced competitors, south of the border. More coal and of better quality was required, and to this end, land was feued from the Duke of Hamilton in the Bo'ness and Polmont areas. It was soon confirmed that the choice of making iron using coke had been the correct one, but there was still a great need for charcoal which was made from prepared bundles of branches known as 'chord' or 'cordwood' and an early estimate of the amounts to be used in the first winter and spring had been, "2,000 chord". Cadell junior at the beginning of 1760 had leased more woods for that purpose, this time at Torwood. Whilst pig iron was made using coke, the same advance had not been made at the forge. Pig iron is brittle in nature with a high carbon content (2.2-5%) and is only suitable for use in castings, so another type of iron known as malleable or ductile iron had to be made. The pig iron was put into a furnace known as a finery along with charcoal, where it was stirred under a blast of air from bellows, which further removed impurities. This refined iron was then put into another furnace called the chafery where it was again brought to a great heat and then hammered. It could then be drawn into rods or bars, or used in the manufacture of sugar pans etc. This was a slow laborious process.

Some of these rods were used in nail making. When the Company acquired the Slitt Mill at Crammond it had also taken over the nail manufactory. With a view to expanding this locally, William Cadell junior brought an English nail maker called John Raybould[26] and six others north, and it is thought that they were settled in the village later to become known as Laurieston. Later, others were encouraged to move near to the works. Nailer rows, that is accommodation with a forge included, were built at Camelon and at Carron. Incidentally, it is recorded in one of Cadell junior's later letters that: "Raybould and Parks have been imprisoned for forging Thistle Bank notes"![27]

Almost anything that could be made in iron was being offered at that time including sad irons, pans and pots of all types, "Cooris" girdles, once made only at Culross in Fife, and farm and garden implements such as spades and hoes. The Glasgow merchants were asked to include Carron goods in their shipments to the colonies, in England, customers were found via Thomas Roebuck & Co. The Company also looked further afield to the Continent and markets already familiar to the Cadells.

In 1761, a further 82 acres of Stenhouse land had been feued from Sir Michael Bruce and that was followed in 1762 by a third feu of 53 acres, making a total of 149 acres.[28] The works site was further expanded, when the old road past John Paterson's house was diverted to the north. There were about 600 men employed by the Company. The following advertisement appeared in the *Glasgow Journal* of January 1762: -

Carron Iron Works Cylinders and Pipes for Fire Engines, Cannon and Cannon Ball, and all other kinds of Cast Iron Goods are made at Carron.

At the end of 1762, there were two blast furnaces with their associated bellows, a boring mill, air furnaces and a forge. The blast furnaces then, were most likely of a square cross-section, made of stone and lined with heat resistant bricks. It is presumed that with the arrival of the second furnace, a second blowing machine would have been installed similar to the original. The first waterwheel, used to drive the bellows, had been fed directly by the water from the furnace lade, but by the time that the second furnace had been "blown in", the Furnace Pool or small reservoir intervened. The water from the Furnace Pool was then transported in a wooden trough to the bellows water wheels. The design of the bellows mechanism was a standard one and there is no reason to believe that the method used at Carron then differed from others.[29] Two giant wood and leather bellows sat side by side, and in the static mode were kept open by counterweights. The waterwheel had attached to its axis two sets of cams, which were spaced accordingly. As the wheel revolved, a finger of one of the cams would then depress an extension to the top 'board' of the bellows causing it to expel air. The cams acting on the other bellows would be set to operate it, just as its counterpart was returning to the open position under the influence of its counterweight. Thus with this alternating action, something resembling a continuous blast was achieved. The forge or smithy was, at the beginning, most likely of a very basic type using hand operated bellows, and it was here that the pig iron was further processed or made into bar iron. A letter of instruction on how to make bar iron was sent to Carron in 1762, from Andrew Holt in Paris, who at that time was accompanying Samuel Garbett's son Francis on his 'Grand Tour [30]. By the end of 1762 however, the forge consisted of three finerys and two hammers [the chaferys] and we must assume that the motive power for these hammers, and for the bellows for the finerys, came from water wheels. The actual location of the forge at that time is not known, the general assumption has been that it was beside the Stenhouse Mill Lade, but that lade was culverted by 1763. It is possible that this forge was the one built to the north-east of the blast furnaces, and after which the Forge Dam of 1765 was named. The boring mill falls into the same category as the forge, and on the works plan of 1773, it is shown as part of that same building. Air furnaces were used to melt pig iron for casting and they operated on the 'natural draught principle', without a blast. One of them was known as a 'Balling Furnace', used to melt scraps [scrap iron], which were brought from Rotterdam in barrels.[31] These furnaces and mills would have been built to a general design of the period, as was the case at established contemporary ironworks. In those days, the River Carron was navigable as far as the Stenhouse Mill Damhead and a wooden, stone-filled pier had been built around 1760 a little downstream from it, allowing 'lighters' or barges to be 'tracked' [towed by men] up to that point, where their cargoes were loaded and unloaded.[32] There were two lighters in use then but these were small, of only 6 tons burden.

Dr Roebuck made attempts in 1762 to manufacture malleable iron using pit coals (Patent No 780), but seems to have had limited success[33] : -

> I melt a pig of any kind of Cast Iron in a hearth heated with pit coal by the blast of a bellow, and I work the metal until it is reduced to nature, which I take out of the fire and separate to pieces; then I take the metal thus reduced and expose it to the action of a hollow pit coal fire, heated by the blast of the bellows till it is reduced to a loop which I draw out under a common forge hammer into Bar Iron.

Some authors have credited Roebuck with being close to a solution though it would be twenty years before a method was found, and not at Carron Works. Also in 1762, William Cadell junior leased seven and a half acres of ground at Carronhill from Carron Company. It was there in 1763, that he built his home Carron Park, spending £1,000 on the venture which included the laying out of the grounds. Another house, Mount Carron, was built nearby for one of the other partners, Thomas Roebuck.

Carron Company was manufacturing cast iron pipes by 1764, supposedly on the suggestion of John Adam who had become a partner[34]; and in the following year Blenheim Palace was supplied with 1,500 yards of piping. It was also recorded that in 1765, the 'Carron', under the command of Captain Porteous, sailed to London with a cargo of 10 guns, plates, sugar pans, sad irons, ovens, stove and kitchen backs[35]. This order was valued at £443-18/-. In the months of June, July and August of that year, the works were affected by an "uncommon" drought, "of a kind never seen since 1723".[36] There was barely enough water for one blast furnace and so there was talk of installing a "fire engine" [steam pumping engine] to return used water to the furnace pool, but nothing was done.[37]

The following year, the Company, or rather Garbett, decided to standardise its housing policy. Until then, it is apparent that some of the workforce had been allowed to live rent free under their original contracts, but there were others inhabiting company houses that had not had that agreement.[38] The rent was to be set at 8% of the outlay in providing the accommodation, and this Garbett hoped, would encourage some of them to build homes of their own thus "attaching themselves" to Carron. It was also thought that it would bring in £1000 per year. The founders always recognized the need to provide housing and to that end, in August 1765, they decided to let out the north part of Carronhill; "to build a village on the north side of the new intended road from Carron to Larbert"; this was probably the origin of the hamlet known as 'Goshen', called after the Biblical land of plenty.

The Works made a profit of £10,213 between January 1762 and March 1765 and by 1766, the weekly output from the existing furnaces was between 35 and 40 tons.[39] Another new furnace, the No 3, was blown in by late 1766 and it was then that a new type of blowing apparatus was introduced to replace the wood and leather bellows.[40] A 'blowing engine', of a type seen by Francis Garbett at a foundry in Rotherham, using three cast-iron cylinders, was to be erected at the No 3 Furnace; John Smeaton was also consulted, but he had recommended using four cylinders. Sam Binns was dispatched to Rotherham with orders to note every detail of this machine and it was erected at the No 3 Furnace by late October.[41] Cadell junior was so satisfied with it that he ordered another two cylinders to be cast for a similar machine for the No 4 Furnace which was then under construction, but which did not come into blast until the following year. Latterly, difficulties were experienced with the crankshaft on this blast engine at No 3 Furnace. One, of Smeaton's design using four cylinders, was tried at the No 1 Furnace in 1768 and another of his, but to a slightly different pattern, was erected at the No 2 Furnace in 1769.[42] Eventually, all four furnaces were served by Smeaton's later design, thus providing a more powerful blast and cutting out the expense of regular repairs to the leather bellows of their predecessors.

William Cadell junior   John Smeaton

Garbett thought that by the time No 4 Blast Furnace was working, one of the others could be kept as a trial furnace and this is confirmed on an early plan. With four blast furnaces, William Cadell junior projected a profit for 1767 of £10,500; instead, there was a loss of £10,000.[43]

With the planned arrival of the additional furnaces in 1766, Garbett searched throughout the Midlands for furnace keepers. The Nos 1 and 2 Blast Furnaces were by then in the hands of William Mathews and William Wild or Wylde; Cadell junior along with a newcomer to the works by the name of Peter Capper, took take care of Nos 3 and 4 until others could be found.[44] Capper, whose father was a friend of Samuel Garbett, appears to have performed the duty of an overseer. He was involved in the nail trade and later worked at Francis Garbett & Co. Sam Evans and John Hadkinson were hired at the Willey Furnace, but Garbett found that Hadkinson was in fact only a pot moulder.[45] Evans, who had a fine reputation as a furnace keeper, then persuaded Garbett that Hadkinson was an honest man and a good worker and if he was allowed to come to Scotland, he would personally train him. Hadkinson was to be paid 15/- per week. Not so favourable was the report sent by Garbett about another keeper called Richard Latt who was already at the works and who had been recommended by another named Giddens. Latt was described as being a vile man. Cadell junior, in reply to Garbett, considered that Latt was in fact the opposite and was a willing worker!

In May 1767, problems were again experienced with the water supply causing the works to remain idle. The lack of water was costing the company £300 a week by June and Cadell was once more pressing for the erection of a "fire engine", even to the extent of suggesting that W. Cadell & Sons would find the money for it.[46] Work was started in June and a culvert, "not above 200 yards", was taken from the blowing engine waterwheels, to an engine pit. This engine pit was sunk to a depth of 8 feet below the level of the wheels and there was a fall of between two and a half and three feet between the wheels, which were situated on the west side of the blast furnaces, and the engine pit. After the water had passed the wheels, it was then allowed to run to the engine pit where it was pumped back into the furnace pool and used again. Cadell was warned to be careful to get the water before it went into the "miller's lead", that is, the Stenhouse Mill Lade, because, "when it gets there, it is no longer our property". That year, James Watt offered to construct this engine for £1000, to a plan he had seen at "Mr. Boltons" [Matthew Boulton's Soho Works], and Peter Capper at Carron had seen some engines at a friend's near Birmingham, where one could be built for £600.[47] Cadell junior recorded that at the time, he had three cylinders at Carron, of 52", 66" and 72" diameters; one of these may have been used, as the "fire engine" eventually erected, did in fact have a cylinder of 72" diameter. It is thought that this engine was first used in the following year. In 1769, it was altered by Adam Smith to operate on the standard principle, and John Smeaton later improved on that, by fitting additional boilers; it had a pumping cylinder of 55" diameter

Many of the workers who came from far off places such as Coalbrookdale, had one common interest - they were freemasons. At first, some joined the nearest lodge, which was at Falkirk and one such man was John Benson, who along with other members of his family were to be employed at Carron Works for many years.[48] He was originally given charge of charcoal production, at that time using the wood from the Duke of Hamilton's estate. His brother William, a clerk at the works, who came to Carron at the same time, 1765, was later immortalised by a piece of poetry, as will be seen. John Benson was admitted to the Falkirk Lodge No 16 in 1765 and two years later, he and several others including Peter Price, mentioned earlier, were permitted to constitute their own Lodge at Carron to be called the Carron Lodge No 138 [later re-numbered 139][49]. It was recorded that one of their first meetings was held "at five o'clock in the afternoon at Mr Garbett's parlour at the Nailery". Benson was later given charge of the Nos 1 and 2 Blast Furnaces and became the blast furnace manager at Carron as early as 1773. He was known as "Baggie Benson" and said to have been, "a bit of a character". He had a son called William, a 'natural child', using the parlance of the day, who lived at Carronshore and eventually became Master of a Company ship, the 'Dynamene'.[50] There were so many Bensons around at Carron in the early days that it led to confusion in later years as to who did what. William Benson the clerk had in total, nine of a family and one of his daughters, Betty, became the wife of William Symington. There were also sons named John and William and, interestingly enough, one called Charles Gascoigne Benson. Another son called Alexander, became a 'writer' at Carron, his name often appearing as a witness on workers' contracts.

The Works experienced a number of difficulties at this time, including shoddy workmanship and never ending reports of wastage, and part of the blame must be laid at the door of the founding partners. Until the end of the decade, Cadell junior appears to have been left in sole charge with Garbett on seemingly endless journeys to Birmingham, albeit some in connection with the works but also to take care of his other business interests. These included, S. Garbett & Company of Birmingham, F. Garbett & Company at Carronshore and Roebuck & Garbett at Prestonpans. He also had an interest in an English slitting mill at Wychnor. If Roebuck had concentrated on the works at Carron, things might have been different. His brilliant mind had conceived the whole concern but, even as the works were being built in 1760, his restless mind was already drifting to new challenges. Garbett eventually recognised the need for at least three partners to be at the works permanently, and in 1767, when another partner was being looked for, he wanted one who was prepared to come to Carron and take part [it was recognised that not everyone would want to come and settle there], and not a "gentleman partner". It was then that he began his attempt to persuade a young man by the name of Ambrose Tibbats of Bilston in Staffordshire, to become a "working" Carron partner. He was convinced that once Tibbats saw the place, his passion would grow. In May 1767, Tibbats purchased one half share in Carron Company, probably from Garbett, for £2,500.[51]

Many more workers came to Carron from all over the country at that time, one John Ball, a collier, had been hired in England by Garbett. He arrived at Carron Works along with two others and demanded that Cadell junior increase his agreed wage of 18/6d per week, to one guinea (21/-).[52] He also suggested that he be put in charge of one of the pits. Cadell junior was astonished at his behaviour: "I could not flatter him with hopes of advancing his wages unless he was of some singular service to the works, and .... that if he was not satisfied with his agreed wages, he was at Liberty to return". This is exactly what he did, taking with him three or four of the Shropshire colliers who worked under James Fish at Kinnaird. Garbett was told to recover the 5 guineas plus travelling expenses paid in advance to Ball. However, on the advice of Garbett, Ball was to return.

With the formation of the Company at a troublesome time in British history, when wars seemed to be an everyday occurrence, it was only natural that attention would be given to the manufacture of the most lucrative product to be made of iron, the cannon. William Cadell junior had, in October 1761, managed to acquire plans of guns of all sizes from Edinburgh Castle[53] and one month later, the first piece of ordnance from Carron, a 6-pounder gun, had been cast. In early 1762, 'Roebucks, Garbett and Cadells', the original name of the Company, made an offer to the Board of Ordnance to supply them with 12 to 42-pounder guns, shot and trucks, but only the offer of shot was accepted.[54] These early attempts were unsuccessful and it would seem that there was more to making a cannon than they at first thought, as by late 1762 Cadell wrote, "We have given o'er making cannon". The following year they attempted to have guns for the merchant service proved at Woolwich, but were told that only guns destined for East India Company service had that privilege.[55] Another endeavour was made in 1764 when a gunfounder from Hampshire was brought to Carron who had previously made guns for the East India Company.[56]

The Board of Ordnance was a Government agency, which tested and ordered guns and other items of ordnance for the Admiralty. In 1764 another offer was made by Roebucks, Garbett and Cadells to supply them with ordnance at £14 a ton.[57] This was probably less than cost price, but those at Carron hoped to make money once a foothold was gained. The Board then invited their other suppliers to match this offer which only Crowleys and Churchills could.[58] A contract was awarded to 'Roebucks, Garbett and Cadells', but the quality of their product was not consistent, with a higher proportion of proof failures than any of their competitors ever had. The Board put up with this for a while, most likely because of the cheapness of the guns or maybe because John Adam, eldest of the Adam brothers and a new partner at Carron, was the Board's building contractor in Scotland.[59] Some of the guns sent to Woolwich had been bored badly, while others still contained moulder's sand. At Carron, the blame for the poor quality and quantity of guns supplied was often attributed, from the mid-1760s, to William Mathews, who was in charge at the blast furnaces and the moulding department.[60] Meanwhile many of the Board's former suppliers went out of business. In 1766, consideration was given to supplying guns to Spain and Portugal, as the Government's contract was not deemed large enough. Garbett however warned of the dangers of exporting to these countries without a guarantee and he even went as far as describing the Court of Portugal then as, "a vile court".[61] The quality of Carron guns was still erratic, as described by Garbett in August 1767:

The 8 guns landed last Monday are very shabby, I was ashamed to see them because they are a disgrace to the Work….Surely Mathews and Wild after what hath passed will not be so base as to hazzard our property & our disgrace by sending more insufficient guns.[62]

Garbett thought that it was time that a partner gave the needful attention to the quality of guns, as a "proofmaster". Judging from the correspondence between Garbett and Cadell junior, it is surprising that the works at Carron did survive. Cadell, as the residing partner at Carron, constantly wrote to Garbett in Birmingham, on the state of the Works, the poor quality of goods and of his concern at the financial transactions. It became increasingly obvious that the business was grossly under-funded. A letter from Garbett to young Cadell dated 18th October 1767, intimated how he was "shockingly disappointed" in all the departments and that everything that had taken up Cadell's time had rendered it impossible for him [Cadell] to give proper attention to the superintendents of these different departments. He continued by saying that all his friends thought that the Works were in a dangerous way, while all the time desperately trying not to offend Cadell. There was a "tendency to inaccuracy and slovenliness" in most of the branches and a remedy had to be found to establish "punctuality, accuracy and neatness". Superintendents could only do this and not the manager, the problem according to Garbett, was how to get that attention from the superintendents. Cadell replied to this letter and agreed with Garbett's assessment, but added that this was what he had been saying all along! Nothing was done to alleviate these problems; none of the other partners came to Cadell's assistance and, as mentioned previously, Mathews at the furnaces was constantly blamed for the poor metal and hence the quantity and quality of the guns and loam goods produced. Cadell wrote: "we are and have lately been very dificient (sic) .... I hope he [Mathews] will soon get the better of these imperfections".[63] At one period, Garbett confided in William Cadell, that the only servant at Carron that he could trust was John Grieve. In 1766, Cadell had received letters from both of the Garbetts, implying that he had been uncivil to Mathews to which Cadell replied that he had been disappointed with Mathews' work, but as for being uncivil, he had treated him more as a partner than as a servant. Cadell's hands had been 'tied', in respect of Mathews, who appears to have been a long-standing acquaintance of the Garbetts. However, by late 1767, as already noted, Garbett's opinion of Mathews' work had changed. It is clear that the strain on William Cadell at this time was very great as of his letters demonstrates:

I have now been above Seven years at this place and indeed no prospect of gain would make me go thro' the same scene of fatigue, vexation, & [disturbance ?] of Mind, as well as [that?] which I have experienced almost without intermission.

The early production difficulties are understandable, especially at the blast furnace where effective operations take place between narrow limits. That is why Cadell junior was very much at the mercy of those 'outsiders', recruited for their expertise. The pig iron produced also depended on the composition of the charge, the temperature of the furnace and the 'burden' or 'burthen [the ratio of fuel to ore] of the furnace. Assaying of the various ores available from Brightons, Bo'ness, Redhousedean, Cumberland etc. was carried out and some of these ores were firstly 'calcined' or roasted, which reduced the amounts of phosphorus they contained.[64] They also knew about washing the ore, which got rid of soluble sulphates, but they were probably unaware of the technical reasons for doing this. The result of assaying in 1768 revealed that, "it appears that our ironstone on an average when well calcined & free of all refuse yields nearly 40 pts. of metal for every 100 pts. calcined stone".[65] Tests on the pig iron were made by fracturing it and examining its appearance, which could be grey, mottled or white, governed by its composition and the rate at which it was allowed to cool. It was the "grey mettal" that was in constant demand for the production of guns. In those far off days and before the advent of proper chemical analysis or the study of metallurgy, it seems to have been trial and error, with the result put down to experience.

By then, Dr Roebuck, who is hardly mentioned at all in the correspondence of this period, had his own difficulties. Back in 1760 when the ironworks was under construction, he was persuaded, contrary to the advice of his friends, to lease a deep coal field at Kinniel. It was the property of the Duke of Hamilton, from whom he had leased Kinniel House, and the promise of large seams of untapped coal was impossible to resist. The agreement also included the salt pans on the banks of the Forth and his plan was to feed the fires of the salt pans with coal from this pit. This concern was known as "The Borrowstouness Coal Company" and the partnership included John Glassford the famous Glasgow merchant, at least at the beginning.[66] It was not long before flooding was experienced at the pit; which necessitated more and more expense on a remedy. A friend of Roebuck, Dr. Joseph Black of Glasgow University, informed him of a young man from Greenock called James Watt who had been experimenting with ways in which to improve a model Newcomen steam engine at Glasgow

Kinneil House

University where he was a technician. Watt was short of funds and in debt, so it was agreed that upon Roebuck settling that debt, Watt would come to Kinniel and finish his experiments; his completed engine would then be used at Roebuck's pit. The first cylinder for Watt's experimental engine was cast at Carron Works in 1766 made to a drawing sent by Watt from Glasgow[67] and is today fixed into the wall of the Carron clock tower. It was not a success due to the inaccuracy of the boring methods used then. He is reputed to have constructed another model of his engine, the cylinder made from tin hammered around a wooden core, which was demonstrated to Dr Roebuck on the dining table at Kinniel House. It was so successful that a provisional patent for it was taken out at Berwick.[68] Eventually, James Watt came to Kinniel House and started work in a small outhouse built for the purpose. A full-size engine, made of parts from Glasgow and Carron, though far from being fully developed, was erected at the Burn Pit in 1768. This engine was known as "Beelzebub"[69] and already Carron Company with this association, had inadvertently entered the annals of history. Watt apparently erected more of his engines at Bo'ness, at Taylor's Pit and the Schoolyard Pit, but these were probably of lesser consequence.

Co-incidentally, in the same year as "Beelzebub" was installed, John Roebuck, because of his worsening financial problems, made it known that he had left the partnership of Carron Company two years previously. He was in debt to many, some of whom included his friends and relations and

James Watt, and his workshop at Kinneil as it appeared in 1913. The little building stands immediately behind Kinneil House and is at present a roofless ruin. Watt worked here from 1768 while Carron Company tried unsuccessfully to manufacture the cylinders required for his improved steam engine he eventually had to part with his other interests at Prestonpans and Birmingham. With the loss of his benefactor, James Watt had to abandon his activities at Kinniel and he took up the profession of civil engineer. In 1770, Roebuck's business and farms at Bo'ness were put in the hands of trustees consisting of his bankers, Mansfield and Hunter of Edinburgh, one of whose directors was Patrick Miller, later to be involved at Carron with the Carronade gun and Symington's experiments.[70] His brother Thomas Roebuck was also a trustee.

> I Doctor Roebuck late Physician at Birmingham Lessee of the Coaling and Salt works at Borrowstoness and others aftermentioned, whereas I have laid out and expended large sums of money in filling and establishing the said Coal and Salt works altho' now brought to such a state as to yield a very considerable annual profit yet hitherto the produce has not been able to repay the debts I have contracted on that account. [71]

Carron Company, the main creditor [for "furnishings" provided to the Coal Company], along with others, signed an agreement acceding to his business being run this way.[72] Accordingly they, along with those other creditors, had to provide finance when requested by the Trustees, whose secretary was John Grieve, formerly of Carron Company, to ensure the continued viability of this coal business.[73] It was not long before they wished they had not agreed, and they were eventually released from the deal upon agreeing to accept Roebuck's and Mansfield & Hunter's offer, of 5/- in the pound, to clear his debt.[74]

Roebuck's friend Matthew Boulton, who operated a successful factory in Birmingham called the Soho Works, knew about Watt's engine, Watt having visited the Soho Works in 1767. He was also aware of the Doctor's personal affairs, for he was owed £1,200. A patent for Watt's engine had been taken out in 1769, with Roebuck owning two thirds of it, but his creditors thought it not even worth a farthing. Boulton knew otherwise and in return for the debt of £1,200, he was given Roebuck's share of the patent for Watt's engine. The engine at Kinniel was taken down and sent to the Soho Works and Watt eventually went there in 1774 ; unfortunately this engine was later destroyed by a fire. James Watt's main improvement to the steam engine was the addition of a separate cylinder - the separate condenser - where the steam from the working cylinder was condensed. By removing the steam and having it condensed elsewhere, to create a vacuum in the working cylinder, it allowed the working cylinder to remain hot and thus saved energy, speeding up the action of the engine. Many more improvements were added by Watt in the coming years. Matthew Boulton and James Watt prospered with their engines although they were never actually built by the partnership. Most of the parts, especially the cylinders, were made by others, including at a later stage, Carron Company, once the Works had learned to bore cylinders accurately. The Boulton-Watt engines were never sold outright but leased on a royalty basis which was one third of the saving made on fuel when using their engine as opposed to those of others. They also refused permission for other engine builders such as Smeaton, to modify their own to Watt's design with the separate condenser. Complete engines known as the "patent type" were made at Carron Works around 1795 but these may have been manufactured under licence to Boulton and Watt, as their patent did not expire until 1800 [the original patent of 1769 was extended]. It has been said that Roebuck sometimes hindered Watt in his quest, but this is not borne out by the evidence provided by Watt himself. In a letter written years later quoted by Robison in *Steam and Steam Engine,* Watt says of Roebuck:-

> To his friendly encouragement, to his partiality for scientific improvements and to his ready application of them to the processes of art, to his intimate knowledge of business and manufactures, and to his extended views and liberal spirit of enterprise, must in a great measure be ascribed whatever success may have attended my exertions.

Dr Roebuck struggled on with the coal business for many years, being paid a wage for his efforts, and he also leased a pottery, founding the Bo'ness Pottery in 1784.[75] After a short illness, he died on the 15th July 1794; his wife Ann being left "unsupported". His body was laid to rest in the Carriden Churchyard where friends erected a tombstone inscribed with his virtues. The text ends with these words: "under this tombstone lies no ordinary man, John Roebuck MD". Historians remember him, not just for his connection with Carron Company which lasted only about 8 years, but also for his many other activities. His contribution to the mass production of sulphuric acid is said by some to have paved the way for the large-scale modern chemical industry. John Roebuck, along with Matthew Boulton and Dr Joseph Black were indispensable to James Watt in his work, which eventually revolutionised the industrial scene. A description of the "good doctor" was given in an article by M H Metcalfe: -

> He was a man of middle stature, square in frame without being stout, ruddy in complexion with finely modelled features, which a bright hazel eye made luminous and pleasant. Attired for the most part in faded black he, when at Carron, and not in chatty converse with the more intelligent of the skilled

workmen whom he brought there from time to time, was often to be found musing on the banks of the river Carron. Freemasonry took his interest, he was a member of Lodge Pythagoric at Bo'ness.[76]

Two years after Roebuck's death, a paper written by Professor Jardine outlining the life of his friend , was read to the Royal Society of Edinburgh, of which Roebuck had been a Fellow. It is from this that the assertions came that John Smeaton had been involved with Roebuck in the design of the early works in 1760. Although no evidence exists to confirm this, and it now seems highly unlikely, Jardine's order of events, that is the progression from the bellows to the iron cylinder blowing apparatus, is chronologically correct. Later biographers have not been so careful with this sequence, some even stating that the blast engines with iron cylinders were first used at Carron Works in 1760. It is probable that Roebuck would have known of him then, as Smeaton in 1759 had just completed the re-building of the Eddystone lighthouse, and had made many visits to Scotland since 1754. Some of these business visits were to Hopetoun House, Edinburgh and Dysart.

Of Dr Roebuck's brothers, Ebenezer was killed in an accident at Carron Works in 1771 when a large piece of iron fell on him. At the time of his death, he was in debt to Francis Garbett & Co. to the sum of £5145; from Bills of Exchange drawn upon him by Dr Roebuck and Thomas Roebuck and accepted by him. Thomas became bankrupt in 1772 but Benjamin continued to have an interest in the Company. In the 1780s, his son Benjamin Roebuck junior, became a partner and remained as such until 1795.[77] More than ninety years passed before Carron Company remembered 'the Doctor' in a tangible way, when three newly built villas at Goshen were named "Roebuck Park". Dr Roebuck had six children, three of whom were the progenitors of branches of the family, far from Bo'ness. Josiah went to Yorkshire, Ebenezer to Canada and John went to Russia. The others were Benjamin, David and Elizabeth.

As far as can be ascertained, no portrait or sketch exists of Dr. Roebuck. However, a sketch of his friend Dr Joseph Black was executed by John Kay of Edinburgh in 1787 and may provide a clue to his appearance. In this sketch, which appears to be allegorical, Black is portrayed contemplating the ragged end of a wall. On closer inspection, this irregular formation appears to be constructed from the silhouettes in profile of seven faces. In the biographical notes, which accompany Kay's portrait, reference is made to Joseph Black's closest friends, of whom there were seven; one was Dr Roebuck who may be represented in the sketch. Around 1912, Henry M

The grave of John Roebuck in Carriden Churchyard

Cadell of Grange, a direct descendant of Roebuck's old partners at Carron, through the auspices of Thomas J Salmon of Bo'ness and two academics in Edinburgh, C.A. Malcolm and James Hill, had the Latin text on the tombstone translated.[78] This was for publication in his book, *The Story of the Forth*, in which he also revealed that years later, valuable seams of blackband ironstone were found on the Roebuck's old property. Twenty years later , due to the diligence of George Pate of the Company with the assistance of H M Cadell, the memorial was restored at the expense of descendants of Dr Roebuck and by Carron Company.[79] At the time, Mr Cadell had a reappraisal made of the translation of the text by Messrs. Gray and Robertson of Bo'ness Academy, who corrected some errors. The stone itself was dismantled and taken to Glasgow where the inscription was re-cut by Messrs Scott & Rae, who later re-installed it in its restored surroundings.[80]

Despite the early loss of Roebuck's influence, and all the technical and other difficulties, Carron Company had survived its first troublesome decade and was by 1770 a well established manufacturing and trading concern. But many problems remained and finding solutions to them would soon become the responsibility of the remarkable Charles Gascoigne.

CHAPTER 3

From Carron to Russia - the Gascoigne Years

Charles Gascoigne was one of the sons of Captain Woodroffe Gascoigne, reputedly of Parlington in the Parish of Barwick-in-Elmet in Yorkshire[1]; however, the connection with this Yorkshire family has been exceedingly difficult to ascertain. The Christian name Woodroffe[2] may have come from Ellis Woodroffe of Hope, County Derby, whose daughter married into the Gascoigne family of Parlington.[3] Captain Gascoigne was an officer in the British Army and is known to have served as a Lieutenant in General Henderson's Regiment, which was stationed at Inverness in 1744, where his daughter Primrose Elphinstone was born.[4] Charles' mother was Grizel, eldest daughter of Charles, ninth Lord Elphinstone and she was born at Elphinstone Tower near Airth in 1704. Charles Gascoigne is thought to have been born around 1738; he later secured employment with the East India Company, courtesy of his grandfather Lord Elphinstone. He is reputed to have made the acquaintance of Samuel Garbett in London in 1757; Garbett, in his role as a merchant, had apparently supplied the Gascoigne household with goods such as candlesticks and dinner plates. It has also been suggested that it was Garbett who found him a position as a joint partner in a firm of drysalters in London, known as "Messrs. Coney and Gascoigne". Gascoigne's partner was one Bicknell Coney, and his half share in the business cost him £1,200[5]. The following year, he took the lease of a house and premises in Fenchurch Street, and his father laid out a sum of money for "building a stack of warehouses"[6]. He also had a one third share in another company by then, called Jorden and Coney, for which he paid £1,126[7]. Charles was probably still living with his parents at this time, a comfortable lifestyle befitting the son of an 'Esquire'. This image, of the ambitious and courteous young man making his way in business, is said to have impressed Samuel Garbett and in 1759, Gascoigne married Garbett's daughter Mary at St Phillips in Birmingham.

Evidence confirms that even before the works at Carron had commenced, Gascoigne had maintained contact with his relatives in Scotland, the Elphinstones, who knew the Carron area at first hand. The family had lived at Elphinstone Tower near Airth until 1754 before taking up residence at Cumbernauld House and Charles Gascoigne, who had been a regular visitor to the house of his grandfather, would have been familiar with the locality.

It may be that it was Gascoigne who suggested the Carron site for the Works
to Garbett!

On the 10th November 1763, Carron Company or 'Roebucks, Garbett
and Cadells', took over the lease of the harbour at Carronshore
[Quarroleshoar] from Thomas Dundas and in that same year Samuel Garbett
feued land at Fulderhaugh near to the harbour, from James Goodlatt Campbell
of Abbotshaugh.[8] Here he built his "Chymical Manufactory", also known
as the Pitch House, for the production of turpentine, and to oversee this
operation, called "Samuel Garbett & Co.", he brought in his son-in-law.
Both Gascoigne and his wife, along with the Garbetts, took up residence at
Kinnaird House, the home of James Bruce. He maintained his business
connection in London.

Under Gascoigne's direction, Garbett & Co. soon diversified and began
to handle the freighting of some of the goods from the ironworks, eventually
building up a small fleet of ships. More and more Gascoigne took an interest
in the affairs at Carron Works, occasionally suggesting to Garbett ways in
which he would improve matters there, much to the chagrin of the other
partners. Charles Gascoigne's only son, also Charles, was born at Kinnaird
House on the 16th February 1765; he also had three daughters, the eldest
born in 1760 at Edinburgh.

From the time that his son-in-law [he was always regarded as a son]
arrived in the neighbourhood, Samuel Garbett had tried to secure a
partnership for him in the ironworks, but the other partners had "absolutely
objected" to this. However, with some difficulty, in 1765, Garbett obtained
their consent, "and by a separate instrument" he sold Gascoigne one of his
own shares.[9] That year, Gascoigne took over the lease of the harbour at
Carronshore from Carron Company, with most of the business from this
busy little port coming under his control.[10] Apart from a small lease still
held by Carron Company and another by the former harbourmaster Alex
Fiddes, he held the monopoly; this angered the local shipmasters who were
required to pay more in harbour dues and who lost business to the Garbett
ships.[11]

When Garbett was absent from Carron, as he was frequently, Gascoigne
was left there as his representative, such was his father-in-law's admiration
for him. He even tried to persuade Cadell junior to allow him to sell Kinnaird
coal in London through his own account instead of the usual channel of the
London agents; this was at first vetoed by Garbett, who thought it unwise,
but he later relented and agreed to the proposal.[12] Another early move by
Gascoigne was to have the Company's insurance transferred to another firm,
which was done with the approval of the other partners, including William

Cadell junior.[13] It became increasingly clear to Charles that there could be a future for him at the ironworks and not at Carronshore, where in 1767, when Garbett's son Francis entered the business, the name was changed to "Francis Garbett & Co."; proof, if it was needed, that Garbett's son would always come first. This may have been one of the reasons for Gascoigne's cold treatment of the Garbett family later.

At Carron, Charles Gascoigne never missed an opportunity to discredit some of the other partners in his father-in-law's eyes. He had also "for many years complained, in the most bitterest terms, of Mr Cadell being allowed to act as manager, and urged the necessity of dispossessing him of that station".[14] But, officially at least, Gascoigne and the other partners, including William Cadell junior, were quite amiable to each other. One event, although not of his doing but which suited his schemes, was the departure of Dr Roebuck. Gascoigne advised Garbett to break his business ties with Roebuck, to avoid being linked to someone in financial difficulties.[15] Roebuck's shares, with the exception of one which had been promised to John Minyer [one half went to Minyer (pronounced Minheer), the other half to Ralph Lodge], were 'unofficially' transferred to Garbett in 1766 to avoid public suspicion.[16] Roebuck was later given the option of being able to re-purchase them at an agreed price, if his affairs improved. The fact that Dr Roebuck was no longer a partner, was not disclosed to the others until 1768, when his letter of transference of 1766 was handed to William Cadell junior. At the first meeting of the General Court, one day later after it had become known, the other partners found difficulty in grasping the fact that Roebuck's name was not recorded as being present, even although he was in the room.[17]

The Cadells, like the others had been required to put more and more of their money into the concern as it grew, quicker than had been realised at the outset, and this put a considerable strain on their resources. Over the years, the capital had been increased from the original £12,000 in 1759, to £80,000 by 1768.[18] In 1769, Garbett, owing to his and the Company's worsening financial position, made a 'call' on the other partners for more money to save the business. Instead of complying with this request, William Cadell junior informed Samuel Garbett that he wished to sell his shares, but was promptly told that no one would buy them with the business in the way it was. Garbett also warned that it would harm the Company's reputation if it was known that the residing partner was offering his stock for sale. Cadell junior felt himself ill-used after all his efforts and voluntarily resigned from the management that year, his position being taken by Charles Gascoigne. His resignation was not it would seem, primarily due to Gascoigne, but to

Charles Gascoigne

the continuing state of the business and the need to provide even more money. An incomplete report[19] on the state of the Works, the finances and the inadequate water supply etc., was written that year. The identity of the author is not disclosed, but he was obviously someone close to one of the partners: "the Stake my Father's Family hold in the works." If this review had indeed been delivered to the partners, it may have been the straw that broke the camel's back, as far as William Cadell junior was concerned. Whilst the author did not condemn Cadell's management, he devoted almost half of his discourse to the need for a new manager: -

> The Business of Carron Company may ably be called a Machine, which is large and unwieldy, without perpetuity of Motion in itself and therefore like every other Machine I'm fully satisfied cannot move justly in Time or Order without a main Spring or Regulator.....The Powers of the Company be vested in a Single hand, by and thro' whom they shall act in their Co-partnery capacity....Who ought to be so entirely independent of each partner as an Individual.

As the new Manager, Gascoigne first turned his attention to the financial stability of Carron Company, arranging for loans from various sources in an attempt to keep the concern afloat. In August 1770, William Cadell junior proposed to sell his Carron Shares again[20]:

[To] *William Cadell snr.*

> I still think it very much for the ease and Happiness of our family to be free of one fourth of our concern at this place, if it can be done on any tolerable Terms.........as the defence of our Property is of such material consequence to the Welfare of our family".

> W. Cadell jnr. August 1770

William was becoming increasingly remote from his involvement in the Works. A disagreement with some of the other partners over the use of his recently acquired land at Banton, hinted at in the letter to his father, prompted the sale and not primarily the influence of Gascoigne. How he felt at that time can be seen from another of his letters: -

I have for many years made myself a slave, spent my money and neglected my family affairs to save Carron and its partners from ruin. I shall continue to give all attention to its welfare, though I will not neglect my family affairs in the manner I have done.

Prior to December 1768, the new partners who had come in since the first establishment were:

Adam and Thomas Fairholme [who had been given shares as security against a loan, but had become bankrupt, the shares then being held by the Trustees of their Creditors], John Cadell, Ralph Lodge and John Minyer [both attorneys at law, of Grays Inn, London], Francis Garbett, Charles Gascoigne and John Adam; although there was no mention of Tibbats, who had bought a half share from Garbett in 1767.

Until then, the share holding had still been in 24 parts, with Gascoigne holding five.[21] By 1770, the shareholding was in 26 parts and the Cadell Family are shown as having 4/26th.[22] They are not down as individuals , that is, as William senior, William junior and John, but as - "William Cadell & Sons".[23] As can be seen from William junior's letter to his father in August 1770, he was proposing "to be free of one fourth of our concern in the place". That is, a 1/26th share, and it was this 1/26th share that was intended, in November of that year, to provide William with the means to obtain the iron mill at Cramond which had become less important in Gascoigne's plans.[24] At the same time, *New Articles of Co-Partnery* were drawn up extending the existing arrangements to 99 years from Martinmas 1770 and fixing the capital at £150,000, consisting of 600 shares of £250 each.[25] Ten shares, entitled one to become a voting partner subject to election, whilst sons of voting partners with the requisite amount of shares had the automatic right. Also, the name of Carron Company, used for many years, was officially adopted. However, one of the clauses of this updated Co-Partnery excluded partners from having conflicting interests to that of the Company, that is private dealings in coal and iron [this would be changed in 1903]. The Cadells refused to agree to this and would not add their names to the Articles because, in 1767, William had purchased property at Banton where rich seams of coal, and later ironstone, were found. Some of the Carron partners were to investigate the effect that this might have on the operation at Carron, and this action further alienated the Cadell family, provoking William junior into offering his share for sale. The three Cadells eventually had their names on this document when it was ratified in 1771; their objections resolved by arbitration, following a proposal from William junior. He suggested that he be given the iron mills at Cramond in return for his 1/26th share of Carron Company stock[26]; this was agreed and in addition he paid £10,585 2s 1d for the stock of bar iron, iron hoops, rod iron and nails held there.[27]

In 1772, Francis Garbett & Co. collapsed with debts of £193,054.[28] By circulating bills under the guarantee of Francis and Samuel Garbett, in which Carron Company and Garbett & Co. drew money from each other, and also by giving financial help to certain partners, Gascoigne had involved his father-in-law in personal debt of £100,000. He had kept Carron Company and some of his friends afloat, at the expense of his father-in-law, although he casually blamed the mishap on the state of the markets. Samuel Garbett's business affairs were so complex that he had no idea that all had not been well. Gascoigne, who was surprisingly appointed Trustee of the Creditors of Francis Garbett & Co., was to repay the debt to the creditors at 20% per annum, but only one of these payments was ever made.[29] That August, he wrote a letter of his intentions to the Standing Committee of partners at Carron:

> I need not tell you how much I suffer nor express the regret I have felt for the Suspicions and Dishonour that must have been thrown on the Carron Company from the Difficulty of distinguishing between the two Companies....I have come to the first Resolution to give up all other connections whatever that can employ any considerable portion of my Time or that can bring me under any possible future predicament.[30]

He also informed them that he had begged the creditors of Garbett & Co. to relieve him of his position as trustee, so that he could follow the business of Carron Company without molestation. (He was eventually replaced as Trustee in 1776 by William Anderson WS, who was himself succeeded in the role by Walter Hog in 1781.) Charles Gascoigne's lifestyle from then on was precarious, always attempting to keep one step ahead of the creditors. He was once arrested in London for a debt due by Garbett & Co., but the creditors in general thought that it would be highly detrimental to all concerned to bring the Carron stock and shipping concern to sale, at the time[31]. He also moved from his residence at Carron House and later rented a house in New Street Edinburgh. The relationship between Gascoigne and Garbett deteriorated completely, but surprisingly, Garbett still continued to give Gascoigne his proxy vote at Meetings of the General Court. The shipping

The original main gate, office and manager's house

side of Garbett & Co. was continued under the trustees until 1778, when its ships were sold to the Carron Shipping Company owned by Gascoigne's cousin, the Honourable William Elphinstone. Elphinstone was persuaded to buy these ships by Gascoigne, who promised Carron Company business. In that same year of 1772, William Cadell senior transferred 12 of his shares to William junior, out of a total of 37/600 which William Cadell & Sons then held under the arrangement of the new Co-partnery, that is, the new modelled shares.[32] William Cadell junior again became a partner.

Away from the financial wheeling and dealing, Gascoigne as the new manager, began to institute a series of initiatives at the Works. One scheme which attracted his attention, as it had his predecessor, was the need to encourage the workers to build their own homes, giving them an incentive to remain at Carron. In 1772, he communicated to the partners his idea to make land available, "in the field to the east, and north-east of the works". The field to the east, is what became known as "Carron Inns" or "East Carron", with its small rows; the land to the northeast around the Stenhouse Mill, eventually became Kirk's Land and Cooper's Land.

As the fame of the works began to spread, many people of note made a point of altering the itinerary of their 'grand tour' to visit Carron and one such person was the eminent American inventor and politician Benjamin Franklin, who came to Carron in 1771. In his wake, there appeared on the list of the Company's goods, "Dr. Franklin's Stoves", or "Philadelphia Stoves", but whether these were designed by Franklin or made as a tribute, is not known. A visit to the Works then could also be an excuse for more sinister activities; for in those days there was no stout enclosing wall, with "stragglers" apparently coming and going as they pleased. The problem was addressed by the manager and several remedies were put into effect. Access to the Works from Carronhill was secured, by having a lockfast gate built at the bridge used by Mrs Cadell, "who often liked to stroll down from Carron Park and walk beside the reservoirs". Much pilfering was in evidence as well as the direct theft of goods and in 1772, Gascoigne had the Works made more secure by having the open spaces between buildings on the periphery walled up and having the place patrolled twenty-four hours of the day. Simultaneously, he laid down the rules for visits to the Works and these appeared in the form of an advertisement, in the newspapers of the time:

Carron Works, 21st April, 1772

We take the liberty of intimating to the public that we have given orders to our servants not to admit any persons to see our Works on Sundays, nor any other day without a ticket, which will be delivered at the Office to gentlemen from the hours of ten in the morning to two in the afternoon.....After this advertisement, we cannot hold ourselves accountable for marks of disrespect which may be shown by servants appointed to enforce this Order to persons who may intrude themselves into the Works without tickets.[33]

Some of these so-called visitors were engaged in industrial espionage, a common enough activity, also practised by Carron Company when it required details of a competitor's product or process. Under an arrangement devised by Thomas Roebuck, and advocated years before by William Cadell junior and Samuel Garbett, some of the partners were given the responsibility for various departments and one such charge was the new "magazine" or warehouse, built at a cost of £211, supervised by Ambrose Tibbats. Here was stored all of the goods that awaited dispatch. According to instructions from Charles Gascoigne, Tibbats was required to keep a record of the goods held there and in his Report Book[34] he described the prevailing conditions then. In October 1772, he wrote of his mortification at the disagreeable appearance of his last inventory [they were done on a monthly basis] and of how he expected the dissatisfaction of the "absent partners":

When I was requested to take the charge of the last iron warehouse I undertook it with great reluctance with the people then employed about it and the Warehouse Gard so much exposed to disorder and Embezelem which we are now almost every week convinced of especially in weight from the scales.

Tibbats was also to be paid £150 per year for his services. James Fish, the overseer at Kinnaird, was given instructions to inform "those people at the Kinnaird and Quarrole coallieries who filled the wagons"; that the gates at Carron would not be opened until six o'clock in the morning, in order to prevent the theft of coal. This would imply that those gates where the tramway entered the Works, had been opened at an even earlier hour, or were permanently open.

Gascoigne next instigated a plan to have the Company incorporated by Royal Charter and this document was drawn up by partner/attorney Ralph Lodge. It was given Royal assent in 1773 and it legally established Carron Company as a Co-Partnery, with powers to sue and be sued.[35] The Company was then able to operate as a company of today would, i.e. a company of limited liability. It also brought much prestige. As shown on the Charter, the main partners then were: -

Samuel Garbett	John Cadell	Francis Garbett
Ralph Lodge	Benjamin Roebuck	John Minyer
John Adam	Ambrose Tibbats	William Cadell snr.
James Balfour	William Cadell jnr.	Charles Gascoigne

The first page of the Royal Charter reads as follows:

> That the introducing and establishing considerable ironworks in that part of the United Kingdom called Scotland, being of no less public utility than national advantage, by giving employment to some thousands and, by extending the exports of Great Britain to Russia, Sweden, Denmark and many other foreign countries, although too great an object for a certain number of persons to engage in; a number of gentlemen, therefore, associated, and advanced in partnership, a capital sum of £130,000 and bound themselves to increase the same occasionally to the sum of £150,000; and they have carried on an iron manufacture thirteen years, under the name and title of "Carron Company".

It was Gascoigne who came up with the Company Seal of the crossed cannon, the Phoenix rising from its ashes and the motto, "Esto Perpetua", meaning, "be thou forever".[36]

Around this time, June 1773, the Cadell family sold all of their Shares of Carron Stock[37] which had been held as follows: -

William Cadell senior	13/600
William Cadell junior	12/600
John Cadell	12/600

The Carron Crest 1773

They were purchased by Ambrose Tibbats, who would later become Charles Gascoigne's main adversary.[38] In addition, the Cadells were granted a Bond of Relief and Indemnification signed by Gascoigne on behalf of Carron Company; this absolved them as individuals and former partners, from a Bond of £20,000 which had been granted by Carron Company to Messrs. Walpole, Clark and Bourne of London in 1769.[39] The Cadells' share of the Bond was taken over by the purchaser of their shares. William and John Cadell next concentrated their efforts in the Grange Coal Company near to Bo'ness and in this venture, they were eventually joined, by ex-Carron Company employees, John Beaumont and John Grieve. At one point, they were involved in a long legal battle over mineral rights, with their neighbour and old colleague, Dr Roebuck. In 1786, William Cadell junior and his brother-in-law Thomas Edington, formerly of Carron Company and the ironmill at Cramond, founded the Clyde Iron Works.

Whatever else may be said of Gascoigne, he faced many difficulties during the early years of his management and was able to overcome most of them. As to the financial state of Carron Company, he bought time, taking advantage of credit from a multitude of sources such as Douglas, Heron & Co. [the Ayr Bank] and the Royal Bank of Scotland. Not possessed with the integrity of his predecessor, he was probably more ruthless when it came to dealing with poor workmanship and bad servants; he had a will to succeed, especially if he stood to reap the rewards.

In the early 1770s Carron Company's cannon manufacturing abilitiy began to be seriously questioned, though there had been complaints from as early as 1766. The standard of Carron guns did not improve and by 1771, the Board of Ordnance was growing increasingly worried by their performance.[40] One at least of the Board's old suppliers, Rose Fuller of the Sussex firm of gunfounders, was wise to the fact that problems were now being experienced with Carron supplied guns and saw the possibility of having his contract restored, but on his terms; the Board in the past had not always been noted for paying on time.[41] Various excuses were sent from Carron such as "a servant has taken leave of his senses." and Gascoigne resolved to improve production. Matters came to a head in 1773 with the Board of

Ordnance having their brassfounder Verbruggan make an assay of the Carron metal which he found to have been badly refined.[42] When tests were made at Woolwich, it was the Company which was obliged to pay for them. The Company was also told that they would no longer make long guns for the Government and that Carron guns would be systematically removed from all ships of the Navy.

With this great loss, markets had to be found elsewhere and at the same time an effort was made to improve the product. New customers were found in Denmark and the Netherlands as well as at home where privateers were sold Carron long guns. The East India Company first took Carron guns in 1773, although Francis Garbett had made the acquaintance of three or four of that company's directors earlier in 1765 in Copenhagen; he thought then that Carron Company would stand a good chance of receiving orders for guns.[43] In that same year, 1773, an order came from Russia and the Company advertised on the 9th of July[44]: -

> Wanted, a vessel of about 120 tons for transporting Cannon to St Petersburgh. The guns are ready, and proposals directed to Carron Company, at Carron, will be punctually answered.

One hundred and sixty tons of cannon were dispatched on board the 'Christian' of Airth under Captain Patrick Cowan of Powside, some of the guns being loaded at Carronshore and the remainder at Greenbrae, in deeper water.[45] Large numbers of guns were sent to Spain after 1773 [although some had been sent there previously] with one James Goold acting as intermediary and later a ship known as 'The King of Spain' was used for this trade. Some time later Goold, who was the Company's agent in Ferrol, took legal action against Carron Company for non-payment of commission. Carron Company of course disputed this claim and began a counter-claim against Goold.[46] The argument hinged on the fact that Goold had misled Carron Company on the method of proving the Carron guns in Spain. The Spanish had used a more rigorous method of testing, or proving, which led to the failure of many of the guns sent there. It was only when William Lowes was sent to Spain to investigate the high rate of failed guns, that it was discovered that the proving method in Spain was more severe than that expected or carried on elsewhere. Also, when Carron Company later changed over to the method of casting guns solid, the Spanish had objected, saying that their contract stated that the guns were to be supplied "con alma", that is, guns cast around an iron bar coated with clay, "the old way". These problems had arisen, according to the Company, due to a poor translation of the contract, which had been supplied by Goold. Carron Company had lost many guns and revenue due to Goold's negligence, hence the refusal to pay commission.

At the Works in 1771, a new cannon boring mill designed by John Smeaton had been erected, but achieved little. It was the practice then to cast the guns hollow, around a central core or newel and to bore and finish them on this machine. Smeaton's device performed reasonably well, but was far from the answer. In October of that year, William Lowes sent this report to the Standing Committee[47] : -

> In the course of assaying, the following Ideas and Observations occurred to me. I am Opinion that We ought to have a chemical Analysis of every Ironstone in Use at Carron, that their component parts may be distinctly known and some Principles established which may be applied to the Blast Furnaces, in order to arrive at an uniform regular Quality in the Metal. The Ideas of Metal adapted to the Different Purpose of Cannon, Sugar pans etc. must be fluctuating, While We are labouring in the dark, ignorant of first Principles and Causes. The Quality of our different mines should be ascertained by smelting them singly.

The idea was there in 1771, but it was not until 1774 that a new assay furnace was built on the site of the old boring mill, allowing the different types of iron produced to be analysed as suggested by Lowes. Part of the blame for this inferior metal was levelled at the ironstone from Dysart and it was decided to dispense with that source. The English ironmaster John Wilkinson invented a machine which bored guns cast solid at his Bersham Works around 1774, and samples of these guns were tested at Woolwich by Verbruggan. He discovered that with guns made this way, the grain of the metal remained more compact, his findings leading the Board of Ordnance to accept only guns made and bored "from the solid". Even although Wilkinson had been granted a patent for his cannon-boring mill [No. 1063], Carron Company and others copied it.

The only known description of this device at Carron comes from an article written in 1818 of a visit made to the works by the Archdukes of Austria in 1815:[48] "the gun is placed in a horizontal position; the borer lies on a carriage, which is advanced towards the cannon; the latter turns round its axis without advancing". It was the ancestor of the modern day lathe. Wilkinson succeeded in preventing some companies from selling guns made on his type of machine, including those who supplied the Board of Ordnance; he attempted to do the same with Carron Company, but to no avail. For many years, visitors to the Works were refused permission to see inside the cannon boring mill, which probably added to the mystique of the process, rather than protecting a great secret. The cylinder-boring mill was apparently changed over to boring cannon, to cope with the demand, and a new mill for boring cylinders [the cylinder turning mill], was erected near to the blast furnaces.

At Carron, the means to produce a better gun had been achieved, by an improved quality of iron and by the new boring mill. In 1776, a lighter gun was being made; its weight having been cut to almost one half of that of its predecessor. Charles Gascoigne was able to say that they were now making guns of all sizes, as light as brass. These were the guns known as the "new light constructed guns"[49] and Gascoigne emphasised their lightness because this had been one of the main areas of complaint from the Board of Ordnance early on, when Carron Company was advised that their guns were too heavy, the mouldings too large and was warned to stick more closely to the "drafts".[50] (Cadell junior had even delivered a copy of the Board's specification to William Mathews in an attempt to remedy this.) The new guns were 'proved' at the Woolwich Warren on the 3rd of August 1776 at the Company's own expense and were to all accounts a success, but the Board of Ordnance was still not convinced. These products sold well enough, but it was the elusive order from the Board that would bring in the big money; the prohibition banning the production of long guns for the Government still held.

It was not until two years later, in 1778, that a completely new type of gun made its appearance at Carron. Gascoigne had some new guns fitted as an experiment, to ships belonging to his cousin the Honourable William Elphinstone. These were the four brigs, 'Glasgow', 'Paisley', 'Stirling' and 'Forth', all previously owned by Francis Garbett & Co., and others including Carron Company's 'King of Spain'. This appears to have been done without the knowledge of the other partners ["the absent partners"] because at a meeting of the General Court held over the 8th, 9th and 10th December of that year, he informed those present that he had constructed a very light species of gun, which he called a "Gasconade".[51] He said that they resembled cohorns and that they had been made on purpose to arm Captain Elphinstone's ships; they were very much approved of by many people who had come on purpose to inspect them and, if it met with the approval of the committee, he could receive a great many orders for them. The meeting, after due consideration, resolved[52] to authorise Gascoigne to accept as many orders for this new species of gun as he could make, but, they were in future to be called "Carronades". The resolution[53] in the Minute Book states:

The Light New Constructed Gun 1776 (above) and the Carronade 1778 (below)

as Capt. Elphinstone run the risk of the experiment of making these guns, he shall be charged for what are necessary to arm his vessels at the price to London Warehouse.

In other words, he would still have to pay for the guns used on his ships, but at a 'wholesale' price! The Carronades soon became popular, especially on smaller craft where, because of their size and lightness, they were easily manoeuvrable. The first order was made, on the 31st December 1778, by an agent in Liverpool called John Zuill & Co., a relation of Patrick Miller, of Mansfield, Hunter & Co., for 16 Carronades to arm a vessel named the 'Spitfire', a privateer of Liverpool. A subtle advertising campaign was embarked upon with the Company inserting in newspapers, details of successes at sea by privateers armed with Carronades. Eventually the Earl of Dunmore persuaded the King to order a thorough trial of these guns at Woolwich. They were accepted by the Board of Ordnance, but long guns of Carron manufacture were still being removed from the ships of the line.

One authority described the Carronade as follows:

> The Carronade was a short, stubby, thin walled gun with a relatively large calibre. It carried a heavier shot than cannon, but at a reduced range. The Carronades were intended to be short range "smashers", most effective at point blank range, about 400 yards for a 68 pound shot and about 200 yards for a 12-pounder. It used a smaller amount of powder than the cannon, but to greater effect. Unlike the cannon, most of the explosive charge was not wasted in 'windage', the space between the shot and the side of the gun. The small amount of powder used also had the advantage of ease of recoil. This substantially lessened the stresses upon its mounting and supporting structure. It was the first new gun invented since the 16th Century.
>
> Encyclopaedia of War Machines

Three men have been associated with the early development of the Carronade gun - Charles Gascoigne, Patrick Miller the Edinburgh banker with a taste for engineering inventions and Lt. Gen. Robert Melville, a soldier. The strongest claim to having invented the gun is thought by many to be that of Melville. He may in turn have got the idea for a short, large bore gun, from a paper written 30 years before by a Cambridge mathematician, Benjamin Robins.[54] Robins had published his theories on the flight of projected missiles and of the effect of larger diameter shot on the hulls of ships and other targets. It has been noted that a model of a Carronade inscribed: "Presented to Lt. Gen. Melville, inventor of the Smasher and

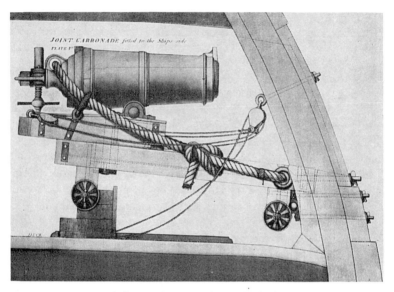

JOINT CARRONADE *fitted to the Ships side*
PLATE I

A Carronade mounted on a ship's side

Lesser Carronades" was supposed to have existed, which would have supported his 'claim', but it has never been found. Samuel Smiles writing in his *Industrial Biography* of 1863, stated that this presentation piece was then in the possession of the Melville family. However, Gascoigne and Miller, who had served in the Navy, also had fairly strong claims to be serious contenders, but no evidence exists to confirm or deny the true identity of the inventor, if indeed this can be attributed to one man.

Many of the early trials of the Carron guns took place on land not too distant from the works, at the Greenbrae Reach on the banks of the River Carron. Early descriptions show that this 'proving' would consist of rapid firing of about 45 rounds of shot, culminating in the gun being loaded to the muzzle with shot and powder, then fired. If it stood up to this, it had proved itself. Some old cannonballs have been found on the mud flats of the river near to this site. The guns were sold by the "pound weight of ball" and there were 12, 18, 24, 32 and 68-pounders. This product was the instrument which changed the fortune and credibility of Carron Company, but it was still at this stage, far from being fully developed. Its success was mainly due to the tactics then used in combat by the Navy - it was in the right place at the right time.

In 1773, along with the request for guns, Gascoigne had also received an enquiry regarding the supplying of a pumping engine for Russia; his correspondent was Admiral Sir Charles Knowles who had been seconded from the British Navy to the Russian Navy as part of a programme of assistance to the Empress Catherine.[55] He replied to Knowles' secretary James Keating, describing the existing "fire engine" at Carron[56] :

> The engine was constructed upon our own plan, but has been greatly improved by Mr. Smeaton..............she raises a column of water fifty-five inches in diameter, six and a half feet high so that the lift of each stroke of the engine gives four and a quarter tons of water.

At first, it had lifted less than 3¼ tons of water per stroke[57] and so Smeaton's improvements would account for Gascoigne's figures. An order was subsequently received to supply a returning engine for the purpose of draining the military docks at Kronstadt; the design for the engine, which had a 66 inch diameter working cylinder and known as the Kronstadt Engine, was entrusted to John Smeaton. The completed engine was dispatched in 1774, along with a supply of coal from the Company's collieries and some men from Carron Works to supervise the installation. Adam Smith, who had been involved with the pumping engine at Kinnaird fourteen years previously, was the engineer-in-charge of erecting this one in Russia. He incurred the wrath of John Smeaton and Gascoigne at Carron, when he began altering Smeaton's drawings.[58] Smith was also reprimanded for "drinking in the company of his workmen". In 1775, this operation at Kronstadt was being overseen by Knowles' successor Admiral Samuel Greig, a native of Inverkeithing, and it was completed by 1776, after a Russian workman had received tuition at Carron Works on how to operate the engine.

Sometime between 1776 and 1777, a Russian visitor who was actually an industrial spy by the name of Nikolai Ivanovich Korsakov, arrived at Carron and was politely escorted around the Works which by this time employed 2000 men but, as was the case with all visitors, he was not allowed to see the place where they bored cannon.[59] Korsakov had actually been in the vicinity, inspecting the Forth and Clyde Canal on the recommendation of John Smeaton, who probably also suggested the Carron visit. One addition to the Works that he would have seen was the newly enlarged 'Carron Dams'. The troublesome and unreliable water supply to the works had been prevalent in the minds of both Gascoigne and his predecessor; the existing resources had become totally inadequate as a back-up supply and the fire engine had only marginally improved matters. Various schemes were looked at but part of the solution was found close to the works; Gascoigne decided that a much larger reservoir was required at Carron. A hint of the impending work

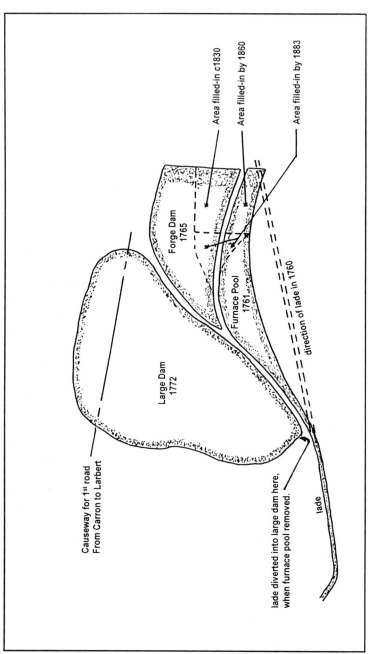

The arrangement of reservoirs at Carron

Causeway for 1st road
From Carron to Larbert

Large Dam
1772

Forge Dam
1765

Furnace Pool
1761

Area filled-in c1830

Area filled-in by 1860

Area filled-in by 1883

direction of lade in 1760

lade diverted into large dam here,
when furnace pool removed.

lade

appears in a letter[60] sent to William Cadell junior by a 'W. Lee' on the 20th of April 1772:

> I am directed by Carron Co. to acquaint you that in consequence of a resolution of the Monthly Committee of the partners of Carron Co. on Monday the 13th instant. That the low ground between your house and the forge pool will soon be inundated. Therefore it will be proper to remove the bricks with all expedition.

From the above letter, it can be seen that a reference was made to the "forge pool" and not the 'furnace pool'; the Forge Dam, the second of the reservoirs, was constructed around 1765. It is evident that the large dam had, by April 1772, been excavated, as it was about to be 'inundated', that is, flooded. The new reservoir was thus created back as far as Carronhill [the site of Cadell's house, Carron Park] on boggy ground; and the banks of the lade were also raised. As far back as 1760, Cadell junior had anticipated the need for constructing more reservoirs on this ground, to augment the 'Carron Pool' [furnace pool]. The arrangement of the three separate dams was adopted for a specific reason. When the Forge Dam was constructed, rather than just extend the existing Furnace Pool, a strip of ground was left, or thrown up between the two reservoirs, to provide a road from the works to William Cadell's house Carron Park[61]. Cadell was also allowed to take the soil excavated from the Forge Dam, to improve the land at Carronhill. The large dam was on average only 3ft. deep, but had a surface area greater that the other two combined; it was used to feed the others via sluices but did not reduce the head of water. A footpath or causeway which incorporated stepping stones, had to be laid across the large reservoir, giving local people a right of way to Larbert; it followed the route of the road proposed in 1765 and built soon after. The present day road around the dams, was built sometime after 1772, but before 1782. John Smeaton designed the convex damhead, built on the River Carron below Larbert Parish Church in 1772; it replaced an older one but carried out the same function, diverting water from the river into the lade.[62] It may have been built specifically to meet the requirements of the larger reservoirs, but it is known that the original 'ware' had been in a poor condition. Apparently, Smeaton had to wait for payment of his fee for this work[63]:

[To] John Smeaton.   7th July 1772.

As we shall soon have the pleasure of seeing you in Scotland - we will defer settling your bill until that time.

The damhead at Larbert required attention in 1789 and Smeaton was again consulted as to the design of a stone apron, the work being carried out by Thomas Bain of Bainsford at a cost of £400. In 1773, as part of another scheme to build a reservoir on ground bought from Spottiswood, the troublesome laird, at Dunipace, Smeaton built a damhead on the River Carron there at a cost of £517. Apparently, the water situation was looked at again by John Smeaton and by James Watt around 1776[64] and the outcome was that a new returning engine designed by Smeaton and similar to that sent to Kronstadt, but with a much larger 72 inch diameter cylinder, was erected about 1780 in place of the old fire engine. Charles Gascoigne was also said to have been responsible for straightening part of the river Carron near Carronshore further aiding navigation, but at least part of this had begun earlier under Cadell junior.[65] He did execute a new lease of land with Bruce of Stenhouse after the river had been straightened nearer to the works and was responsible for that section, the alteration aiding navigation on the river west of Carronshore where barges were still being 'tracked' to the works.

Another major initiative which greatly interested the Company was the the scheme for the 'Great Canal'. In 1764 Smeaton was given the task of completing a survey, and the first proposal was for a shallow narrow canal. Those at Carron, headed by Charles Gascoigne, pressed for the eastern end to be fixed at or near to the Works, but as interest in the project grew, the scope of the proposal changed in 1768 to cater for much larger vessels. Both Smeaton and another group, Messrs. Brindley, Yeoman and Golbourne, commissioned by Carron Company, agreed to extensive "cuts" being made between the Works and the Canal, but the latter gentlemen also suggested that the Canal enter the River Carron at the Greenbrae Reach.[66] Smeaton was opposed to connecting this larger Canal into the river at this point, where, in his view there was already enough congestion with ships waiting for the tide or proceeding to Carronshore, a situation which would be aggravated.[67] As it became obvious that the wishes of the ironworks were not foremost in the thoughts of the Canal Company, Carron Company had its own plans prepared which showed possible cuts or canals complete with locks, linking the river at the Stenhouse Damhead to the river at the Carronshore Harbour and to the Great Canal at Bainsford. These were sent to the meeting of the Forth and Clyde Navigation Company on the 5th November 1771.[68]

By 1772, after Smeaton's new boring mills and mill race were completed, Gascoigne had constructed two small canals within the works, connecting Blast Furnaces 1 & 2 and 3 & 4 with the Boring Mill and warehouse. They were used to transport goods to and from these departments. At the river entrance to these canals at the Stenhouse Damhead, two lock gates were built, in anticipation of the proposed 'cut' between the works and the Great Canal. At the time, he had surveyor Alexander Shepherd draw a plan of the works to show the improvements[69]. However, by April of that year, the plan for the cuts was no further forward and Gascoigne informed the other partners that after eight General Meetings and Committees of the Canal Company at which both he and John Adam had been in attendance, nothing had been concluded upon. It was resolved [Resolution No. 420] : "to empower Mr Gascoigne to stake out the line of the proposed cut, to prepare estimates of the expense and to receive proposals for executing the same." On the 16th April 1772, Gascoigne wrote to John Balfour in Edinburgh asking for the following advertisement[70] to be inserted "three times in the publick papers": -

Persons willing to undertake the digging and finishing the whole or any part of a navigable Trench or Canal may see the nature of the work and deliver their proposals in writing upon application at the Company's Compting house any day after the 1st of May next. Labourers already engaged with the proprietors of the Forth and Clyde Navigation or by the Gentlemen farmers in the neighbourhood will find employment for eight months certain upon application as above.

CG.

This ambitious scheme for the cut linking the works to the canal at Bainsford never materialised, but one was later made between the river and the Great Canal, or the Forth and Clyde Canal as it became known, and a weir had to be erected across the river, to direct water into it. A few years later, after disagreements between the Canal Company and Carron Company, it was closed permanently.

In October 1782, Gascoigne proposed to the other partners that a small canal be constructed between the works and the river near to Carronshore; it would utilise part of the mill lade which was the tailrace of the cannon boring mills. The idea had come from John Smeaton who suggested it could be made at small expense and with the assistance of a single gate [lock]. Barges were in fact already used in this mill lade, but only the smaller variety that had already been used in the river. They would be towed from the river into the Stenhouse Mill Lade and from there into the lade from the boring mill [the "miln race"] and then into the works. Shepherds's plan of 1772/ 1773 also indicates that a loading basin had been constructed inside the works, next to the mill race of the Boring Mills; goods could be transferred from the two small internal canals via this basin, to the lighters in the mill

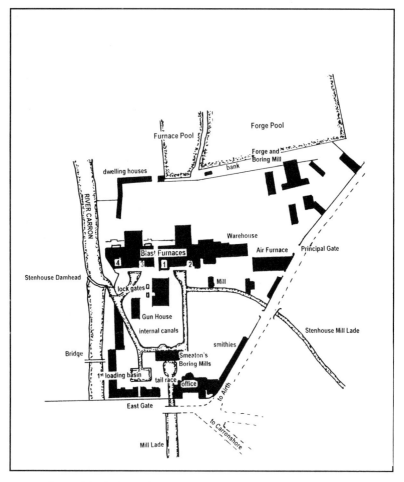

Carron Works in 1773 based on a plan drawn by Alex. Shepherd
at the instigation of Charles Gascoigne

race and vice-versa. The new canal, or 'navigable cut', began inside the
works at the tail-race of the cannon boring mill where a stone-lined loading
basin was built; it then continued along the route of the mill race to a point
above Carronshore where it entered the river via a lock. That lock was later
built of stone in 1824/1826, a fact discovered during excavations by local
archaeologist Geoff Bailey in late 1994. Barges of 40 tons burden were then
utilised, hauled by "well-built youths". By this method, goods were taken
from the Works to the harbour and the larger sea-going vessels.

Charles Gascoigne had, as did the others who followed him at Carron, a passion for acquiring property, the trademark of success. He once owned the farmlands of Tamrawer near Kilsyth which eventually came into the ownership of the Company, but nearer to the Works he was known to have feued the estate of Abbotshaugh, until at least the late 1770s. The house of Abbotshaugh, not to be confused with a later house of that name situated nearer to Dalderse, stood on the south side of the River Carron almost opposite the wharf at Carronshore, but the estate also encompassed the land on the north side which had been part of the Gairdoch estate or 'Lands of Gairdoch'. All of this he feued from James Goodlatt Campbell "of Auchline and Abbotshaugh", who was a grand-nephew of the last Laird of Abbotshaugh [or Ebishaw], James Goodlatt. Not far from the site of the old house of Gairdoch stands Carron House, built by Charles Gascoigne. Its purpose was to provide storage space and office accommodation for Samuel Garbett & Co., and private apartments for the Gascoignes. Carron House probably also housed the Garbett Family.

In 1776 the shareholders in Carron Company were as follows:

Partner	Shares	Partner	Shares
Samuel Garbett	96	Francis Garbett	55
Ralph Lodge	55	John Minyer	27
Benjamin Roebuck	55	John Adam	27
Charles Gascoigne	137	Charles Gascoigne	11
Ambrose Tibbats	54	William Lowes	11
James Balfour	41	John Balfour	14
Undivided stock	17	Total	600

The largest of the two blocks of shares in Gascoigne's name, were those held by the Trustee of the creditors of Francis Garbett & Co. and Charles Gascoigne, after 1776.[71] With the collapse of Francis Garbett & Co., both Garbett and Gascoigne had their sequestrations held in suspense, but Gascoigne was finally declared bankrupt about three years later.[72] During the period, around 1776, with all the uncertainty of the litigation surrounding Gascoigne and his relatives, the other partners took the unprecedented step of making the manager's contract renewable on a yearly basis - "That Mr Gascoigne be appointed Cashier and Managing Director for the year ensuing".[73] He was also "away from the works" on many occasions; for instance, in 1778, it was decided "In case of Mr Gascoigne's absence from the works, Mr John Balfour shall be empowered to sign the books and draw the money".[74] Another stated: "Mr Gascoigne's salary to be restricted to

£300/annum until a new article be executed with him."[75] At the same time, the General Court of Carron Company resolved [resolution 807] to accept the re-conveyance of Gascoigne's shares to the Trustee of his creditors, 37 shares having already been transferred to Ambrose Tibbats in Trust for Gascoigne's daughters. The Court also acknowledged that: "this would disqualify Mr. Gascoigne from acting as managing Partner.................which would be a great inconvenience to their business". By the following resolution [808] on the same day, the others had permitted him to buy 10 shares of unissued Company stock, thus allowing him to remain as a partner. The shares to be held by Carron Company in trust and as protection against predators. It will be observed that it was deemed necessary by the majority of the partners that Gascoigne continue as manager, even under the circumstances surrounding his private life. They needed his ability but not his liability and accepted the Honourable John Elphinstone's offer of £5,000 security for Gascoigne's management.[76] In 1777, Carron Company raised two petitions against Samuel Garbett.[77] The first was over a debt incurred by John Roebuck, of £4,000, which was said that Garbett had assumed when he purchased Roebuck's shares. The second concerned another debt, of £11,000, over the purchase of Dalderse Estate, which Gascoigne had persuaded the Garbetts to acquire.

In 1779, during the litigation, Gascoigne stepped up his assault on his father-in-law and circulated pamphlets to the creditors of Francis Garbett and Co.; it showed the state of the accounts between Dr Roebuck and Samuel Garbett and it also included private correspondence between Garbett's clerk at Birmingham, James Alston, and Roebuck's clerk at Bo'ness, Mr Downey. James Alston informed Garbett that these were "an abridged version of the accounts and that most of Gascoigne's statements were based upon hypothesis or conjecture"; he also apologised for his "accord". Amongst other accusations, Gascoigne alleged that Garbett had made a false entry in his books at Birmingham in order to give his accounts a better appearance and that he had also 'pocketed' £3100, by placing an additional value on the Prestonpans Works.[78]

Garbett's "Answers", on May 14th 1779, to the first petition took the form of a document running to 58 pages plus an Appendix of excerpts and copies of letters from and to Samuel Garbett, Charles Gascoigne and others, which added another 33 pages. Garbett opened with:

> The respondent [Garbett] would have been greatly surprised at the unjustifiable abuse thrown out against him, in a petition to your Lordships, signed by three of his partners in Carron Company, and at the extraordinary liberties they have

taken with facts contrary to evidence in their own possession, had he not been sensible of their deep connections with the real author of those atrocious calumnies, and acquainted with the reasons which they have, on that account, to give all the aid to such a cause, which can be derived from their names. The petitioners affect to keep Mr Gascoigne out of the question;

Garbett also stated that the petition had been taken out against him, in the name of Carron Company, when he and his family held more than half of its stock, so the respondent [Garbett] was made to be the chief accuser of himself. He then explained the facts, from his point of view, of his acquisition of Dr Roebuck's stock, the state of his accounts at Birmingham and Prestonpans, and the fact that Gascoigne had been lending money from his account which, along with other mysterious dealings had, he alleged, led to the collapse of Francis Garbett & Co. in 1772. Most importantly he showed that he had not accepted Roebuck's debt with the purchase of his shares. He also stated that he and his son had been forced to leave Scotland, by friends of Gascoigne, in an effort to keep them from discovering the true facts. The President of the Court of Session found Garbett blameless on the first petition, but on the second he proposed that all assets of the Garbetts and Gascoigne be put into a common fund for the benefit of their creditors. [79] As a result, Garbett transferred all of his property in England and Scotland to a trustee; he had previously dealt with his shares in the same way, in 1772. Samuel Garbett was eventually declared bankrupt in 1782, one year after it became public knowledge that Gascoigne himself had debts of £60,000. [80]

Away from the personal wrangles of the leading lights at Carron the business continued to develop with some of the country's most talented designers engaged to decorate the Company's range of products. Samuel Haworth and his father before him, were noted carvers in the City of London, carrying on business on a large scale at Denmark Street, St Giles-in-the-Fields. [81] Samuel employed about thirty assistants, many of whom were Dutch or Flemish carvers and his premises were occasionally visited by King George II. [82] He was invited by the Company to design and carve in wood, portraits of King George III and Queen Charlotte, to commemorate the granting of the Royal Charter to Carron in 1773 [83]; these were later cast in iron to decorate the Company's "fine goods". Possibly as a result of this connection, his son Henry Haworth was invited to come to Carron Works in 1779, the year in which Samuel died, to create carved wood masterpieces to be used as patterns and thus transferred into iron for dog grate recesses, hobs, panels and other ornamentations such as balustrades and balcony work. Henry lived at Forge Row, the residence of the 'aristocrats' or key workers

Willam Haworth   Henry Haworth

employed at the works then. His time at Carron was precious; he caught a
chill whilst attending a ball at Linlithgow in 1781, died shortly afterwards
and was buried in Larbert Churchyard.[84] In a Carron Company publication
of 1900[85], the author claimed that Henry Haworth had been responsible for
the design of the Bruce obelisk in Larbert Churchyard, but as this memorial
in cast iron was erected in about 1785, four years after Henry's death, that
work had most likely been executed by his successor. His place at Carron
was filled in 1782 by his brother William, a more detailed carver and equally
gifted designer. He too made his home at Forge Row where in 1802 his
annual rent including window tax, was £10, the top figure paid then for a
company house.[86] Both brothers, who were painters as well as carvers,
learned their craft at the Royal Academy in London under the guidance of
Sir Joshua Reynolds. William Haworth died in 1838 after 56 years service
to the company, and was also interred in the churchyard at Larbert. The
name of Haworth and their creations lived on at Carron for many years, as
can be seen from the Larbert Parish Records. At a meeting of the Carron
Friendly Society in 1888, attention was drawn to the presence of old John
Kerr, a grandson of the first William Haworth. His father, Walter Kerr, a
shipmaster who was lost at sea in 1825, had married William Haworth's
daughter Margaret in 1816.

Other creations by the famous Adam family of architects and designers
featured in the production of the well-known dog grates, matching pierced
fenders and mantle-pieces. The designs appear to have been sent up to the
works from London, brought by John Adam and carved by the Haworths at

Examples of the design work of the Haworth brothers

Carron. Many of the Haworth designs were still being used this century, incorporated into fireplaces such as the No. K4C 'Shrine' Interior Grate. Even Samuel Haworth's carvings of King George and Queen Charlotte, along with those of his sons, could be found on the No 318 Hob Grate, still available in the 1930s. At an exhibition of historic wood carvings held at the Victoria and Albert Museum in 1963, the Carron Company's Haworth carvings were proudly displayed. Many of these are now in the collection held by Falkirk Museums.

In October 1781, Carron Company intimated to James Bruce that they intended to give up the lease of Kinnaird Colliery.[87] Bruce agreed to take the farm and the colliery off the company's hands, on their paying him £600, rebuilding the house at Back-a-Dykes, returning his colliers agreeable to the lease and assisting in the removal of the nuisances from opposite his windows. This move may have stemmed from the fact that Bruce had earlier taken legal action against Carron Company for allegedly erecting the Kinnaird pumping engine in the wrong place, causing flooding at his pit. The plan [RHP 702] showing the position of the engine pit and the new road at Crosshillmuirhead etc. is dated 1779 and recorded as appertaining to Bruce's action against Carron Company. Bruce himself took over the running of the coalfields at Kinnaird for some years, but the lease eventually reverted to Carron Company. Likewise in 1788, the coal lease at Carronhall was surrendered, but as with Kinnaird previously, the contract was renewed later when Lady Eleanor Dundas entered into negotiations with Carron Company.[88] One of the reasons why the company bought so much land at this time, was for mineral rights, the land not necessarily to be used, but to make it clear to others, that it could be used, if required.

In 1784, Admiral Greig in Russia renewed his acquaintance with Gascoigne when an order for 432 guns of the light new constructed design, was placed with the Company.[89] A ship was purchased especially for this trade and it was renamed appropriately, 'The Empress of all the Russias'. By then, the Russian authorities had become increasingly convinced of the need to construct or improve suitable foundries for the production of cannons in their own country. Under the direction of the Empress Catherine, Greig was entrusted with the task of enlisting British expertise in this field and to that end, Russian technical specialists were sent to Britain, to Boulton's Soho Works in Birmingham and to Carron.[90] It was Gascoigne who was chosen to help, probably because he was reputed to be the inventor of the new Carronade, but more likely because of his past dealings with Greig. He was approached by Mikhail Stepanovitch Stepanov, a student at Edinburgh University, who acted as intermediary in negotiations between Gascoigne and Semen Vorontsov, the Russian Ambassador to London.[91] At first, much to the anguish of partner Ambrose Tibbats, orders were received for machinery to be used at blast furnaces in Russia. Tibbats, always suspicious of Gascoigne's motives, including the fact that he was also misappropriating money from the Company's funds, duly reported everything to his friend Samuel Garbett in Birmingham. Gascoigne's supporters within the partnership refused to believe this, assuming that the money had been borrowed and would be repaid; those same partners could see nothing wrong with this new Russian trade. It was only when plans for guns and gun boring equipment were sent out to Russia, that the Lord Advocate became interested enough to summon Gascoigne to appear before him to explain his actions. Charles Gascoigne was accompanied to this interview by his cousin Lord John Elphinstone. After confessing to his naiveté in sending 'sensitive' items for the manufacture of instruments of war to a foreign power, he was pardoned.

In March of that year 1786, the bold Gascoigne attended the wedding of his daughter Anne which took place at St Cuthberts in Edinburgh. She became the wife of Thomas Hamilton, 7th Earl of Haddington.[92] Hamilton, possibly wise to Gascoigne's status, refused to enter into financial negotiations with him, with regard to the wedding arrangements.

At a meeting of the General Court of Carron Company held on the 28th April 1786 under the chairmanship of John Adam, Gascoigne informed the other partners that in consequence of the uncertainty of his own situation, he had entered into a correspondence with Sir Samuel Greig,

> for going over to Russia to assist in Regulating the foundry of guns in that Kingdom.[93]

He continued:

> The treaty was now so far advanced, that I find it impossible, either consistent with the interests of the Company, or what I owe myself, to avoid going over there this summer.

He asked the permission of, and leave of absence from the Court, but he expected to return to Carron before winter. It was resolved[94] that Mr Gascoigne should leave for Russia to supervise the erection of the apparatus sent there from Carron Works[95], as had been the practice more than 10 years previously with the installation of the returning engine at Kronstadt. He left for Kronstadt in May 1786 on board the 'Empress of all the Russias', taking with him some 12 Carron workmen including one Charles Baird and another by the name of Alexander Wilson.[96] When this ship returned, preparations were at once made for another voyage to Russia with Carron goods. The Cadells, it is said, found out that more workmen from Carron were to sail with her and they informed Ambrose Tibbats who just managed to remove two of the Carron employees "by force", as the ship slipped its moorings.[97] They were Archibald and James Heugh who, along with Captain Andrew Strathearn, were charged with enticing away servants of Carron Company who were James Harley, John Eadie, John Swan and William Muirhead.[98] The Edinburgh Evening Courant made much of this incident:

> Too much attention cannot be paid to so dangerous a traffic, and it cannot be doubted that an immediate scrutiny will be made into this transaction, by the gentlemen to whom that business belongs, as the commerce and manufactures of this country will be most materially affected by it.

Strathearn had escaped with his ship and was declared a fugitive. Both Heughs were given bail and their case came up at the High Court in Edinburgh in July 1787. Neither of these men appeared and a sentence of outlawry was pronounced against them. Carron Company arranged with their agent in Russia to have this ship sold; six of her crew returned in

November, on the 'Jean' of Leith. Someone informed Gascoigne in Russia of this incident and he at once dispatched a letter to Carron:

> I hasten to assure you upon my word of Honour, I have no hand directly or Indirectly in the affair of Strathern .... he would not be the agent I would have employed .... had such a stratagem entered my head as that of seducing Carron Company's apprentices or moulders of any sort of denomination .... it would certainly have been gun moulders and men not Pot Moulders Apprentices and Boys that I should have pitched upon.[99]

He also expressed his sorrow, over the fate of the Heughs. Gascoigne and the others connected with aid to the Russians in the military sense were initially ostracised by the rest of the British community living there but this was soon overcome. By September 1786, Gascoigne was re-organising the Alexandrovski Works at Petrozavodsk on Lake Onega, on the same lines as Carron. He also built another factory of lesser consequence, at Mariupol, on the Sea of Azov. In November, Benjamin Roebuck junior received a letter[100] from Gascoigne which he handed to John Minyer, who put it before the General Court. Gascoigne stated how the Company had prospered under his management and that he had left it in good hands and: "It must be some years before Carron Company can get wrong again". In referring to his critics, he retorted that "even if those malicious Wights who have preyed upon my good name obtain their wishes of preventing my return. For my own part, I can live in any part of the world, and if it's necessary I can die here". He then got to the main point of the letter:

> you my dear sir [Roebuck jnr.] as the only Partner of Carron Company that probably can (and certainly is qualified) to come here and view things with his own eyes. If therefore your business at home will permit, and Carron Company agree that you shall come here for a few months next summer.

The partners found it unnecessary for Roebuck to go to Russia. For a while, Gascoigne was still 'represented' at the twice-yearly meetings of the General Court of Carron Company, courtesy of his 'proxy', which had been entrusted to John Balfour.

It was only after the Company's reputation began to suffer as a result of her Russian trade - the attitude of the general public towards Russia was changing - and when it was obvious that the manager did not intend to return, that all contact between Carron Company and Gascoigne ceased. It will probably never be known if Gascoigne's original intentions were to remain there; it might have been the opportunities in a new land or the threat of his creditors at home, or had it been due to "those malicious Wights"? His excuse for not returning as he had promised was that the icy winter had set in, preventing him from sailing. Certainly, from the tone of the two letters mentioned previously, it can be argued that here was a man who planned to return, being concerned enough about his reputation to take action - in the form of a denial of guilt with respect to the Strathearn case, and in the need for a qualified eye-witness as to what he was doing in Russia, as requested of Benjamin Roebuck junior. It has also been suggested[101], that Gascoigne's initial contract for his work in Russia indicates that he was dictating terms to the Russians, rather than looking for an easy alternative to his situation at home. Apart from his salary, he was on a percentage [50%] of production cost saving, over a basic level[102]. But of course this was Charles Gascoigne! He prospered in Russia and in the years following had many honours bestowed upon him by the Empress and by her successor. When he first went there, it was as a contractor; he ended his career as a member of the Russian Government, being known as 'Actual State Councillor' Karl Karlovich Gaskoin.[103] His salary in Russia in the year 1789 was £2,500, whilst the man who replaced him at Carron Works was being paid £700. He is said to have had a hand in every technological advance made at that time in Russia. Early on, the British government had fretted over the possibility of Gascoigne manufacturing 'carronades' in Russia[104], but it is interesting to note that for one who was reputed to be the inventor, Gascoigne apparently never attempted to make them there. He remarried after the death of his first wife Mary Garbett and died in St. Petersburg in 1806.

Back in August 1786, when the party from Carron Works arrived in Petrozavodsk , the Alexandrovski foundry there[105] was found to be in very bad order and the business in decline. The Russians were only turning out one good gun per week. and Gascoigne set about the task of improving this performance. Under his direction, Charles Baird was given the responsibility for the Blast Furnace Department. His brother James, who joined him from Carron in October 1787, attended to the erection of the boring mill machinery. The cast iron axle for the waterwheel for this mill had been made at Carron Works and this was coupled to five gear wheels, some of which also came from Carron, giving ten different 'movements'. After making some other improvements to the carriage, bar and cutter, James thought that this was the most complete boring mill in Europe. Of the 260 guns cast there in January 1790, only 7 failed at proof. At Carron, according to James Baird, where the machinery was pretty tolerable, a failure rate of 1 in 10 guns was regarded as accaptable. One test for the straightness of the bore was to insert in the gun, a turned cast iron cylinder 3 feet long and of a diameter one twentieth below that of the bore itself, that is the 'windage'.

By 1790, the Alexandrovski Foundry had 4 blast furnaces, an assay furnace, 7 air furnaces, a forge and a boring mill and was probably comparable to that at Carron. The blast furnaces used charcoal, which could point to a lack of coal in that area then; it may be remembered that coal had to be sent out from Carron to Kronstadt to fuel the returning engine of 1776. New blowing engines had also to be erected, as the Russians were still using the old bellows method, which had ceased to be used at the Carron Works almost twenty years previously. One advantage that these works had over their counterpart at Carron, was the greater availability of water. At the boring mill for example there was a fall of 11 feet, which probably accounted for the improved results there, compared with those at Carron.

Charles Baird and his brother James had obviously held important positions at Carron Works, within the Blast Furnace Department and at the Boring Mill, and it was no doubt for their skills that they were chosen to help at Petrozavodsk. Charles Baird eventually 'struck out' on his own, becoming involved with many undertakings including other foundries and the provision of steam passenger ships, the first in Russia. He, like Gascoigne, was honoured for his services.

In 1792, Gascoigne's cousins, the Elphinstones, tried to settle his debts with Carron Company and to this end they offered to sell his Carron Company shares which they, after an arrangement with Ambrose Tibbats, held in trust for his daughters.[106] This move was apparently blocked by Samuel Garbett, the grandfather of the young ladies. Of Gascoigne's family, Marie his second daughter, was married to Baron Poltoraski in Russia. She was in a delicate state of health, lonely and homesick and so wrote to her friend Helen Paterson of Carronshore in 1795, asking her to join her in Russia as a companion. However, before Helen arrived in Russia, Marie had died. Anne, after the death of her first husband, remarried in St. Petersburg in 1796, to James Dalrymple of North Berwick; still known as the Dowager Countess of Haddington, she offered her 12 Carron Shares for sale in 1825 and died in England in 1840. In 1803 in St Petersburg after only a few days acquaintance, Elizabeth Primrose married George Augustus Pollen who had previously been MP. for Leominster.[107] When the couple were shipwrecked off Memel in 1807, she survived, but George Augustus was drowned; his body was not recovered for some months and he was eventually interred at North Berwick. She died at Wimbledon in 1856. In 1920, in the Company's Shares Register, it was recorded that 12 shares were held by the "Trustees of the late Mrs Elizabeth Primrose Pollen", Gascoigne's last surviving daughter[108]

Gascoigne's son Charles is presumed to have died at an early age as no mention has been found of him beyond the registration of his birth. Gascoigne did on at least one occasion return to Scotland incognito, but was recognised by his old creditors at Tyninghame and was forced to flee back to Russia via Sweden.[109] As Tyninghame was the seat of the Earl of Haddington, it would seem likely that Charles must have been there to visit his daughter, the Countess.

After his death, Gascoigne's accounts with the Russian Government were found to be complicated and unsatisfactory and were only finally settled in 1825 when his daughter Anne petitioned the Russian Government who agreed to write off his debts to the Russian Crown.[110] She then arranged for his bankruptcy in Britain to be discharged. His career at Carron, especially with respect to the manufacture of ordnance for the Navy, was obviously greatly enhanced by his connection with the powerful Elphinstone family and in particular his cousins, William and George. William Fullerton Elphinstone had allowed Gascoigne to install the first Carronades on his ships, and he later became a director and sometime chairman of the East India Company, a major customer of Carron Company. George Keith Elphinstone "greatly distinguished himself" in the Navy and for his services was created a peer by the title of Lord Keith, and afterwards Viscount Keith. He was an Admiral of the Blue [third in seniority] and a member of the Admiralty Board. After the Siege of Sevastopol in 1856, Russian cannon, some bearing the name of Gascoigne, were taken as war booty and are now in Canada.[111] One however can be seen in England, at Ludlow.

With Gascoigne out of the way, Samuel Garbett renewed his direct contact with Carron Company as a partner [his shares still held in trust], until his death in 1803. Most of his time had however been spent successfully, in his hometown of Birmingham. Ambrose Tibbats, as well as being a partner, had also owned a firm of carters, "Ambrose Tibbats & Co.". He was given the business of bringing coal from the pits on the south side of Falkirk, to the works. As late as 1802, he was still a partner but was living at Aston Newport, Shropshire. He died in 1815.

When Gascoigne had first assumed control at Carron at the beginning of the 1770s, the works operated with 4 blast furnaces, each supplied with the cold blast of air from the blowing engines of Smeaton's design. These water-driven machines had four cast-iron cylinders, their outlets joined by pipe-work to produce a continuous blast. Smeaton further improved this blast by installing an 'air chest' between the blowing engines and the furnaces. This was a reinforced chamber of two sections, filled with water and acted on by atmospheric pressure, causing the air supply to become balanced or regulated. Gascoigne was at the forefront of 'water communication' and may be remembered for his many contributions at Carron such as the straightening of the river, the creation of the large dam, the two small internal canals at the works, the fight for the Great Canal, the cut between the River Carron and the Forth and Clyde Canal, and finally, the private canal or navigable cut. Water-wheels were in abundance - by the late 1780s there were no less than 18 of these - all taking their power one way or another, from the river. The furnaces themselves, of which two had been rebuilt in 1776 and 1777, were 45 feet high with open tops, the flames reaching heights of 10 feet. There was

> an open area of great extent built in the form of a terrace and on a level with the upper apertures of the fireplaces [furnaces], appointed to the reception of the supplies of ores and coal.

So wrote Barthelmy Faujas de St. Fond, French Commissioner of Mines, after a visit in 1784. With the creation of the Forge Dam, a new forge and boring Mill was erected to the east of the dam; it was here that bar or malleable iron would be made for the next one hundred years. Coke was processed in large heaps 60 feet by 15 feet by 10 feet high, there were about 12 of these 'coke fires', two being fired at any given time. The ore was also 'calcined' in the open, before the use of kilns for that purpose. This area was later occupied by railway sidings. These ores were stored in sheds, which are noted on the works plan as "shades".

In 1771, two new boring mills were erected on the east bank of the Stenhouse Mill Lade, both designed by John Smeaton.[112] One was for boring cylinders and the other, as noted previously, for boring guns. The years of 1774/1775 may be regarded as momentous as far as the art of boring is concerned, especially at Carron. Until then, at the cylinder-boring mill, every manufacturer had faced the difficulty of attempting to bore cylinders with parallel walls and with an accurate diameter. The two foremost exponents in this field were John Smeaton and John Wilkinson. The problem with both of their designs was that the heavy cutting tool which resembled an iron cartwheel with cutters placed around its circumference was pushed through the cylinder being bored, or rather, the cylinder was pulled into the cutter which was rotated by the action of the waterwheel. The immense weight of this cutter caused it to cut more into the lower part of the cylinder, giving an uneven form. Smeaton at first tried to solve the problem by turning the cylinder through 90 degrees every four cuts, but the remedy found was to support the cutting wheel at the opposite end of the drive, keeping its weight off the cylinder. Both men arrived at this solution, but in a different fashion. It was Wilkinson's machine that was used to bore accurate cylinders for James Watt's steam engines.

The Works then were still in their infancy and lessons were learned the hard way, as their more experienced competitors had done previously. By 1776, Carron Company had to some extent acquired the technology in making better quality iron products, especially guns. Also around 1776, the wooden trough which took water from the Furnace Pool into the works, was replaced by a stone version, at Gascoigne's suggestion. In the same period, another development took place near to the works at the Stenhouse Ford. This ford was the only means by which the Company's carts could cross the River Carron on their way to and from Falkirk, although a wooden footbridge existed a short distance upstream from the ford, according to an early plan[113]. Unfortunately there had been a few instances of drowning there and therefore it was decided to build a bridge. Some of the money required was raised by the performance of a play at the Theatre Royal in Edinburgh; it was organised and performed in, by one Nicholson Stewart of Carnock. Other donations came from the Earl of Zetland and Carron Company and the foundation stone of the triple arched bridge was laid by Sir Michael Bruce of Stenhouse on the 19th of April, 1775.[114]

All Carron business, until the re-organisation of the works in the 1870s, was conducted from an office, built at the time of Gascoigne[115]. "Office", was the description given to two entirely separate entities; there was the Compting House [Counting House] reached by a flight of stairs at the rear and there was the Manager's House, which faced the main road but was situated behind a small enclosure or court fronted by an iron railing. At Gascoigne's suggestion, the vaults of the Counting House were fitted with iron doors, to protect all documents in the case of fire. To the right of this enclosure was the main gate, which replaced an earlier one further south. Stretching into the works at this point was the Smithy Row. The surrounding area too was soon caught up in the activities generated by the ironworks. Opposite the works, the Carron Inn was constructed in 1777 replacing an earlier "Ale House" shown on a plan of 1763[116]; it was "built up and fitted out" at the Company's expense, a sum of £236-12-11d. A contract dated 22nd January 1778, was drawn up between Thomas Stuart (or Stewart) vintner and Charles Gascoigne for Carron Company, in which Stewart was to pay a rent of seven and a half per cent on the outlay.[117] He at one time had owned one of the breweries at Carronshore and may be the same man mentioned in other documents as, "servant of Charles Gascoigne". The Inn was purchased by Carron Company in 1792 for use as a bank, but reverted to its original purpose. Local tradition has it that here, "the King of the Potters" hired workmen with their contracts sealed over a dram. [Potter was the name given to moulders who specialised in making pots]. The Inn passed through the tenancies of Messrs Smith, Burgess, Horne and Aitken but appears to have ceased to be used for its original purpose on or before the turn of this century. It was altered internally for housing like so many other buildings in the vicinity. As late as the 1950s, according to a local source, the distinct smell of wine could be detected in the old cellars. An underground passageway was supposed to exist between there and the old stables. The fame of the Inn rests however with its most famous visitor of which more later.

Another attempt was made to find the elusive method of making malleable iron with coke and this time it was Gascoigne's turn, but he was no more successful than Roebuck had been. However in 1783, a man called Henry Cort, a contractor to the Admiralty, had stumbled on such a method using a reverberatory furnace. It was called the 'Puddling Process', and it utilised rollers to shape the metal, as opposed to hammers. He offered to demonstrate his process to many ironfounders, including Carron Company, with a view to earning royalties. At first, the offer was turned down by Gascoigne who thought that he had discovered his own method, but in 1786, he met with Cort in Edinburgh and it was agreed that he should come to the Carron Works, use Carron labour and pay for the materials used.[118] Cort's process was not adopted at Carron, being said to be "wasteful of iron", which it was. It was adopted by some, who made more from it than poor Cort did. After his death and the expiry of the patent, it was used by all and later improved by Joseph Hall in the early 1800s, who replaced the bed of sand used by Cort, with a bed of broken slag.[119] Hall's improvement considerably increased the yield, thus reducing the amount of wasted iron. As late as 1797, malleable or bar iron, was still made at the Works by the "Shropshire Process", which involved the use of clay pots which kept the iron apart from the charcoal used.[120] The metal was then further processed using waterwheel-driven tilt hammers, at the Forge Mill beside the Forge Dam. This mill was still shown as the "Malleable Iron Works", on the first Ordnance Survey map of 1860. It was demolished around 1873.

In 1760, part of the agreement between Sir Michael Bruce and Carron Company had allowed for the use of the Stenhouse Mill Lade. The Company was given permission to alter this Lade to their requirements and to utilise it for water power and for water transport. However, they were not to restrict the flow of water to the Stenhouse Mill. To what extent the Stenhouse Mill Lade was actually being used for then is difficult to ascertain, but it is presumed that some water wheels were installed, for the boring mill and forge. The spent water from the bellows wheel at the blast furnace went directly to this Mill Lade. By 1763, that part of the Stenhouse Mill Lade between the damhead and the road to Airth had been "arch'd over", that is, it passed through a culvert. This in itself points to the supposition that this Lade played no major part in operations at that time. The River Carron, east of the works, still meandered through two loops, as can be seen in Figure 1.

Charles Gascoigne can rightly claim the responsibility for most of the water communication projects in and around the vicinity of the works, and by 1772, he was at the height of his power in that field. The straightening of the river, by making cuts across the two loops already mentioned, had just been completed, as had the installation of Smeaton's new boring mills. To direct water to the two water wheels associated with these mills, the Stenhouse Mill Lade was diverted within the works - it has to be assumed that the early culvert of 1763 had been opened up for this purpose. At the same time, Gascoigne constructed two internal canals, to carry goods from the blast furnaces to the boring mills. The tail race from these mills was taken out of the works in the form of a mill lade, its waters joining the Stenhouse Mill Lade before it entered the now straightened river. It was soon found that it was possible for small boats or lighters to be used between the river and the mill race inside the works. However, a loading basin had to be built on the internal canal, and south of the mill race. Goods could then be transferred from the internal canals via the basin, to the boats waiting in the mill race. The details can be seen in Figure 2.

This arrangement was not totally satisfactory and may be regarded as a stop-gap measure, whilst Gascoigne awaited the decision of the Canal Company with regards to the Company's need for a cut or small canal between the works and the Forth and Clyde Canal at Bainsford. A cut was in fact made, somewhat further east of the works than had been anticipated, but it had a short life. In 1782, John Smeaton proposed that the existing Mill Lade from the tail race of the boring mills could, in part, be converted into a canal from the works to a point on the river just above Carronshore. This was accepted and a new stone-lined loading basin was also built within the works, the change can be seen in Figure 3. A plan dated 1826, suggests that a project was underway on the river below West Carron, and that the Stenhouse Damhead had gone. It is believed that this entailed the construction of the weir with its associated aqueduct or culvert into the works. To allow room for this culvert, the north bank of the river was gradually filled with slag and refuse and also used to support a new road to West Carron Village, completed in 1830. Within the works, what remained of the Stenhouse Mill

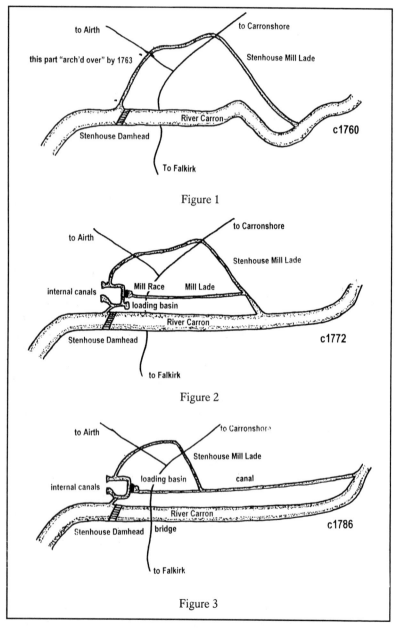

Alterations to the river , Stenhouse mill lade, mill race and canal at the Works

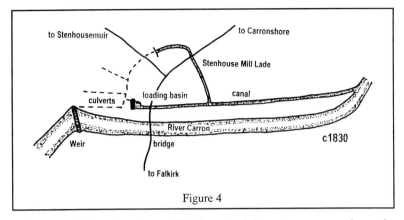

Figure 4

Lade, passed through culverts. The layout of the water courses shown in Figure 4 remained as such until the early years of the 20th century, when the canal and loading basin fell into disuse. The remainder of the Stenhouse Mill Lade was piped-in, in the early 1950s, and the canal met the same fate in the early 1990s.

Of the great engineers connected with the early development of the Works, John Smeaton of was the most important. Most of his work for the Company was executed within the first twenty years of Carron's existence and his advice was often sought - "we see and move but through you"[121]. Some of his achievements have already been touched upon, but there were others. It is apparent that he was first consulted by those at Carron around 1766, in connection with the new blowing engines. Smeaton was a master in the design of industrial water wheels, being at the forefront in the use of cast iron axles and gearing in the drive from the wheel. Six of his wheels were erected at the Works. A high breast wheel of 27 feet in diameter and an overshot wheel of 20 feet in diameter, were erected at the blowing engines; at the boring mill of 1771 he installed 2 lowbreast wheels, each of 18 feet in diameter and set in a divided water course[122]. Two, identical to those at the boring mill, were installed at the clay mill around 1777[123]. The type of wheel used depended on the type of work required and also on the fall of water available; for instance, the supply of water to the wheels for the blowing engines arrived at different heights, due to the topography of the site. The overshot, where the water entered the wheel at the top, only gave 55% of power, or 'duty'; the high breast, where the water entered slightly lower, improved on that. The low breast, or breast shot, where the water entered the wheel below the axle, was the most efficient at 80%. The water wheel was still used at the gun-boring mill as late as 1815 and at the cylinder turning mill until at least 1848, because it was reckoned that the steady motion of the wheel was preferred to that of the steam engine.

Five steam engines designed by Smeaton were built at the Works[124]. Three were returning engines (for Kronstadt, Carron and Chacewater) and two were winding engines (for Long Benton and Walker Collieries). The returning engines were all of a similar design, with the exception of the size of the working cylinders. The engine at Carron had a 72-inch cylinder which was 8 feet deep. Its 30-foot beam operated four pumps which raised 40 tons of water per minute from a depth of 36 feet. A tragic event occurred at that engine in April 1786 and was reported in the Edinburgh Evening Courant:

> On Tuesday last, a most melancholy accident happened at Carron work. The boiler of the fire-engine which throws the water back into the reservoir broke, by which two men were scalded to death in a shocking manner.

Smeaton's engines, efficient as they were, were only improved versions of the old Newcomen Engine. His last major work at Carron was the tilt hammer[125] for the clay mill forge, in 1785. An 18-foot diameter water wheel drove, through gearing, a hammer-beam crankshaft which powered three tilt hammers. John Smeaton died at his home at Austhorpe in Yorkshire, in 1792.

From the earliest days, the Works attracted the attention of travellers in Scotland who came in large numbers to witness the extraordinary sights and sounds of this new industry:

> We arrived about 9 at Carron and breakfasted [presumably at the Carron Inn] - Would my dear Miss P, it were possible to give you any description of the vast works which are carried on here, at all adequate to what we saw & heard - it would fill you with astonishment & horror as it did us.

These are the opening lines of a journal[126] written by Jacob Pattison, physician, after a visit to the works at the time of Gascoigne in 1780. Many descriptions of the early works were given in letter or journal form, by the visitors . The description of this lesser-known visit given by Pattison, is by far the most revealing: "Every person we met seem'd to have some congruity with the place - they were dark, gloomy & smelly." He recorded that permission had to be obtained from one of the 'directors' before being allowed to enter the place, permission, so he had been told, which was seldom refused. [That would not always be the case when, during the Dawson era, Samuel Smiles was told in no uncertain terms, that there was no time for that sort of thing at Carron.] A man attended Pattison, "thro' all the works".

He was firstly taken to the stores, where some of the general products such as boilers, cauldrons and pots were duly displayed. The sight of the cannons and carronades and the other instruments of death - ball, grape and cannister shot - filled him with horror. In particular, the star shot shocked him most of all:

> It consists of eight pieces of Iron adapted to each Star, fastened at one end and having knobs at the other, slightly connected by a fillet of thin Iron - each of these pieces is about 12 or 14 inches long - The knobs are closed and first put into the Cannon - as soon as they are discharged they separate, yet by the single, they whizz along & I should think would rarely fail of doing execution. We are told that they are now coming into Fashion and are charitably supposed to be used mainly for destroying the Rigging, the French may politely design no more - but the English are barbarians.

He had been informed, quite correctly at that time, that the Company had got into difficulties over the performance of the Carronades; this information had not been received within the works: "altho' we in vain endeavoured to get it confirmed". Jacob was then "fortunate" to see the casting of 32lb cannonballs. His description of the event is enlightening, but his fascination was confined to a man who was employed to "regulate" this furnace on a daily basis. This required him to enter the partially cooled chamber, still "insufferably hot",

> for 15/- a week, most of which money he is obliged to expend in liquor to keep any fluids at all in his body........his visage & appearance is that of a skeleton - his eyes are shrunk, his voice hollow.........he is very near dried up, & I think it is not difficult to foretell his fate - the heat will certainly one day catch him like tinder, or touch paper & crackling, he will disappear.

Pattison next saw the place where they cast cannon, noticing that the guns were cast in a vertical position. He was also told that these guns were bored by a method not long in practice [bored from solid] and as a result, fewer guns burst during proving. He joined another party of visitors making the same tour, but only he and one or two of the group were prepared to enter the building which housed the blowing engine:

> [We].....followed our guide up a dark entry, over bits of old Iron & cannonballs, & soon arrived at the bellows [sic], the noise of which prevented our hearing each other speak when near them.

There next followed a complete description of Smeaton's apparatus, which used four large cylinders of cast iron.

> This vast body of air is thus driven with the greatest violence into a tube of only two inches & one half in diameter, into the Furnace, with a noise that nearly stuns you.

Towards the end of his journal, he again returned to a description of the employees, which is not surprising considering his profession:

> the appearance of those within are truly diabolic, most of them half naked & as black as the region that they live in - they are said not to be long lived - this is little to be wonder'd at, as most of them seem half parched.

The unexpected departure of Charles Gascoigne was a major blow to Carron Company though the remaining partners probably found comfort in his assertion that "It must be some time before Carron Company can get wrong again." The business in the mid 1780s was without doubt in a healthier and more secure condition than when he had assumed control fifteen years earlier. By the time it became clear that he was not intending to return, his formidable successor was already in charge at the Works. That man was Joseph Stainton and he and his immediate family would retain control of the Company for the best part of the next hundred years.

CHAPTER 4

The Carron Family
Staintons, Dawsons and Maclarens

Joseph Stainton, reputedly a watchmaker to trade, came to Carron Works in 1780 from Keswick in Cumberland. He was born in the township of Underskiddaw, the first child of John and Ann Stainton; his father was a shoemaker to trade. Joseph was baptised at Crosthwaite Church in Keswick on the 23rd of November 1755 and it was at Crosthwaite School near to the church, that the young Joseph received his early education. He was one of seven brothers and sisters; the others were: John [b.1761], Dinah [b.1764], Ann [b.1767], Sally [b.1770], Betty [b.1772] and finally, Henry [b.1774]. After he left the Keswick area aged 25 years, he never returned and so nothing of him, his family or any relatives who followed, is known about by the people of that town. Carron Company imported iron ore from Cumberland from the earliest times and this may provide the connection. Another family from Keswick called Banks, were contemporaries of Joseph Stainton at Carron and it is possible that they arrived at the works at around the same time.

Joseph began life at Carron in the relatively lowly position of clerk in the Counting House, but must have quickly shown an outstanding ability. When it had been agreed that Gascoigne could go to Russia, the General Court of Carron Company resolved that

> The court having taken into account their most serious consideration the manner of conducting the Company's business during Mr. Gascoigne's absence .... to allow the present overseers still to conduct the business of their different departments. That Mr. Gascoigne should, by orders of the General Court give a power of attorney to Mr Stainton to conduct the business of the Compting House.[1]

Joseph was next given permission to "draw bills on London, Edinburgh and other places, including the Bank of Scotland" and then allowed to sign leases of Company property to others. He was gradually given the authority previously only held by the managing partner. Most of the other partners were obviously too involved with their own private affairs and were only too relieved to be able to hand the day to day business over to someone else. After having been at Carron for only six years, this was a tremendous

Robert Burns at the Carron Inn from a 1950's publication

achievement, but from other correspondence, it is apparent that Joseph
Stainton had quickly become the confidant of Charles Gascoigne, to the
extent of having knowledge of things far beyond the environs of the Counting
House. Stainton's first report to the Court informed them that he had executed
a lease with Sir Michael Bruce of Stenhouse for the privilege of getting
sand from Stenhousemuir and also that he would have to grant a contract of
excambion [an exchange of land] for the Club Room, with the membership
of the "Carron Club" [The Carron Friendly Society]. Subsequent reports
tell of how well the business was progressing! During the second year of
Stainton's 'temporary' management, arguably the most famous visitor to
the Works made his appearance.

   Robert Burns spent the night of Saturday 25th August 1787 at the Cross
Keys Inn in the High Street of Falkirk, where he is reputed to have 'scored'
the words of the following verse, on a window pane: -

> Sound be his sleep and blyth his morn,
> That never did a lassie wrang,
> Who poverty ne'er held in scorn,
> For misery ever tholed a pang.

This was "quoted from memory" by George Boyack in an article for the
Fifeshire Journal of 4th November 1847.[2] To "preserve some remembrance

of these lines", a friend of his, Adam Dickson, a Falkirk schoolmaster[3], thirty years previously, had incorporated the first two lines into a ballad. He stated that as far as he knew, this had never been recorded in any edition of the life of Burns.

The following morning, with his companion Willie Nicol, classical master at the Royal High School Edinburgh, Burns left the Inn early, stopping at the graveyard of the Old Parish Church where they saw the tomb of Sir John de Graeme, friend of Wallace. Crossing the Great Canal, they arrived at Carron. At the Works they approached the porter's lodge beside the main gate, but were refused entry. They had apparently made three mistakes; it was Sunday when visitors were not allowed into the Works, they did not have a ticket of admission and Burns himself was said to have used a fictitious name. Vexed at this treatment, the two men retired to the Carron Inn nearby, where Burns vented his fury by scoring a few lines of poetry on a window pane:

> We cam na here to view your works
> In hopes to be mair wise,
> But only, lest we gang to Hell,
> It may be nae surprise;
> But when we tirl'd at your door,
> Your porter dought na hear us;
> Sae may, should we to Hell's yetts come,
> Your billy Satan sair us.

All he recorded in his journal of the visit was: "Carron .... breakfast".[4] The room in which Burns dined was situated on the first floor and it was here that the poem was seen by William Benson[5] the clerk, brother of John, the blast furnace manager, and was duly copied into an order book. He was a clever and enterprising man who would later hold two company shares and part ownership of a boat called the 'Jamie and Jenny'. Benson penned a reply:

> If you came here to see our works
> You should have been more civil
> Than to give a fictitious name,
> In hopes to cheat the devil,
> Six days a week to you and all,
> We think it very well;
> The other if you go to church,
> May keep you out of Hell.

The porter was not to blame for having the two travellers turned away from the Works; he had only followed Charles Gascoigne's explicit instructions laid down in 1772 designed to make the place more secure. In later years tickets of admission to the Works could be obtained at the Carron Inn! The companions left Carron and made their way to the old church of Larbert. There in the churchyard, they saw the "fine monument in cast iron" erected over the grave of Mary Dundas, wife of James Bruce of Kinnaird , who had died just two years previously. The monument had been cast at Carron Works to a design by William Haworth. Burns may have been informed about this example of Carron workmanship by someone at the Carron Inn and decided to see it for himself; he did not have to stray far from his planned route.

On or about the 4th October of that same year, Burns returned to Carron, on his way to Stirling.[6] He was accompanied this time by Dr James Adair who later recollected that "We visited the Ironworks at Carron, with which the poet was forcibly struck".[7] He added: "The resemblance between that place and its inhabitants to the cave of the Cyclops, which must have occurred

The memorial raised by James Bruce of Kinnaird for his wife and which later marked his own grave. It was made in Carron and included a decorative panel designed by William Haworth. The memorial, which Burns visited in 1787, was refurbished in the 1980s and moved to a different location in the churchyard

to every classical reader, presented itself to Burns."[8] William Harvey, in *Robert Burns in Stirlingshire*, written in 1899, was in no doubt that Burns had been admitted to the Works during this mid-week visit. He also stated that one remark of the poet had been preserved: "The blazing furnaces and melting iron realized the description of the giants forging thunderbolts". This was the description given by Barthelmy Faujas de St Fond after a visit to the works in 1784. Strangely enough, Carron Company never tried to make capital from this second visit; in Company publications, for example in 1909, the two visits were confused or treated as one as one, with Adair accompanying the poet in August 1787. If Burns had been within the Works it certainly was not recorded, or perhaps not known about, by those in control at Carron.

In 1788, just one year after Burns' first visit, Joseph Stainton had his salary increased to £300 in recognition of his appointment as manager That same year, he bought land from Sir Michael Ramsay, son of David Ramsay of Lethendy, of Mungal House. On it he built Mungal Cottage and it would remain his home for the rest of his life. In 1791, he purchased ten shares of unissued Carron Company stock and became a partner, with his salary increased to £500.[9] At the same time, James Maclaren, a clerk at Carron and who later married Joseph's sister Betty, also obtained shares, but only managed to acquire six, four short of that needed to become a partner.[10] Stainton in his new position began to apply his skills to improving and consolidating the financial position and profitability of the works, personally supervising all operations from the birth of a new product to its dispatch. Joseph was often seen on horseback, galloping down to the wharf at Carronshore where he supervised the loading of the ships. He is accredited with giving the shareholders the best return on their investments, since the formation of the company. An advertisement[11] of 1788 proclaims the variety of goods available at the beginning of Stainton's management:

CARRON WAREHOUSE – To be sold at the Carron Warehouse in Queen Street, all kinds of Cast Iron Goods, manufactured at Carron, such as

Bath Stove Grates Box, Tailors, Hatters & Sad Irons, Pots and Pans, Cylinders and Camp Ovens, Bushes Barrs and Bearers, Girdles and Frying Pans, Doors and Frames, Smoke and Register Stoves, Skittles and Saucepans, Boilers, Kerbs and Drying Stoves of all dimensions, together with Tinned Tea Kettles, Goblets, Round Pots, Fish Pans and Stew Pans and many other articles. At the same place are sold, Oil of Vitriol, Aquafortis and Pearl Ashes of the best quality, together with Patent Liquor for the use of Calico Printers. Likewise London Porter either in hogsheads or bottles for home sale or exportation.

All of the departments within and without the works were scrutinised; no waste was tolerated, not a penny spent needlessly and the problems of theft and pilfering which so troubled Stainton's predecessor, were brought under control using his own special methods. Joseph would send his "beagles", a group of armed men, after known offenders who, if they were lucky might end up in jail.[12] On the other hand, they might end up on a 'man o' war' and never be seen again. Such was the power of the manager at Carron. One example from the year 1799 involved two apprentices, John Brooksby and Michael Bell, who having absconded from the works, were caught in Glasgow and thrown into jail.[13] It was only when security was found "for the faithful performance of their indentures", that a letter was sent from Stainton to the Lord Provost and Magistrates of Glasgow, requesting their release. In this respect, every workman or apprentice who entered the Company's employment had to sign a contract and this was at the instigation of Stainton. As an example, there was Charles Gascoigne Benson, son of William Benson the clerk mentioned earlier, who signed a contract to become a ships carpenter.[14] This was on the 28th April 1800: "bound as apprentice and servant to the said Carron Company......both by night and by day for seven years". This was signed by the apprentice, his father and by the manager himself. Interestingly the apprentices and workmen invariably signed their names rather than making a mark or cross, indicating that they had received some basic form of education.

Joseph Stainton has been described as an "awfu pushin man", but his epitaph said that he was "firm but kind". In 1795 he purchased the twenty Carron shares held by Benjamin Roebuck junior and this marked the end of the Roebuck connection with Carron Company.[15] He sold four of these shares to James Maclaren, who subsequently became a partner. It was then that Henry Stainton aged 21 years, youngest brother of Joseph, was brought to Carron along with his cousin, Thomas Crosthwaite. They both assumed the position of clerks and James Maclaren was later sent to Liverpool as Company agent, the first member of this 'family' to be placed in a position of importance. Joseph's other 'activities' have tended to overshadow the significant technical advances made during his period of management. For instance, the Carronade so often associated with Gascoigne, Melville and Miller, which started life as a simple but flawed design, was improved out of all recognition under the management of Joseph Stainton. He was also involved with William Symington at Carron , in his effort to design steam engines and to provide the revolutionary steam power to propel a boat.

Symington came to Carron Works in 1788 at the request of Patrick Miller, a director of Mansfield Hunter & Company who gave loans to the Company,

William Symington

and who himself had been a trustee of Dr Roebuck and reputedly had had a hand in the prototype Carronade. An engine was built at Carron in 1789, at a cost of £363-10-6d and it was installed on a boat at Carronshore. This boat had been provided by Miller and was named 'The Experiment' and was tried on the Forth and Clyde Canal.[16] Joseph Stainton and some of the other Carron partners witnessed that trial but Miller was not impressed and withdrew from the enterprise. Symington had various static steam engines built at Carron to his design, including three for Kinnaird colliery.[17] He also brought many orders for engines to Carron Works and was held there in high esteem. Later in 1801, Symington was asked by Lord Thomas Dundas of the Forth and Clyde Canal Company to build an engine for another boat, to be used on the Canal. As before, the engine was made at Carron and installed in the craft at Carronshore. It was successfully tried out on the Canal, but the Canal Company refused to allow it to be brought into service there, as it was feared that the wash from the paddles would damage the canal bank. The Canal Company then ordered that the vessel be dismantled, the hull to be used as a 'ballast boat'.[18] Symington is then said to have had the engine installed in a larger boat, but the Canal Company would not change its decision. He finally gave up his attempt to make marine engines. The proof, that these boats, propelled by steam power, had actually existed and taken part in trials, was provided years later in 1824, when affidavits to that effect were signed by Symington, Joseph Stainton and Henry Stainton among others.[19] It would seem that the boat built for Dundas was to be called 'Charlotte Dundas', on completion, but as has been seen, Symington actually built two boats in that attempt. The fact, that he had in his time been involved with three different boats, one in 1789 and then two, from 1801, is mentioned in the affidavit signed by Joseph Stainton.

The success of the ironworks was not due solely to the leading figures like Symington, Gascoigne and Stainton, but also to the ordinary and sometimes extraordinary workmen who were so adept at solving the many problems which they faced in those pioneering days. One such man was William Anderson. He was born in 1733 and was one of the first to secure employment at Carron Works. William apparently took a great interest in the erection of an early pumping engine and promptly constructed a working model of the engine which attracted great interest. Shortly afterwards he became Superintendent of the Engineering Department. It would appear that the water supply to the working cylinder of this same pumping engine had to be regulated manually, which required constant observation to prevent disaster in the form of a complete malfunction; William came up with the idea of a header tank or cistern fitted with a ball cock valve, saving money and ensuring the safety of the machine. He was also responsible for laying down the tramway from the works to the harbour at Carronshore. Ingenuity and hard work paid off, allowing William to purchase the farm of Gutterhead[20], which he operated with the help of a farm manager, whilst still attending to his duties at Carron. Family tradition tells of his high religious beliefs, which in turn, led him to place a large notice in his workshop, warning of the perils of taking the Lord's name in vain, a common occurrence amongst some of his colleagues. On another occasion, Joseph Stainton sent for his superintendent to attend to a breakdown of an engine. This event took place on a Sunday which precluded a visit from William, who stuck to his rule, never to work the Sabbath. At the stroke of midnight, William, fearing instant dismissal from the Company, set off on horseback from Gutterhead and arrived at Carron, only to be confronted by an angry and verbal Joseph Stainton. William told the manager:

> Mr Stenton[21], I hear what you say. As you know, I refused to make an agreement to work on the Sabbath. I have a Master to serve higher than the company, and if you cannot continue me this liberty, I regret I must leave the company's service.

Stainton, who could appreciate courage, and also the value of this man, replied: "You have upset me a bit, Anderson; maybe I have been hasty. Away and get the d-m-d thing set agoin." Not many of the Company's servants would have had the courage to confront Joseph Stainton. William Anderson rode daily on horseback to and from the Works, except on Sundays, until he could do it no longer.

> One star-lit night, in his 94th year, he stood in front of his door and silently and alone looked round on the familiar scene – the brilliant night-sky, his own fields and garden, the distant fires of Carron. Who can say what were his communings as he surveyed all for the last time. Turning in, he sat down in his chair beside his family, and without a word or a quiver passed away.[22]

That was August 1826. He outlived manager Joseph Stainton, by one year.

Many of the Company's products found their way to the London market where at first, they were handled by Thomas Roebuck & Co. This operation was then taken over by a specially set up firm called "Adam and Wiggin". William Adam was the youngest of the Adam brothers and John Wiggin had formerly been a clerk at Carron. This firm suffered with the collapse of Francis Garbett & Co. in 1772 and the business of the London Agency was henceforth carried on by Wiggin alone. He absconded with the Company's funds there in 1777 and William Lowes, a partner who was a clerk at Carron and mentioned previously in connection with his observations on the production of iron, was sent to London to pick up the pieces. Lowes also departed with the Company's funds, probably due to the fact that he was in financial difficulties. His Carron shares were then held by his creditors. Robert Sinclair succeeded him, but by 1784 the agent was a gentleman by the name of William Hood.

It was during the period of Joseph Stainton's management, that a completely new warehouse complex was established on the north bank of the river Thames at Castle/Upper Thames Street. These premises were built up over the years, beginning with No 15 acquired from one Thomas Williams for £7,500 in 1795. The warehouse was erected there, on the site of Baynard's Castle. The adjacent property at No 14 cost £6000 and was purchased from Owen Williams in 1823; it became the residence of the London Agent and until 1851, it was the domain of Henry Stainton and was known as 'Carron House'. No 16 Upper Thames Street was acquired in two parts in 1836; one from a "Major Mackay and others" at £1,600 and another from a Miss Charity at £5,000.

After 1796 when long guns were again being manufactured at Carron for the Board of Ordnance[23], the new gun moulders shop, No 8 foundry, was built, to cope with the increased production of these guns and the Carronades; a workshop for the construction of steam engines also appeared about this time. No plan of the works exists from the Stainton period, but one, of the Stenhouse Estate in 1826, shows the outline of the works. The angular northern boundary seen on the plan of the works of 1773, has expanded out in a curve of the road to Stenhousemuir, defining the limits of Carron Works until the 1870s. Most of the buildings occupying that expansion - smithies, workshops and warehouses - were built in Joseph Stainton's time. Some of the buildings housed steam engines signalling the gradual replacement of the water wheel. Around 1797, Carron Company purchased the estates of Jacktrees and Crowgarth in the Parish of Cleator in Cumberland, to 'corner' a market in iron ore which supplied their competitors. The hematite ore was brought to Carron via Grangemouth.

A Carron Company 5 shilling note issued in 1797 and used as legal tender

In 1800, William Cadell junior purchased 2 shares of Carron Stock from John Minyer[24] and in the following year, he bought 8 shares from the trustee of the creditors of Francis Garbett and Co. and Charles Gascoigne [Walter Hog, manager of the British Linen Bank][25]. Cadell paid £2700 for these shares, which were part of 91 shares offered for sale at a public auction. These 91 shares were in turn, part of 101 shares, which stood in the books of Carron Company in the name of Charles Gascoigne. Although William Cadell then had the necessary 10 shares to be eligible to become a voting partner, it would seem that he refrained from attempting to achieve this objective. It was around this time that the General Court of Carron Company introduced 'promisory notes', of 5 shillings and upward. They were legal tender in central Scotland until the use of banks became more common.

A lesser known brother of the Staintons called John, found his way to the district and in 1803 was known to be living at Croftandie, one of the Company's farms near Shieldhill. According to correspondence in the letter books, he sometimes acted as 'middle man' in the sale of farm implements to people such as William Dawson of Keswick and John Callander of Reddingrig, but his main occupation was farming. In 1810, Henry Stainton advised brother Joseph against employing John at the works, describing him as: "one who will not exert himself".[26] John had a son of the same name, who was born in 1792 and in 1808 became Dux of the Royal High School in Edinburgh. He was called to the Scottish Bar in 1818, but later his career was said to have been marred by "an unfortunate incident". John, the younger, who became a Carron partner in 1815, died in 1832. According to the census of 1841, John senior, his wife and daughter Elizabeth were all living at Mount Carron and John was recorded as being a farmer.

Another two of Joseph Stainton's relatives came to Carron from Keswick at the beginning of the 19th century. They were Joseph and William, the sons of William and Dinah Dawson. Dinah was a sister of the Stainton brothers who had married William Dawson of Keswick, a cloth manufacturer, in 1787. Other members of their family included Margaret [b.1790], John [b.1796], Henry [b.1799], Anne [b.1801] and Thomas [b.1807]. Joseph was born in 1788 and William in 1794. When the two brothers arrived at Carron, Joseph the eldest immediately commenced his training at the works whilst William, who was of school age, continued his education, at the self-supporting school at Bainsford.

By 1802 the main or voting partners were, Joseph Stainton, Samuel Garbett, John Minyer, James Maclaren, William Adam, the Honourable William Elphinstone, Archibald Tod Esq., John Tod Esq., Andrew Dalziel (Professor of Greek, Edinburgh University), Charles Selkrig Esq. (accountant) of Edinburgh, James Balfour and Gilbert Hamilton.

Joseph Stainton's younger brother Henry appears to have been well liked by the workforce at Carron where he was affectionately known to all as "Mr Harry". However others seemed to take a different view judging from the tone of a letter written by company secretary James Balfour to Joseph Stainton. The following lines were written, almost as an afterthought:

11th March 1802.

I had almost omitted to say that it gave us all very great pleasure to find your brother was to become a partner, and if we engage with the Clyde Works, he may even be more essentially useful than he is at present.[27]

Although Henry had the necessary shares to enable him to become a partner, the vote on this took place at a special meeting of the partners in October of that year. The reference to the Clyde Works alluded to talk of some form of partnership or arrangement with Carron Company. Balfour cannot hide his thoughts on Henry's usefulness at Carron.

In 1806, Joseph Stainton acting through an intermediary John Tawse, writer in Edinburgh, purchased the Lands of Biggarshiels near Biggar, Lanarkshire. For this, he paid the princely sum of £11,500, and from the 19th November 1806, became known as, "Joseph Stainton of Biggarshiels"[28]. It is surely only coincidence that these lands had once belonged to the Earl of Wigton, an ancestor of one of Stainton's fellow partners at Carron, the Honourable William Elphinstone. That very same year, Joseph also bought Mungal Mill on the west side of the road from Falkirk, not far from his home.

A goods list thought to date from the later years of the 18th century, shows just how comprehensive was the range of products turned out at Carron. The list would be added to as a new line was introduced with few items becoming obsolete quickly at that time. In the main section ordnance dominated, from cohorns, carronades, cannon of the "Light New Construction", to the guns of Government Pattern, which were manufactured from 1796 onward. Smaller items of war such as eight different types of shot and hand grenades, as well as carriages for the carronades, also feature on the list. The general goods ranged from the basic culinary items which included tea kettles, tinned goblets, French pots, sauce-pans and 'skellets' to kitchen heaters, perpetual ovens and "cabbin stoves". Parts for mill and ginn wheels; pipes, cylinders, pistons and boilers for steam engines; carpenter's tools of every description; agricultural implements such as 'common spades', hoes, 'plows', picks and cart-axles as well the more famous fine goods into which category came the polished cast iron fenders, ornamental jambs (with medallions) and pedestal stoves. Included were the ubiquitous sad irons, brewers vats and sugar pans, which had been the first

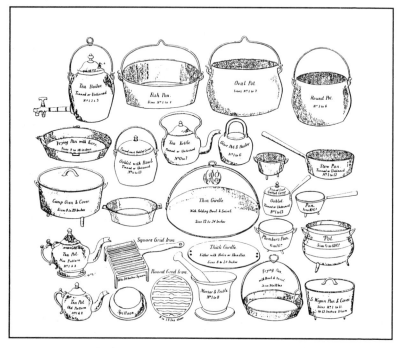

A selection of Carron domestic ironware of the period

of the Company's products . After a few years, James Maclaren took charge of the warehouse at London and was succeeded at Liverpool by Joseph Stainton's cousin, Thomas Crosthwaite. When Maclaren died in 1808, Henry Stainton filled his position at London and young Joseph Dawson took his Uncle Henry's position at Carron as assistant to Joseph Stainton. It is almost certain that with the two Stainton brothers in control, at Carron and at the main agency, the schemes were devised that did not become public knowledge until nearly half a century later when both men were no longer alive to answer for them. It is clear from what has been written about the brothers, that these very shrewd men often displayed a black sense of humour - perhaps unintentional. When the Napoleonic wars drew to a satisfactory conclusion, Joseph came upon some Carron workmen who were celebrating the event. His advice to them was that instead of rejoicing, they would be better off going home and putting on their black coats[29] [To mourn the passing of a war that had brought much business to the Company and had helped to keep them in employment.] He was once heard to say that: "Bony [Napoleon Bonaparte] did not fecht half"[30], in other words, according to Joseph, the war and Carron Company's lucrative trade, should have lasted a lot longer! Henry, when trade was poor thought the best hope for an upturn, was: "if another violent revolution came along".

Moving goods and raw materials to and from the Works was always a matter of great concern to the Carron managers, hence the construction of waterways and anxiety with regard to the Forth and Clyde Canal. On the 18th May 1810, an Act of Parliament was passed with several clauses in it giving the Road Trustees, one of whom had been William Cadell junior, the power to facilitate the heavy traffic conducted by Carron Company between their Works and Falkirk[31]. A problem existed at Bainsford with its narrow Main Street where many of the houses had outside stairs, but to widen the street would have been a costly exercise. This was overcome by the Company which decided to build a tramway from the Works, the Bainsford section running behind the houses on the west side of the street, known even today as the Wagon Road. This was another 'narrow gauge' wagon way, which was connected into the existing coal fields tramway where it left the Works at the road to Stenhousemuir. It was constructed along the front of the Works and crossed the river by means of an iron bridge which was fixed to the western side of the old stone bridge. This iron bridge rested on extensions to the original piers of the stone bridge. The southern terminus was a loading basin at Burnhouse, on the Canal. According to George Dott in an article on the Carron wagonways written in 1949, the colliery tramway had double tracks by at least 1795. The section built to the Burnhouse Basin at Bainsford also used double tracks. (*New Statistical Account for Scotland: Stirlingshire, Larbert Parish, 1845*). A photograph exists of the old bridge at Carron (see page 134) prior to its demolition to make way for the new bridge in 1905; it shows the termination of double tracks on the south side of the river, which appear to be in line with the old iron bridge which carried Carron Company's tramway over the river. It is the author's opinion that these belonged to the Carron tramway. These rails were fitted to stone setts, twenty inches square and eight inches deep and were still in existence until 1905, although long out of use. The wagons were horse drawn and it is thought that one horse was used to pull four wagons, under the control of a driver or 'waggoner'. One of the early waggoners was John Leishman, known locally as "the Shaver".[32] He was killed on the tramway near to the Lady's Gate after his horse was startled and one of the wagons was pulled on top of him.

Around that time, the Company began working limestone on the Newbigging Estate in Fife, and sometime between 1808 and 1828, a wagonway was erected between the quarry and the old harbour of Newbigging. Part of this network incorporated a gravity haulage device, or 'sterlie', for lowering loaded wagons down a steep incline which at the same time caused empties to be raised[33]. In 1844, the mine at Nine Lums was began and a new tramway laid down[34]. Ships once carried the limestone from the harbour to the River Carron, but that task later went the way of the mainline railway.

In 1815 another Dawson brother called John came to Carron and, after completing his education at Edinburgh University, immediately commenced his training at the Works. Five years later, in 1820, Sir William Bruce of Stenhouse, according to an old story, heard of the plan to capture the Carron Works and the ordnance stored there[35]. This was during what became known as the 'Radical War' and Stenhouse was to be taken first and the attack on the works to be directed from there. Dragoons were already guarding the works and he then arranged for some of the locals to protect his home, even to the extent of having a couple of Carronades taken up to the house. Henry Stainton it is said, decided to test the defences at Stenhouse, and late at night made his way up through the gardens hoping to steal into the house. When he appeared from behind some shrubbery, he was startled to find one of the 'guards' confronting him with a loaded gun and demanding to be given the 'countersign' or password or he would shoot. Henry, who could hardly draw a breath by this time, turned to flee shouting: "For God's sake don't fire, I know nothing about your countersigns; but I am Mr Harry". He ran as fast as his legs could carry him, not stopping until he had put the Forge Row between him and the heights of Stenhouse.

It was in 1820 also, that Joseph Stainton brought some of the Irish workforce from Wilsontown to Carron[36]. They were settled at the Nailer Row, Carron, which had been built for the nailers under the direction of William Cadell junior, more than fifty years previously. This Irish community suffered harsh treatment at the hands of some of the local youths though they were by all accounts peaceful and easygoing.

Gradually, another side to Joseph Stainton's management style was emerging. After so much success in improving the operation of the Company, at first to the great satisfaction of partners and shareholders alike, he began to assume an autocratic stance over all matters concerning the running of the Company. The monthly meetings of the managing partners, a procedure laid down in the terms of the Co-partnery, soon took on an unusual format. Joseph often appeared armed with proxy votes, which he assumed gave him overall say; by 1813, the half-yearly meetings of the General Court had stopped altogether[37]. He bought more shares as they became available, some of which he sold or transferred to relatives such as Henry Stainton, John Stainton junior, his sister Betty Maclaren and Joseph Dawson who became partners, augmenting the power of the Stainton family within Carron Company[38].

He added to his property in 1815 when he acquired Merchiston Hall, formerly known as Mungal House, from the estate of the late Captain Charles Napier. With this came the superiority of some of the houses on the west side of Main Street Bainsford. The farms of Langdale, Broomyknowe, Lethandy and Mungal Mill, all within the vicinity of Mungal Cottage, were bought by him in 1816 and by this time he also owned Bellsdyke farm and a workshop in Vicars Loan, Falkirk. A man of property indeed! Carron Company's shareholders were not oblivious to what was happening and some of the partners, those outside the 'charmed circle', were becoming suspicious as to the true extent of the profitability of the company. But not surprisingly, there was little dissent shown when Joseph was around. On the 14th January 1821, at the age of 66 years, Joseph Stainton married Jean Headrick in the Parish Church of Larbert[39]. She was just 19 and was the daughter of a carpenter at Carron called William Headrick. Their children, Caroline [b.1821], Joseph [b.1823] and Lucien [b.1824], all entered the world at Mungal Cottage; the eldest, Caroline, was baptised within Carron Works at "Mr. Stainton's House", which was then the manager's official residence[40].

Another famous visitor who came to Carron at this time was James Nasmyth, son of Alexander Nasmyth the portrait painter, and the man who later invented the steam hammer. He visited the Works around 1823, when he was 16 years of age[41], in the company of Robert Bald the celebrated mining engineer and later recorded his impressions:

> When seen partially lit up by the glowing masses of white-hot iron, with only the rays of bright sunshine gleaming through a few holes in the roof, and the dark, black, smoky vaults in which the cumbrous machinery was heard mumbling away in the distance - while the moving parts were dimly seen through the murky atmosphere, mixed with the sounds of escaping steam and rushes of water; with the half-naked men darting about with masses of red-hot iron and ladles of molten cast-iron - it made a powerful impression on the mind.

He recollected that on the walls of the house of the manager at Carron, there was a collection of old armour, dug up from the field of the Battle of Bannockburn. There were swords, daggers, lances, battle-axes, shields and coats of chain-armour. The manager at the time was of course Joseph Stainton and the house referred to would have been the manager's official residence, at the entrance gate to the works. "I have often regretted that some of our artists do not follow up the example set them by that admirable painter, Wright of Derby, and treat us to the pictures of some of our great ironworks". Nasmyth later visited St Petersburg in 1843, where he met Francis Baird and General Alexander Wilson, the sons of the Carron men who went there with Charles Gascoigne in 1786.

Joseph Stainton died at Mungal Cottage in 1825 and was, with the exception of his son Lucien who had only lived for ten months, the first member of this family to be interred in a private area of the Larbert Parish Churchyard, the 'Carron enclosure'. Only a few yards from the grave of Joseph Stainton is that of William Cadell junior, first manager of Carron Company, who died in 1819. Later, in 1826, at the instigation of Henry Stainton and to the annoyance of some of the partners, an obelisk was erected over Joseph's grave with suitably inscribed words proclaiming his virtues:

> Joseph Stainton of Biggarshiels.
>
> By economy, diligence and scientific skill he relieved the company from embarrassment and placed it in unrivalled prosperity. Firm, but kind, in the exercise of authority, The thousands whose labour he controlled, Partook of the general sorrow which prevailed at his death.

The names of the rest of his family who were later buried there, were added, including that of his wife who had remarried, to a John Anderson of Edinburgh. She was laid to rest beside her first husband and her sons, in

The Carron Enclosure in Larbert Old Parish Churchyard

1885. All of Joseph's property was entailed, held in trust for his son Joseph junior, two of the trustees being Jean Headrick his widow, and his brother Henry. Joseph junior died in 1845 at the age of 22 and his daughter Josephine became the heiress. Joseph Stainton's successor at Carron was Joseph Dawson, who was assisted by his brother William. With Joseph Stainton gone, some of the partners and shareholders with long hidden grievances, now turned their anger towards the new manager, at first demanding that his salary be reduced, as in their view he was not as experienced as his uncle. How wrong they were. Three shareholders, Thomas and John Tod and John Romanes began to ask questions at the General Meetings over the profitability of the company and on the way it was being run, having perused the printed copy of the Co-partnery. On this account, Henry Stainton advised Joseph on how to handle them: -

> Give nothing to startle them, only a few general items at the meeting, from which they could obtain nothing of importance. It is necessary to keep all information from these gentlemen to prevent them doing mischief; but it may be necessary to remember that in dealing with the fools of this world, flatter not fight, they are not to be guided by reason.[42]

John Tod and John Romanes were Writers to the Signet in Edinburgh, but Stainton and Dawson outwitted them just the same. One compromise was obtained; Henry Stainton's salary was set at £2,000 instead of a previous arrangement of 5% of the profit on all goods sold through the London warehouse[43]. Two years later in 1827, another concession was made, John Tod and George Ross were allowed to investigate the Company's accounts, but were always refused permission to see the full accounts.[44] These people it is said, eventually lost heart and sold their shares in 1833 to the Dawsons.

Any malpractice in which Joseph Stainton might have engaged was probably small , compared to that begun in earnest by Joseph Dawson and Henry Stainton. The account books were systematically altered giving a 'trial balance' with a lower profit and thus a lower dividend, before being shown as abstracts, to shareholders. The difference between this and the true figure was set aside to enhance reserve funds, to be used in times of trouble or other unforeseen circumstances, on the proverbial 'rainy day'. Joseph Dawson was also responsible for the covert stockpiling of huge amounts of pig iron. The Works just kept on turning out pig iron whether there was a demand or not, to the benefit of those employed at the furnaces, but possibly not to the shareholders. This in itself was a calculated risk, that with the backing of the hidden funds, most of which should have been paid out in dividends, the Works could then weather the storms that claimed others. It kept the Works and the workers productive, and of course the stocks of pig iron could always be drawn on when there was an upturn in demand. It may have been the original intention of the management of Carron Company at that time to protect and ensure the viability of the Company independently of "market forces". However, it must be said that advantage was taken of this successful arrangement as the years went by. By convincing shareholders that their return on investment was poor, it was then a relatively easy task for members of the 'family' to relieve those unsuspecting speculators of their shares. In this way, Joseph was able to buy undervalued shares which he then sold or passed on to others, such as his brothers, William, Thomas and Henry, who became partners[45].

Henry Stainton also accumulated shares and was for many years until his death, the main shareholder. He was married to Miss Sarah Tomkinson of Lewisham on the 20th May 1817 at the Church of St. Benet, Paul's Wharf London, adjacent to the London Warehouse[46]. The Staintons set up home there, at the house within the warehouse. Henry also purchased Springfield House at Rushey Green, Lewisham that year, but this only became public knowledge when he moved there with his family in 1822[47].

Another dubious scheme alleged to have been operated by Joseph Stainton and later by Joseph Dawson and Henry Stainton, was over goods sent to the London Warehouse, in particular the large amounts of ordnance made during and after the Napoleonic Wars. Greater numbers of individual goods were sent than were invoiced for and claims were also made by Henry for goods that were supposed to have been damaged. Hence, the production figures for ordnance may be higher than those recorded. Monies raised this way were put into a special reserve fund held by Henry in London, known as the "Board of Ordnance Account".

Some tenacious shareholders, one of whom was voting partner and advocate John Jardine, were still suspicious of the true status of the Company and gave Henry and Company much cause for alarm. But it was not until 1839, when a disenchanted clerk at the works called John Carmichael leaked to another shareholder who was a friend of Jardine, the details of the various managerial procedures, that a compromise had to be reached[48.] James Gibson Craig, the Company's law agent and also a partner, acted as intermediary between Henry Stainton and John Jardine and always tried to avoid litigation. It was stated later that he had gone as far as writing to the manager at Carron, informing him that he believed that the way the Company was being run, with respect to the continual refusal to allow the books to be examined properly, was illegal and contravened the Articles of Co-Partnery. Eventually Gibson Craig had to side with the Jardine faction and at the meeting of the General Court of Carron Company held in April 1840, the outcome was that the partners were told of an increase in profits, with the dividend which had stood at 9% for the previous 35 years, being increased to 11% with a bonus of 10%[49]. The manager was also warned against keeping such large sums in reserve. The dividend thereafter settled at 12% until 1853[50]. Those who disagreed with the Stainton/Dawson policy, that is, with Henry, were regarded as "poor fools" or "the catspaw" of others.

Incidentally, John Carmichael who exposed these questionable practices, had been brought to Carron by Joseph Stainton, but when Joseph Dawson had taken over, his salary was reduced from £100 to £80 despite being given a heavier workload, causing the clerk to take his revenge. John Jardine was the son of Professor Jardine of Glasgow University, who had written the tribute to Dr Roebuck in 1796[51]. He was married to the only daughter of James Bruce of Kinnaird and his wife, Mary Dundas of Carronhall.

Within the Works, new developments had taken place. In 1828, the 'hot blast' method, where heated air was used for the blast at the furnaces instead of cold air, was invented by James Beaumont Neilson. His experiments were carried out at the Clyde Iron Works, where William Cadell junior

The top of an old blast furnace, probably built around 1835

once had an interest. The greater temperatures achieved within the blast furnace allowed for the exploitation of blackband ironstone and cheaper grades of coal. It has been said that those at Carron were slow to appreciate the benefits that this brought, but according to the *New Statistical Account of Scotland*, published in 1845, that may not have been the case: "At a date when Joseph Dawson had been manager for ten years [1835], two of the old furnaces were pulled down and rebuilt on a 'new construction', adapted to the application of the hot blast". It is now thought that these two were built to the design of the 'first' cylindrical type of blast furnace, although still with open tops. The evidence for this comes from a photograph published in 1953 in the Company magazine, *Carron Cupola*. It shows the 'bridge' of 'an old open-top furnace', presumably at Carron Works, either the No 6 or the No 4, resembling a lighthouse in appearance, with a circular platform at the top enclosed by railings of wrought iron. Until then, the blast furnaces would have been those built in 1766, 1776 and 1777, with the exception of a fifth furnace built in the 1790s. The photograph may have been taken, along with many others, before the works were reconstructed last century. William Jack, writing in 1885 about this period at Carron, stated that after Neilson had invented his hot blast method, he had to take action against many who had infringed his patent [a payment of 1/- per ton of iron produced using his method], but he could do nothing about Joseph Dawson at Carron who used a hot blast which was principally of his own design. He also went as far as suggesting that Neilson had got his idea from a local blacksmith called John Buchan who had devised a simple means of heating the blast of air from his forge bellows; Neilson had, according to Mr Jack, apparently visited this forge, thought to have been at Carronshore. He published this story in the trade journal *The Engineer* on the 25th September 1885, and later that year in a series of articles for the *Falkirk Herald*. With the advent of the hot blast furnace, it was found that raw coal could be used in the charge instead of coke, but at Carron, for some years, they still processed coke using the old costly method.

In 1830, Thomas Crosthwaite died and his position at Liverpool was given to another Dawson brother, Henry, while his brother Thomas was established at the Glasgow office. At Carron Works, the main departments came under the direction of the other Dawson brothers, Joseph, William and John. Apart from his managerial duties and the supervision of all things connected with the blast furnaces, Joseph Dawson was also responsible for the operation of the pits at Carronhall and at Kinnaird which he is said to have visited on Sundays for some reason[52]. An old Carter at Carron by the name of Michael Hardie had once complained to Joseph Dawson that he would need to get: "a wee thing mair for cairting up to the cinder hill, because I have further tae gang noo". "Hoots man", said Joseph, "ye dinna need tae gang ony further, jist build it up; ye're a lang way frae the roof yet". A similar story was also recounted by Gillespie in *History of Stirlingshire*, but he referred to a large pile of pig iron instead of the cinder hill. Perhaps he was alluding to Joseph Dawson's clandestine stockpiling of pig iron, without actually stating the fact. Incidentally Joseph, although born in Keswick, reputedly spoke with a broad Scots accent.

In charge of the pig iron department in those days was John Dawson who, with a team of labourers, skilfully graded the iron produced at the blast furnaces[53]. John was also responsible for miscellaneous departments including paying the people who harvested the fields at the Mulloch and at Old Roughlands. Even the welfare of the swans on the dams was his responsibility, as was that of the workers when, from 1840, he became involved with the organising of the Carron Victualling Society. John was later to occupy Mount Carron, where he lived with his wife Jane whom he had married in 1830. In his spare time he was a keen entomologist. John Dawson is something of an enigma. He has never been identified, or even mentioned, by other authors who wrote on this subject, apart from one footnote in J C Gibson's *Lands and Lairds of Larbert and Dunipace*, which referred to John's collection of moths, such was his low profile compared to that of his brothers. It is not known if he was ever a partner - he was always referred to as a 'clerk' which in those days also meant head of department, but there was never a bad word said of him.

William Dawson's domain was the lower part of the works, where he was assisted by James Mitchell who had charge over the blacksmiths and the grate and range mounting shops, and by William Adams, who was in charge of the green sand moulding shops[54]. Mitchell and Adams were also clerks. At 7.00am, in his long-tailed coat and his tall hat, William Dawson could be seen "flying around", by 8.30am he was at the blacking house supervising the moulder boys getting their 'blacking' and making sure they didn't take too much, or spill it. At 9.00am, he saw to it that those same boys got their 'peas meal' and by 9.30am he was in the file room at the square, serving out the files. At 10.00am, keys in hand and followed by his blacksmiths, he was off to the barns at Carron Inn where he gave out the rod iron. Back at the Works, he would then set about examining the fine goods for the London market. All products had to pass his rigorous inspection, "they had to be correct, or to the left hand side they would go".

Smeaton's old blowing engines had by this time been replaced by the more powerful steam variety. The first of these is thought to have been built to a design of William Symington, then followed by one built by a man called McDonald in 1828 and another, known as the 'Watt engine' but probably built at Carron to the patent design of Boulton and Watt. Within the confines of the 'Watt engine' there was reputed to be an illegal still or distillery.[55] It was known then as a 'little pat' or 'wee still' and was apparently quite safe there as "the managers never went into places like that". However, its downfall came when rivals decided to set up their own at the base of Smeaton's returning engine and Henry Stainton got to hear about it. He had it destroyed and subsequently made a raid on the other still, with the result that it too went the way of its competitor!

In those days within the ranks of the 'key workers', there were a few stalwarts who warrant some attention. Edward "Neddy" Banks was the cashier and he had apparently come to Carron from Keswick, with his father John, his mother, sister and grandmother. His father was a contemporary of Joseph Stainton and when he died in 1801, he was buried in a railed enclosure in Larbert Churchyard, a sign of some status. Neddy Banks died in 1849 aged 80 years. John Carmichael, mentioned earlier, and his son, also John, were clerks along with Charles Green and John Campbell. These men and the three Dawson brothers, are listed in the Falkirk Almanac of 1836, as the "managers" at Carron. These clerks had their place of work at the Counting House and their homes were at Forge Row, where they all had a "family servant". At that period in time, the 'Row', where the most important employees lived, faced on to the road to Stenhousemuir. This road ran from where the clock tower is today, and cut through the site of the present works to the northwest corner of the forge dam. Other occupants of Forge Row were Henry Jobson of Manchester, who was employed as a designer and the Mastertons, ancestors of whom appear to have been employed by the Company almost from the beginning. The head of this family was Alexander who was a patternmaker. It was most likely his father, John Masterton, who signed a contract with the Company as a patternmaker - "from the 14th of February 1811, bound for 21 years"[56]. The contract was signed by Joseph Stainton and witnessed by William Dawson and Alexander Benson. The Mastertons were probably inhabitants of this district before the establishment of the ironworks. In property writs held in the Company archives for lands at Bothkennar, mention is made of the "Maistertouns"[57]. The ordinary tradesmen and labourers inhabited every conceivable piece of property available. At Carron, there was Stable Row, later known as the Carron Inns, the Barber Row, Cooper's Land, Kirk's Land and the Nailer Row. There was also the Clubroom*, which had existed since at least 1786 and had been school and meeting place; it too housed a few families. Among the occupants

Forge Row c1890 from a painting by the author based on contemporary records.

of some of those dwellings, as was later recorded in the census of 1851, there were paupers, that is people with no visible means of support. Some were widows, with children of school age and there were others, former employees, who had either retired or were unable to work, but were still allowed to live in their Company houses. Dwelling houses were still in abundance on the periphery of the works and at the old village of West Carron. Carronshore and Stenhousemuir had a large number of their population employed at the Works and even Carron Park, the one time residence of William Cadell junior, played host to Carron workers, although it was still the property of the Cadell family. Many of the workers however made the effort and built their own houses, as Samuel Garbett had hoped, all those years before.

In 1840, Joseph and William Dawson both lived at the "manager's house", next to the main gate at Carron Works. The following year, William Dawson at the age of 45, married Margaret Taylor, the daughter of a local saddler; she was aged 21. He then leased ground from the Company which had been feued from Sir Michael Bruce. This was at Carron where Carron Parish Church later stood, but at that time there was a small farmstead called Blacktown, previously Mill Quarter, and a house formerly John Melvin's, both of which had existed before 1759[58]. Blacktown was the name he gave to his new house, built to the east of the old house; the farm remained in the possession of Carron Company. His children were born at Blacktown House: William [b.1842], Dinah [b.1843], Anne [b.1846] and Dinah Margaret [b.1847]. Dinah died aged three years in 1846, and one year later her new born sister was named Dinah Margaret, which was a combination of the Christian names of her grandmother and mother. The family at that time had four house servants to look after their needs, Elizabeth Walker, Christina Johnston, Marion Johnston and Margaret Duncan.

A partner at that time, although not actively involved at the works, was James Maclaren junior, a son of James Maclaren, late of the London Warehouse. He was married to Caroline, daughter of Joseph Stainton and they had two sons, Ambrose and James Joseph and were then living at Hurst Green in Sussex; they later moved to Constable Burton in North Yorkshire. Henry Stainton bought more property in 1825, this time it was the farm of Stonehouse near Skinflats. In 1838, he acquired the old Ogilvie policies known as the Lands of Gairdoch, which by that time had encompassed Abbotshaugh, Dalderse, Carronside, Coblebrae, Langlees, Backrow, Upper Gairdoch and Yonderhaugh. There was one local farm on the east-side of the Carron Road between the River Carron and the Canal, which Henry, and later William Dawson, never managed to obtain. This was Millflats, always in the possession of a family called Ritchie. Later in the 1880s, it was bought by the Trustees of the late William Dawson.

These people then were the major players at Carron Company, in the middle of the 19th century. Joseph Dawson, with the connivance of Uncle Henry, still continued the clandestine practice of share manipulation and by then, the majority shareholding was in the hands of these families. Henry genuinely believed that they should have total say in the running of the Company and not the "speculative writers in Edinburgh", who just happened to have bought shares as an investment. In 1844, the Inspector of Taxes at Stirling began to ask questions about the apparent non-profitability of Carron Company compared with others which were not doing one quarter of the business. John Jardine again hounded the management; he too felt that the profits were much lower than they should have been, considering the business that was being done.

Joseph Dawson, known at Carron as "auld Joe", or "the auld maister", died on the 5th of January 1850 and he was interred in the private cemetery at Larbert. His obituary stated: "his death has cast a deep gloom over a wide district, ... many a tearful eye will testify the deep regret which all feel, that one possessed of so many valuable qualities has been snatched from among us". These were genuine expressions of sorrow. A monument, of Peterhead granite, 26 feet high and sculptured by A. McDonald of Aberdeen, was erected in the Carron enclosure at Larbert Churchyard in 1858. Henry Dawson "of Liverpool", at his own expense, later arranged for a stained

glass window to be placed in Larbert Parish Church, in memory of his
brother[59]. The management of Carron Company passed to William Dawson,
with brother Thomas, who had been the Glasgow agent at 125 Buchanan
Street, acting as assistant. Almost at once, Henry Stainton wrote to William,
possibly at William's instigation, explaining the existence of a hitherto
unknown part of the operation. In this letter, of April 1850[60], he set out
before his nephew the details of a fund,

> long ago put into my hands for safe and secret custody, being originally the
> outcome of the Board's account, the regular produce to be added to the principle
> as my judgement may direct.

He listed the individual constituents, showing how the total of £96,046 was
arrived at. There then followed an important statement:

> The whole being the property of Carron Company stands in my name and it is
> entirely unknown to anyone here besides myself.

This secret fund, although acknowledged by Henry, as belonging to Carron
Company, was the one known as the Board of Ordnance account, mentioned
previously. A description of Henry Stainton's life by an anonymous observer
throws light on the intensity with which he went about his business and the
secretive side of his nature which emerged only after his death.

> Henry Stainton was a remarkable man whose whole time and thoughts were
> directed to the study of natural history and zoology as a recreation and to the
> making of money as a very serious profession. He lived at Lewisham near
> Blackheath and amused himself with amateur waterworks and the care of tame
> deer and wild fowl. He used to rise at six every morning summer and winter, and
> spend the first two hours of the day amid his cascades, canals and pets. The rest
> of the day from eight in the morning till late at night was, for many years devoted
> to iron, and all his business transactions were recorded with great care and
> minuteness. Even Sunday was entirely devoted to thoughts of business. He never
> went to any place of worship but spent the day on his islands and ponds ruminating
> over new patterns and original designs for castings and grates. Although known
> to be very wealthy and living expensively, he shunned society.

Henry Stainton died in 1851 and his personal estate was sworn for probate
at £400,000, a very substantial amount of money for the time[61]. He was
survived by four daughters, Elizabeth, Sarah, Charlotte and Caroline and by
two sons, Henry Tibbats and James Joseph; another son Ambrose Tibbats
had died in childhood[62]. It can be seen from two of these names that there

was a connection with Ambrose Tibbats, the former Carron partner. On the 2nd May 1815, Henry Stainton had been appointed Trustee for the estate of the late Ambrose Tibbats and by 1825, he was using the voting power of Tibbats' Carron shares. The eldest son and heir, Henry Tibbats Stainton, was given his father's position as manager of the London warehouse, where he had succeeded the late Ambrose Maclaren as assistant. Upon later examining his father's private papers, he discovered details of sums of money entered under the headings of "Sundries" and "Porterage of Wares" and was at a loss as to what these meant[63]. He conveyed his unexplainable findings to William Dawson at Carron who arranged for brother Henry to leave at once for London.

It transpired that when Henry Stainton's salary had been fixed at £2,000, all those years before in 1825, he had decided to wreak revenge on those who had brought this about and subsequently drew his income which amounted to almost double his salary, from these hidden accounts already mentioned. It is not known whether Henry also withdrew his legitimate salary because, as someone remarked later: "it appeared as if he had been working for nothing"[64]. Joseph and William Dawson had been required to examine the account books of the London office twice-yearly, but it is doubtful if this was carried out properly if at all, because Henry Stainton: "had been regarded as such an honest man"[65]. It was now apparent that Henry had been defrauding the Company of funds over a period of many years. James Maclaren junior, who is thought to have been a member of the legal profession as well as a Carron partner, advised William Dawson to inform the other partners and shareholders.

Carron Company then demanded from the trustees of the late Henry Stainton, who included Henry Tibbats Stainton, the Dawson brothers and James Maclaren junior, the payment of a sum of money equal to the difference between Henry Stainton's salary and that of what he had taken[66]. With interest, this amounted to £108,491. The matter was placed in the hands of the Company's lawyer, Gibson Craig, Dalziel and Brodie and an action brought in the Scottish Courts. As an interim measure until the claim was settled, the company refused to release the shares formerly belonging to Henry Stainton, of which there were 101. In 1854, an action was begun in the English Courts by the Executors of the late Henry Stainton against Carron Company; it was for the transfer of these shares and it brought the affair to the attention of the general public.

The state of things then is recorded in a private correspondence of James Maclaren junior, written in April 1854[67]. In this letter, he implied that Henry Tibbats Stainton had been willing to see that justice was done to those

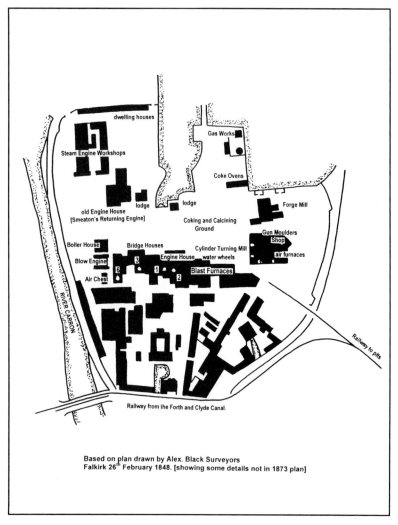

Based on plan drawn by Alex. Black Surveyors
Falkirk 26th February 1848. [showing some details not in 1873 plan]

The Works in 1848

shareholders who had sold their shares in ignorance of the Company's affairs.
He also stated that he had advised against the action taken against the
Company with its inevitable publicity, but the true instigators of this had
been Henry Stainton's daughters, who refused to believe that their father
was guilty of these misdemeanours. He also referred to the time when Henry
Stainton had been a trustee of the late Joseph Stainton junior [Maclaren's

brother in law] and had arranged in 1844 for Stainton junior's 58 shares of Carron Company stock to be sold to Carron Company as undivided stock [held by the Company itself]. As a very low price had been got for these, Maclaren felt that Stainton junior's daughter Josephine had a claim against Henry Stainton, that is, his executors, for the mismanagement of the shares.

Henry Tibbats Stainton was, in 1856, removed from his post as London agent and replaced by Henry Dawson, with one Robert White as his assistant[68]. This treatment may have been the reason for his revealing the details of the buy-out of shareholders by the members of the family[69]. There then followed a series of suits from shareholders past and present demanding remuneration for false returns on their investments. In 1858, a compromise was reached whereby the Company received £159,889, in return for the transfer of the 101 shares to the trustees[70]. During another litigation, the details of Henry's secret reserve fund, that is the one communicated to William Dawson in 1850, were revealed. Carron Company then refused to transfer the shares and in 1859, commenced a new action in the Court of Session, claiming the additional sum of £106,000[71].

In those turbulent times, the business of running Carron Company went on as the various parties awaited the outcome of the legal business. For instance, in 1855, William Dawson was occupied with the acquisition of land for Carron Company and for himself. He purchased the lands of Mungalhead to give access to a modern railway between the works and the main line at Burnhouse and, on a private note, he bought the estate of Powfoulis and assumed the 'title', "William Dawson of Powfoulis" though he continued to live at Blacktown.

After the compromise of 1858 was annulled, the sum of £159,889 received from the trustees of Henry's estate was ordered to be paid by Carron Company to the Accountant General, to form an account known as "the Compromise Fund"[72]. Earlier, during another suit, an order had been obtained requiring Henry Stainton's heritable property in Stirlingshire to be sold. This was the "Lands of Gairdoch", consisting of many local farms as mentioned previously, and was to be disposed of at a public auction. The property was bought by William Dawson in 1859 for the sum of £59,000, William being then addressed as "William Dawson of Gairdoch and Powfoulis". The £59,000 paid to the Royal Bank of Scotland was then ordered to be paid into an account known as "the Real Estate Fund"[73]. The executors of the late Henry objected to this in an action brought before the House of Lords, but the outcome was that Carron Company's case was upheld and Henry Stainton's accounts, and the accounts of Carron Company, were to be investigated back to 1808, the year when he took up his post in

London. The enormity of this task was summed up in a report in the Falkirk Herald of October 1859, the centenary year of the works:

> the books of the concern have been thrown open, ... accountants have been engaged for several weeks past,.........they have only, it is said, overcome twelve months in nearly as many weeks, so that the result of their labours will be remote, and what that result may be, it would be rash to predict.

One piece of information found during this investigation, which seems to have gone on until 1861, was the following which was attributed not to Henry, but to his brother Joseph: -

> Statement of sums carried by Joseph Stainton from the credit of General Charges to his own credit in Carron books during the ten years preceding his decease.[74]

Principal from 1815-1824	£41,532 -12-10d
Interest at 5% to 31st Dec 1860	£84,255 - 4 - 2d
Total	£125,787- 17- 0d

This statement was authorised by Gibson Craig, Dalziel and Brodie W.S. 1861. The date of the beginning of the transfer of money from the Company to Joseph Stainton's account was 1815, the year in which he acquired Merchiston Hall; in 1816 he had then purchased the four local farms. This "statement of sums carried", would seem to explain how he was able to finance these transactions.

On the 1st April 1865, the trustees of the estate of the late Henry Stainton agreed to pay to Carron Company the sum of £100,655 with interest at 5% until payment, in addition to the £220,000 [Compromise Fund plus the Real Estate Fund] already held by the Accountant General[75]. This strange episode drew to a close, apart that is from the actions brought against the Company and individuals such as William Dawson, by shareholders eager to settle old scores. In one such action, "Maclean v Carron Company", it was alleged that the actual profits in the 10 years from 1829 to 1838 were £294,000, but the apparent profits were only about £119,000.[76] The Trustees of John Jardine, who had died in 1850, raised an action in 1861 in respect of his 16 shares, 8 of which were sold to Carron Company in 1851, 4 to William Dawson and 4 to Sir Michael Bruce of Stenhouse [one of the few outsiders who for appearance sake were occasionally allowed to purchase] in 1853[77]. They claimed damages of £80,000 as the amount lost on these sales, in consequence of the fraudulent doings of the Company. It was also alleged that the value of wrought iron concealed in 1851 was £60,000 and pig iron was £95,000[78]. The case was settled by compromise on the final day of the trial. Eventually, it was believed that around £240,000 was paid by Carron Company to shareholders past and present[79].

The repayment of the large sums to the Company, in no way diminished the life-style of Henry's beneficiaries but, to be fair to Henry Tibbats Stainton, he had been entirely innocent of the ways of his father and soon took his rightful place as a partner at Carron. In his private life, he was a world authority on moths and butterflies and owned a huge collection of specimens and books which he kept at his home Mountsfield House, which had been built for him at Lewisham by his father. He wrote many books on Entomology and was also a Fellow of the Royal Society.

In 1883, a book called *Some Professional Recollections by a former member of the Incorporated Law Society* was published and it contained the story of the Stainton-Dawson case; the author it would seem, wished to remain anonymous. It was claimed that at the time, Carron Company bought up as many copies as they could find and had them destroyed. In 1912, H M. Cadell of Grange carried out extensive research into the affairs of the Staintons and Dawsons and this he intended to include in his book, *The Story of the Forth*, in chapter ten, dealing with the history of Carron Company. However, he had second thoughts following the intervention of George Pate of the Company and decided not to include what he had found: "as their publication might hurt the feelings of several worthy people connected with the Company". This probably meant, J J S Maclaren the grandson of Joseph Stainton, F L Burder and R C Clarke, both grandsons of Henry Stainton and Alexander and Henry Mitchell Dawson, grandsons of Henry Dawson, who were all totally innocent of the ways of their ancestors. Cadell's witty summary of the situation was as follows:

> By 1850, only 118 of the 554 shares issued were held by outsiders. Of the remaining 436, the family held 328 or more than half, and the Company, (another name for the family) the balance.

One small piece of evidence which confirms the care the family took to keep matters away from prying eyes was the fact that some of the Minute Books had their pages stuck together with sealing wax fixed with the Company's seal, to prevent tampering.

Despite all the legal and financial wrangling, Carron Company had continued to expand and remained profitable despite the rise of a number of competitors, some of whom were on the Company's doorstep. Many men who had learned the art of the foundryman at the works decided to start their own enterprises, the first of them being George Sherriff. After his time at Carron he moved south to secure employment with Boulton and Watt in Birmingham. His knowledge of steam engines then took him to St Petersburg where, under the direction of Charles Gascoigne, he was responsible for the erection of a steam engine, to drive the stamping machinery at the new Royal Mint undergoing installation in the Peter Paul Fortress. On his return to Scotland, he established the Dalderse Iron Foundry on the banks of the Forth and Clyde Canal, in 1804[80]. Sherriff's works were doomed to a short life and closed in 1810, just as another came on the scene.

Some "enterprising gentlemen", most of whom were employed at Carron Works, started their own business, calling it the Falkirk Iron Works. It began under the management of John Hardie, and some of their first employees came from the defunct Dalderse Iron Works. Using skills learned at Carron, they too manufactured guns for a time, small 'carronade' types of 12 and 18-pounders, for use on merchant vessels. The only known occasion of Carron Company taking legal proceedings against its employees, occurred around 1833, when some Carron moulders broke their contract to take up employment with this new firm[81].

In 1848, the foundry came into the ownership of the Kennard family, who had been partners in the original set-up for many years[82]. They extended the works and gradually expanded on the production of light castings. Like their counterpart at Carron, the Falkirk Iron Works also manufactured shot and shells during the Crimean War. They had a similar product range to that at Carron - register grates, ornamental castings of all descriptions etc. and had customers world-wide. By the 1880s, the workforce numbered 900 and by then the Falkirk Iron Works was the second largest in Scotland. However, with the exception of the Camelon Foundry in 1845, the majority of the independent foundries followed in the thirty years after 1850. A founding partner of the Camelon Foundry was one R W Crosthwaite, a relative of the Staintons and Dawsons of Carron Company. He had a hand in the foundation of no less than four of the local foundries including the Union Foundry in 1854, the Burnbank Foundry in 1860 and the Forthbank Foundry in 1869[83].

Thanks largely to Carron, the Falkirk area became the centre of the nation's iron founding business, but despite the challeges, Carron still reigned supreme in the closing decades of the 19th century. How long this would remain the case depended on how far the Company could adapt to the new conditions of competition and the changing technology.

CHAPTER 5

The End of the Old Regime and the Reconstruction of the Works

In the year of 1866, Carron Company launched what was to become one of its most famous products, the ubiquitous Carron bath. At that particular period, demand for this utensil was slowly increasing though the original baths were nothing like those we know today, being of a painted or 'japanned' finish. They continued to be manufactured as such until near to the end of the century; some of the painted designs featured imitation marbling or wood graining, water lilies, waves and lines.

In 1867 tragedy struck the family of William Dawson with the death of his wife Margaret followed shortly afterwards by the sudden illness and death of his son William junior at the age of 25 years. William died at the Dawson residence at Kirn, Argyllshire. He had been groomed to follow in his father's footsteps, carrying on the tradition of partner/manager and his death changed the mode of management within the Company. For William Dawson, apart from his personal sorrow, there now remained the serious predicament of who would be his successor. At the age of 71, he was in poor health, and his brothers, although slightly younger, were not going to provide the answer; there was no 'Charles Gascoigne' standing in the wings eager to step in. Also, times had changed and although Carron Company was still regarded as one of the main ironfounders in Britain, other companies had appeared with the vitality of youth and the desire to move forward with the help of new technology.

From the early 1850s in England and in Wales, there had been many advances made at the blast furnaces, the 'core' or 'heart' of the iron foundry. After the spread of the 'hot blast' from 1828, the first cylindrical furnaces were built [two at Carron Works are thought to have been in this category] - tall cylinders of firebrick encased in another shell of plated iron. It was not until the 'bell and hopper' was tried at Ebbw Vale in 1850, that the practice of closing the furnace tops was generally adopted[1]. This became the standard blast furnace in Britain, but it took longer to be adopted in Europe. Next came E.A. Cowper's version of the Siemens regenerative principle which took the waste gases trapped in the enclosed furnace, and used them to provide fuel to heat the blast[2]. Immense savings were made by utilising these new methods. The leaders in this field with these new advances were

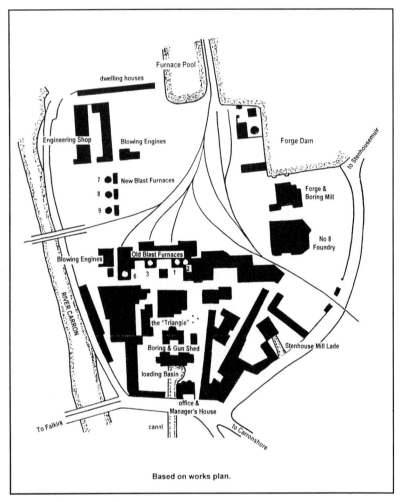

Plan of the Works in 1873

the ironfounders of Cleveland, Northumbria headed by Lowthian Bell[3].
William Dawson must surely have been aware of all of these developments,
which added to his dilemma.

Young Andrew Gordon had just completed his engineering training at
the Summerlee Works at Coatbridge, under the direction of Walter Neilson
who was a relative of J B Neilson, the inventor of the hot blast[4]. It is not
clear as to what level of training Gordon had been given since most of the
records of the Summerlee Works were destroyed by fire, but his reputation

must have been considerable, attracting the attention of William Dawson. Gordon was brought to Carron Works as chief engineer around 1870 and his first task was to modernise the blast furnaces[5]. Until about 1840 there had been five, two of which as noted earlier were erected in 1835 using the hot blast method. By 1870 there were four in use, all of the open-top variety built at least forty-five years previously, one of which still operated by a 'cold blast'. Under Gordon's plan, three new ones were to be installed in a completely new position, in an east to west configuration. Gordon also had the advantage of having the new railway that could be utilised to bring in construction materials.

First, the new site had to be cleared and on it stood the returning engine erected by John Smeaton around 1780. In 1868, Carron Company had offered to the Patents Museum, the forerunner of the Science Museum, an engine which they described as the "old Roebuck-Watt pumping engine"[6]. This offer was refused due to the size and weight of the machine. This may well have been the Smeaton Returning Engine and if so, it would suggest that the site, possibly for new furnaces, was to be cleared two years earlier than it was. According to one report, the date of 1776 was found to be inscribed on the cylinder of this engine, leading Gordon to believe that this was when it was erected, but it most likely referred to the date on which the cylinder was cast. He had so admired this work of Smeaton, that he wanted part of the cylinder mounted into a wall at the works, as a memento. Someone else would take up this idea, but not with this cylinder, possibly due to the fact that it was 72 inches in diameter[7].

Gordon's furnaces were fifty-two feet high, and sixteen feet in diameter at the widest part. The heaters, or the apparatus where the air for the blast was heated, were brick buildings containing a network of cast-iron pipes, through which the cold air from the blast engine was passed. These pipes were heated and caused the air passing through them to become hot as it went to the 'tuyeres' or nozzles fitted into the sides of the furnace. After delays, Gordon's first furnace went into blast in early 1874, the others followed. They were numbered 7, 8 and 9 and the whole operation cost the company, £26,000. It was reported in a newspaper article at the time[8], that great surprise was expressed by various people associated with the iron industry when it was learned that these new furnaces were to be built on the modern principle, that is, giant iron cylinders lined with firebrick and with enclosed tops, the charge being fed by the 'bell and hopper' or 'cup and cone' arrangement. However, on the 1873 plan of the works which indicates the three new blast furnaces with their associated heaters, these heaters are shown as the cast iron pipe type, which suggests that neither of these furnaces then were of the closed top regenerative type. But it may be that one was converted after 1873, generating the newspaper response.

In 1873, William Dawson, suffering from partial blindness and a slight disablement, decided to retire from the management and he handed over that responsibility to his younger brother Thomas who was aged 66. Thomas had been William's assistant for some years, but he appears to have been given this position on the understanding that the day to day operations at the works were to be the responsibility of Andrew Gordon[9]. Thomas had only been "manager" of Carron Company for a few months when he died suddenly at his home in Uddingston. In December 1873, Gordon was named as his successor, the first non-partner to be manager since Joseph Stainton had replaced Charles Gascoigne in 1786. The 'old procedure' had gone forever. Andrew Gordon is generally recognised as being the first professional manager of Carron Company and it is sometimes said that he was brought there for that specific purpose, which is not entirely correct.

Just as the new furnaces were coming on stream in 1874, William Dawson died, in his eightieth year, at Blacktown House. He had been a wealthy but reclusive man who shunned society, never taking part in local affairs; the works at Carron, his family and his property, dominated his life. William Dawson's last resting place is a mausoleum built by a local stonemason and builder, James Law, in the style of a Greek temple; within it stands a statue sculpted in flawless white marble. The mausoleum is situated in the northwest corner of the private enclosure at Larbert Old Parish Churchyard. William's two daughters, Anne and Dinah Margaret, became the major shareholders of Carron Company. These two ladies it is said, had led very sheltered lives under the influence of their father, this would now change. After his death, they took up residence at Powfoulis House. Also, William had in his will, laid down provision for the founding of a charitable trust and on the demise of his line of the family, the proceeds of the estate were to go to the Trust[10]. This was the 'Charitable Trust of the late William Dawson', more popularly known as 'The Dawson Trust'.

Even then, Carron Company was still a relatively prosperous concern and as such there appeared to be no real reason for change though this was not a view shared by critics of the management. But William Dawson in his later years, had seen the writing on the wall and had left the future of the Works in very capable hands. The new blast furnaces had only been the beginning. In the following year, 1875, Andrew Gordon recommended to the General Court that the whole of the works be modernised as soon as possible and this was accepted[11]. However, many of the changes that were about to take place, had been proposed as early as 1873. Some parts of the works dated back to the time of Charles Gascoigne, with additional workshops from the Stainton period scattered about in places that bore no relation to their closely connected functions. More importantly, most of the buildings were just worn out and in a dilapidated condition - the newest of these were reputed to be the No 8 Foundry and the Engineering Shop, both of which are shown on a plan of the works dated 1848, as the Gun Moulding Shop and Steam Engine Workshop. Much of the credit for the re-building of Carron Works has gone to Gordon's successor, but the original idea was his. Where he finished and what was completed by his successors remains a grey area, but some clues can be found from sources external to the Company. For example, a short article in the *Falkirk Herald* of 25th November 1876, reported that

> The public road on the north side has been diverted in a considerable sweep, and the future boundary of this part will consist of a substantial wall with the chief entrance and offices intervening. Indeed, these are so far forward that a short time will suffice for their completion.

This confirms that it was Gordon's plan for the extended area of the works and for the 'front building', whose clock tower is inscribed with the date 1876. The rebuilding was then thought to be costing £100,000, but that figure was soon surpassed. The old office and counting house and many other old buildings were reported as having been demolished in 1877, again, according to the *Falkirk Herald*. Robert Gillespie, who wrote about the works in the third edition of Nimmo's *History of Stirlingshire*, seems to imply that the clock tower had been erected first, an irony considering that it is the only part of that building still in existence today.

In 1876, Anne Dawson, William's eldest daughter, married Thomas Brodie WS, who was the son of John Clerk Brodie the Company's law agent and a partner. Anne soon transferred ten of her Carron Company shares to her husband and, because his father was already a partner, Thomas automatically became 'one of them'. He adopted the middle name of Dawson and was henceforth known as Thomas Dawson Brodie. In the late 19th century, various partners were, at different times, being referred to in the press and elsewhere as "chairman", or "head" of Carron Company. Thomas Dawson Brodie was one of these gentlemen, but however, the office of chairman was not made official until 1906[12]; before that time, various partners were elected as chairman or 'proeses' of the meetings of the Standing Committee or General Court. Brodie was for many years, Company Secretary. He was a partner in the law firm of J C Brodie and Sons which

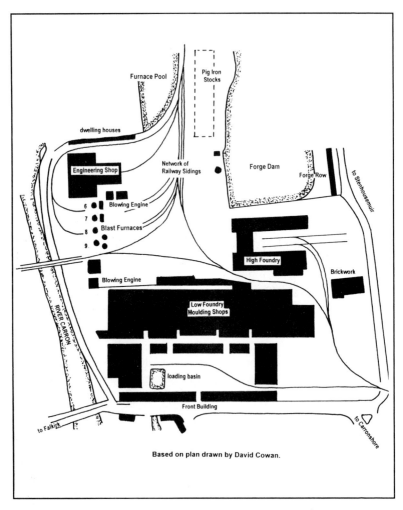

Plan of the Works in 1883 based on a drawing by David Cowan

had formerly been known as Gibson Craig, Dalziel and Brodie, but he was also a man of many parts. In the twenty years he spent as a partner of Carron Company, he bestowed many gifts to the local community and was regarded as a 'true friend'. Gairdoch Park was given to the people of Carronshore, as were all of the instruments for the Carron Works Brass Band. He also donated money towards the building of the Grangemouth Public Library, adding to that given by Andrew Carnegie. For many years, farming was his interest and he kept some very fine animals at the Powfoulis home farm. A keen

Sir Thomas Dawson Brodie

sportsman by nature, he was Honorary President of the Bainsford Bowling Club and a member of the Stenhouse and Carron Curling Club.

In 1879, John Dawson died at his home Mount Carron, but unlike his two older brothers, he was interred outside the private enclosure at Larbert Churchyard, probably due to a lack of space. Never one to reach the heights achieved by his four brothers, he had remained as a clerk during his time at Carron Works. At that period, the clerks, the cashier, the overseers and the masters of the company ships, were the highest earners, apart that is from the manager himself. That very same year, Andrew Gordon was replaced as manager, the reason unknown. His successor at Carron would have to be capable of carrying on, not just as a manager, but as the guiding light behind the modernisation that was taking place.

The new manager was David Cowan who came to the Company from the Tharsis Copper and Sulphate Company of Spain, a subsidiary of the St Rollox Works, Glasgow. He was a Civil and Mining Engineer and well qualified to carry on the re-construction of the works, a task for which it is said he was specifically chosen. When he came to Carron, he was given "a house and free coal"; the house was 'Mount Gerald', situated on the old Crosshillmuirhead Road between Alloa Road and Bellsdyke Road. Within weeks of taking up his post, he was faced with industrial action by the moulders, brought about by the company lowering prices and thus, wages[13]. It involved a strike, during which, one or two of them decided to keep on working and this eventually led to some ugly scenes outside the works. The manager was warned that a similar demonstration was to take place on the following day and he promptly called in the police. The informant had been correct and the mob appeared the next day as forewarned. When the non-strikers came out of the works, they were harassed and shouted at by the demonstrators, who then followed them to Stenhousemuir under police escort. On arrival there, some of the non-strikers were assaulted and windows were broken at their homes, resulting in arrests being made. Court appearances took place over a period of two days with the offenders being fined; the whole episode lasted five weeks. In 1881, Cowan again had to contend with striking moulders. This strike occurred due to the implementation of new regulations introduced at the time of the reconstruction of the works, which brought a fear of reduced wages. Cowan explained that prices were only dictated by market forces. He offered "no strings attached" advances to those suffering hardship during the strike, but this was refused. At that time, the weekly wage of a moulder was on average, 24 shillings per week; pattern-makers earned 21 shillings, wrights and blacksmiths 20 shillings and labourers 15 shillings.

Much of the modernisation of Carron Works was completed by 1883 and this had included the expansion of shipping warehouses. An additional blast furnace of the regenerative type, the No 6, had been added to the others, but possibly in Gordon's time. It was given the number 6, because it replaced the old No 6 which had still been operational when the three new ones were constructed, hence the numbering out of sequence. These were the first blast furnaces in Scotland to have regenerative hot stoves equipped with a chequer brick interior; David Cowan did not claim the credit for these, which adds to the belief that it was Andrew Gordon's work. Cowan still had much to do at the blast furnace department. The two furnaces with the closed tops each had a weekly output of 220 tons as opposed to 180 tons from the others[14]. By 1886, Cowan was about to modify the furnaces to a standard height of sixty-one and a half feet [those at Cleveland had achieved heights of one hundred feet, although a safe height was apparently also dictated by the quality, or type of coal used] and also convert another to the regenerative principle[15]. Other improvements included the provision of reverberatory furnaces equipped with a supply of 'gas' from the two closed-top blast furnaces, augmented by a supply from specially built gas producers[16]. There was also an arrangement for supplying materials to the

Furnace Bridge, by means of a gantry with a hydraulic hoist fed by the railway wagons. A network of pipes provided a high-pressure water supply around the works, which was used to operate hydraulic hoists at various workstations and also doubled as a water supply to fire hydrants. To facilitate the movement of goods around the works, a narrow gauge tramway was laid down - the horse-drawn bogies actually ran to a timetable.

Cowan also instigated a new procedure, the introduction of weekly meetings between the General Manager and his Heads of Departments. At these Tuesday morning gatherings, difficulties could be brought to the managers attention and matters of general interest to the company could be discussed. In this respect, each Head of Department then knew how his counterpart performed and of the possible problems experienced by him; he was responsible for his own department, but that department was indirectly being supervised by the others and under the oversight of the General Manager.

Also in 1886, David Cowan presented to the Institution of Civil Engineers, of which he was a member, a paper he had written about the re-organisation of Carron Works. He described, with the use of a series of plans, the changes that had taken place within the works. Cowan was a proponent of the plan to divert the River Carron which had been suggested by his contemporary, William Jack, one year before in 1885. Cowan used a drawing of the works, "soon after commencement" [based on what is now Register House Plan 44494], superimposing a drawing of the modern works, which shows the river on two different courses[17]. The early plan has been identified by the author as that commissioned by Charles Gascoigne in 1772[18]. It was drawn by surveyor Alex Shepherd and presented to Gascoigne in early 1773[19] (see page) and it does show the river flowing closer to the works. Jack and Cowan both suggested, that the river had once flowed through the area where the new blast furnaces were built. William Jack, while a little off the mark in suggesting that the river flowed as far north as the furnace site, appears to be correct with the rest of his statements. If the river had been diverted, and that would have needed to have been a 'rivers width' to the south, then that event had to take place between 1772/1773, the date of Shepherd's plan of the works, and 1775, when the first road bridge was built. In the absence of plans or records detailing such an operation, it has remained an enigma; however there is usually no smoke without fire. Another unrecorded operation did take place on the River Carron, in the 1820s. The results of what took place then, can be appreciated more from later aerial photographs[20] of the works. The river was restricted or reduced in width, with some ground on the north bank reclaimed between

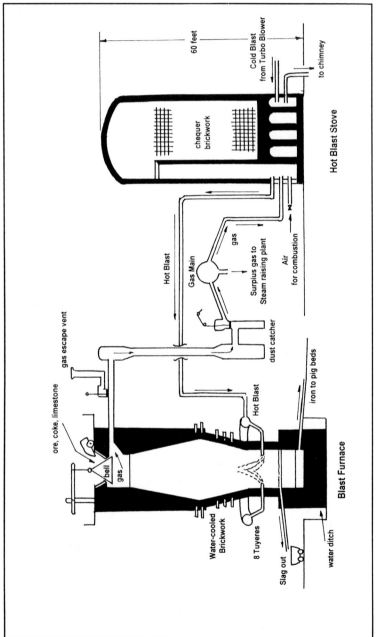

Blast Furnace Unit at Carron Works

the road bridge and the entrance to West Carron village. Slag and refuse from the Works was dumped into the river from the north side, but a part of the northern side of the river was left untouched[21]. On a plan of 1826[22], this is shown as a cut or branch of the river, flowing east from the site of the present day weir and parallel to the river. This part was left for a reason; after the construction of the weir, the culvert from the weir to the works was built in this ready-made trench:

> The large aqueduct which connected with the lock or sluice at the entrance of Wester Carron was constructed to fill the place of the river, whose bed was being filled in with the slag and other refuse from the works, thus forcing the river to make a channel for itself more to the south.[23]

The purpose of the culvert is thought to have been to feed the private canal and to provide water for steam, especially for the blowing engine of Macdonalds, erected in 1829[24]. This water was then raised by pumps, situated beside the blowing engine house[25]. The road to West Carron is somewhat convex in shape, 'bowing' out into the river on the reclaimed land. It was constructed, along with its walls on either side, in 1830[26]. After this operation, the southern boundary of the works took on the convex form, rather than the straight outline shown on the early plan of 1772/1773. The line of the old works southern boundary can be traced from the position of the old Engineering Shop [Steam Engine Workshop of around 1800] and the Blowing Engine House. Another investigation into the river diversion was undertaken by Robert Mitchell of America in the late 1980s. His goal, after very extensive research, was to find the old Stenhouse Damhead and thus the stones from Arthur's O'on. He was convinced of the diversion of the river, but his evidence does not appear to be markedly different from that of the others. After the reconstruction, the major departments were as follows:

The Blast Furnaces. These were large cylindrical chambers of plate iron, thickly lined with firebrick and supported on eight cast-iron columns. The interiors tapered towards that part called the 'bosch', the point of maximum temperature; below that was the hearth where the molten iron and waste, called 'slag' or 'scoria', collected. The outlet here was plugged with clay and was taken out when the furnace was tapped. The molten iron was allowed to run into a channel traced into sand and called the sow, its tributaries being called pigs and hence the description 'pig iron'. (The local hostelry known as the Carronbridge Inn was a favourite haunt of the furnacemen and was given the sobriquet, "the Soo Hoose".) The slag which settled on

The Carron blast furnaces after the reconstruction

top of the iron, was also drawn off, from the 'slag notch', deposited in 'slag ladles' and dumped outside the works. At the top of the furnace was the furnace bridge; the four furnace bridges connected via walkways. Here, on just two of the furnaces by 1886, were the large circular hoppers with the 'bell' at their centre. The hopper was filled with the materials, i.e. limestone, iron ore and at that time, raw coal, which constituted the 'charge' and at the appropriate time the bell was lowered allowing this charge to drop into the furnace. Below the level of the bell, the waste gases were drawn off via 'dust catchers' or filters and taken to the hot blast stoves and other departments. According to later diagrams of these furnaces, the walls of the bosch were water-cooled as was the base of the hearth and there were eight 'tuyeres' or nozzles to inject the blast into the furnace. Eventually, all four blast furnaces were of the closed-top variety. The more efficient heaters were large cylinders similar in size to a blast furnace, and they contained refractory bricks set in a 'chequer' layout. When not in use, these bricks were heated by the waste gases of the furnace; they in turn heated the air from the blowing engine when they were eventually brought into service. The standard procedure at each furnace was to have a heater in use and one being heated, allowing for a changeover and a constant supply of a hot blast. At that time, the blast for the furnaces was obtained from two vertical blowing engines with 78 inch diameter blowing cylinders, and from a beam engine, which appears to have been used with the old furnaces, with a 102 inch diameter blowing cylinder[27]. All were steam-driven, supplied by eleven double-flued Lancashire boilers. Later blowing engines were of the turbine type, driven by super-heated steam. Near to the beam blowing engine, were pumping engines for raising water from the culvert which led from the weir at West Carron to feed the steam raising equipment for the blowing engines[28].

The High (or Heavy) Foundry. Built not far from the brickworks on a north to south line alongside the Forge Dam, the building was 154 feet long and 80 feet wide and incorporated into its southeast corner was the old No 8 foundry or Gun Moulding Shop. It was equipped with two overhead cranes which could bring molten iron directly from the two cupolas. Sugar pans, dyers' pans, stills and large heavy castings were made here and so came the name often used, the 'heavy foundry'. Access to this foundry was by a gate in the northern part of the boundary wall, on the road to Stenhousemuir.

The Low (or Light) Foundry. This was situated directly behind the main office block and was where various light castings such as ship's cooking apparatus, ranges, stoves and rainwater goods were made; it was also known as the moulding shops. The buildings were arranged close to a railway loading bank and the loading basin allowing goods to be dispatched either by rail or canal. The name 'Low Foundry' was given because of its location at the lower level of the works.

The Front Building. Built by J & A Reid of Stenhousemuir, this building which is sometimes referred to as the office block, also contained a warehouse at one end and offices at the other on the first floor with a workshop beneath. In the centre was the clock tower, incorporating the main entrance gate. To the left of this gate was the staff entrance and on the right was the 'business' or 'managerial' door, latterly of the revolving type. A boardroom was also provided, complete with boardroom table and a set of appropriately inscribed chairs. The walls would later be adorned with portraits of the 'great and the good' of Carron Company, beginning with that of William Dawson, which always took the central position, mounted slightly above the rest.

The Brickworks. These were situated at the north end of the works parallel to the 'new road' to Stenhousemuir. Here, bricks were manufactured from clay from the Company's own mines. Before this new facility was opened, a brickfield with kilns had existed on the south side of the lade and

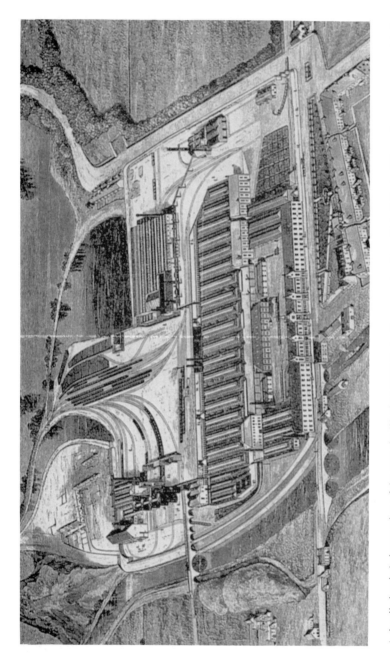

A detailed artist's impression of the way the Works would look after reconstruction. Not all the buildings shown were completed.

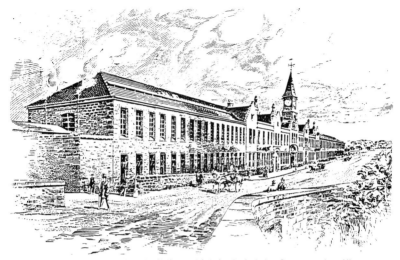

The new front building building which included the Company's offices

a clay mill and refractory brickwork also stood where the Burder Park is today at the spot where Smeaton's last machine for the company, the tilt hammer, was erected. Various types were made, including the refractory bricks used to line the furnaces and heaters, and those for grates, ranges and stoves. Carron Company also made their own general building bricks. Many of these products were also sold externally.

At the same time as the reconstruction, the internal railway system was expanded, and a plan of the time, "Shewing the works after reconstruction", indicates the myriad of sidings, all marked as to their purpose - so many wagons of coal in one, wagons of coke and iron ore or limestone in others. The gradients of some of these sidings are also shown, to assist the shunting operation. Track also went to the rear of the blast furnaces to deliver the various minerals used and to the front, where the 'slag ladles', were filled with the waste product. All waste - slag or scoria were known locally as dander - was deposited at the Cinder Hill, which once stood at the entrance to West Carron village. The Cinder Hill was later removed to allow for the expansion of the village; an area to the west then became the Slag Heap. The only buildings to survive from the older Carron Works were: the No 8 Foundry, the Engineering Shop, the so called 'Thief's Hole' and the row of dwelling houses on the western boundary of the works, which faced West Carron. The Thief's Hole is thought to have dated from the 1770s!

Funding such a massive reconstruction was no simple matter even for a company as big and powerful as Carron. Finance for the project came at

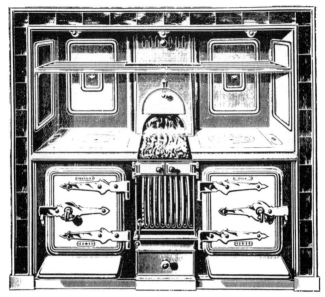

The Palace Open and Close Fire Range

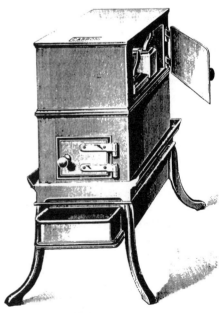

Laundry Stove   Tailor's Stove

first from Company reserves, the greater part of these being the large stocks of pig iron etc., which had been 'put by'. In a period when there was a downturn in sales, money was raised from every conceivable source, by selling stock held for investment, by loans raised against property and latterly from loans arranged by Brodie & Co the law agents[29]. Given this financial climate it is perhaps surprising that such an extensive reconstructiuon programme was allowed to go ahead at all. It is possible that the new manager was able to persuade the partners that only by such massive investment could they hope to retain their markets into the next century. After 1890, every department was carefully scrutinised - in other words they were to be, in modern parlance, 'profit centres'. In 1961 the economic historian R H Campbell said that the Company was "economically integrated", in other words, departments bought from other departments within the organisation. For instance, coal was sold from the Mining Department to the Furnace Department at a charge "corresponding to market prices", but sometimes these costs were higher than what could have been obtained from outside sources. This would lead to the position where efficient branches, such as the Blast Furnace Department, appeared to be inefficient due to this economic "loading". This anomaly was still being practised in the 1970s, when certain departments could have purchased materials from outside the works at a reduced cost. Even in depressed times when there was no market for their produce, the furnaces continued to work, to use their quota of coal from the collieries which showed a profit whilst the furnaces showed a loss. To be fair, it was sometimes a no win situation where there was great difficulty in closing down a pit, for safety and maintenance reasons, when the demand for pig iron fell for awhile. This was an example of being forced to depend on a supply from within come what may, there were also times when it was an advantage, but the choice was non-existent.

The period between 1849 and 1884 was also a prolific one for design, and beautiful productions came from the drawing boards of Carron Employees: G Frew, W Pearson, A Turnbull, G Smith and J Smith. Over 200 of their collective designs were registered with the Designs Office.[30] The major products of the 1880s included: stable fittings; 'Restaurateur' cooking apparatus; ranges; register stoves for dining and drawing rooms, library and parlour; ship fittings; wrought iron forged; stamped, turned and milled work as used by the Admiralty. The 'Carron' Brand of pig iron was so malleable, they advertised that castings made from it could be punched or sheared. They could also handle special and heavy castings, of up to 30 tons. In 1888, Carron Company's products were exhibited on Stand 586 at the Glasgow International Exhibition.

Dining Room Grate Number 341

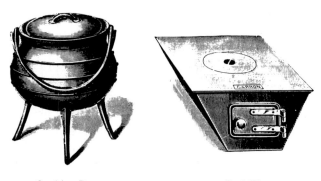

Cooking Pot   Bath Flat

Whilst employed at Carron Works, David Cowan was also involved in other schemes which gave great benefits to the community. He championed the formation of further education, which in those days was referred to as 'art classes', and these were held in the evenings at the old Carron School at East Carron. Cowan was also an original member and convenor of the Falkirk and Larbert Water Trust founded in 1888 and here he used his knowledge of Civil Engineering to aid the acquisition of a water supply from the Denny Hills. Cowan's philosophy was expansionist, always advocating the need to expand to maximise profitability. It may have been the reaction to this policy which jarred with the partners who expected greater results from the new plant, that led to his resignation in 1892. By that time, he was living at Kersehill House in Etna Road. He left Carron Company to become an engineering consultant in Glasgow and spent his latter days at Cove, Dumbartonshire and then at Abernethy where he died on the 10th January 1921, in the house in which he was born.

The benefits of the new works were slow in coming, a problem that would have to be tackled by the next manager. John Frew was promoted from within the Works where he had been the blast furnace manager, but his term in office was marred by periods of ill health. From time to time, he was assisted by Thomas Bamforth, a native of Sheffield who was the foundry manager, and by George Pate. Pate had come to Carron in 1893 from the iron and coal masters Merry and Cunninghame of Lanarkshire and Ayrshire. He took up the post of Company shipping agent at Grangemouth, as successor to William Jardine and, in 1895, he was appointed pig iron and coal sales manager. Carron Company sold much of their pig iron and coal externally, and at that time the markets for pig iron became very competitive, as a result of other firms introducing cheaper grades.

It was due to Bamforth that the works were to expand again. Following an upturn in trade, a new foundry was erected for the production of black castings, on a site south of the river Carron on land that had been part of Mungal Mill Farm. It was named Mungal Foundry and was estimated to cost £22,089, but it was soon given the name "Klondyke", after the Yukon goldrush of the time. The moulders at "Old Carron" had to load their sand and moulding boxes on to railway wagons bound for the new works. Years later in the 1950s, Mr Andrew Graham recalled the event:

> After loading the wagons, branches were cut from nearby trees and stuck into the sand, handkerchiefs were tied to the tops of the twigs and it was all aboard for Klondyke.

The removal wages paid were, "5/- a day per man, 4/- a day to older assistants and 3/6d a day to younger men". The first cast was made on the 1st March 1898 and on that day the workers were given beer or lemonade, and biscuits and cheese; the more enterprising of those present went back and rejoined the queue, for a second helping. Manager John Frew, who had incidentally been the first occupant of Carron Grange, built as the manager's residence between 1895 and 1897[31], resigned from his post in 1899 due to ill health. He died later that year and his successor, Archibald McLellan, came from an outside firm.

Carron Company reached the end of the century in reasonably good heart. Although they had lost both Andrew Gordon and David Cowan, the architects of the new Carron, their legacy was a completely modern plant well capable of maintaining the supremacy enjoyed by the Works for nearly 150 years

Note: The pictures of Sir Thomas Brodie on page 115 and of James Joseph Stainton Maclaren on page 130 are included with the permission of the Scottish Record Office. The reference numbers are GD 58/21/2/55/18 and GD 58/21/55/13 respectively. The original drawing of *A Light Constructed Gun* on page 182 is also used with permission and has reference number GD 58/8/87.

CHAPTER 6

Carron Company in the 20th Century

As the new century opened, the major part of the shareholding of Carron Company was still in the hands of a relatively small group of people, mostly descendants of the Stainton, Dawson and Maclaren families. The largest proportion was held by the two Dawson sisters. A closer look at these related families may explain the pattern of control within the business.

By this time, Anne Dawson Brodie was Lady Dawson Brodie, but she was also a widow. Her husband Sir Thomas had at one time been Deputy Keeper of the Privy Seal of Scotland and had been knighted in 1892, four years before his death at Idvies House near Forfar. He was interred at the Dean Cemetery in Edinburgh. In acknowledgement of his generous actions in the neighbourhood, Sir Thomas had in 1889, been presented with his portrait by Sir George Reid, and also with an illuminated address; the presentation had been subscribed to by many gentlemen and tenants of the estates in the district. The Dawson sisters were also extremely philanthropic towards the less fortunate of the district and beyond - in 1876, they had a large walled garden created at Carron House and extensive greenhouses built where they cultivated orchids as their late Uncle Thomas had done and often flowers from this garden would brighten up a hospital ward, or the sick room of some local person. Many were grateful for the help given, often anonymously, by these ladies. Two facilities, which benefited from Dinah Margaret Dawson's generosity, were Falkirk Infirmary and the Falkirk Victoria Memorial Nursing Association. Indeed the Infirmary which started life in Thornhill Road illustrates very well the important part played by the family in supporting such community activities. When the original cottage hospital opened its doors in August 1889 it was Sir Thomas Dawson Brodie who performed the official opening ceremony. Eleven years later when the first big extension was completed his widow, Lady Ann, performed this duty and in 1906 a second new building was opened by Miss Dawson of Powfoulis[1].

As far as Carron Company was concerned Miss Dawson could never be regarded as a 'sleeping partner', but as one who took a great interest in the affairs of the ironworks, even to the extent of helping financially at difficult times, a method the company depended on from time to time as their borrowing capacity from outside sources was limited by the terms of the

James Joseph Stainton Maclaren   Miss Dawson of Powfoulis

Charter. She was also very religious, perhaps influenced by the evangelical movement which had appeared in the late 1870s in her father's home town and become the annual "Keswick Convention". It is still going strong today. In 1902, she paid for the building of the Dawson Mission at West Carron and for the provision of a missionary there and a "bible woman" at Carronshore, where the missionary's house was built. The Falkirk Town Mission also took her interest as did the Howe Mission at Stenhousemuir and the Kinnaird Mission, which were at the time largely maintained by her. Her own place of worship was Bothkennar Church but she also followed the activities at Larbert and Airth Parish Churches. Her sister, Lady Anne, who never really recovered from death of her husband, died at her townhouse in Ainslie Place Edinburgh in 1903; all flags, on Company ships, at the Works and at West Carron, were lowered to half-mast. Dinah Margaret then became the major shareholder and in 1904 she made land available for the creation of the William Dawson Park, named in memory of her late father and brother. This new recreational facility served the occupants of the then recently erected housing in Carron Road, Bainsford. Mostly in the form of tenements, these houses were built on ground which had once been part of the Lands of Gairdoch, like others on the east side of the Carron Road right up to the Forth and Clyde Canal.

Miss Dawson herself died at Powfoulis House on the 15th May 1910 and was interred in the Dawson Mausoleum at Larbert Churchyard. A plaque, in memory of Anne and Dinah Margaret, was mounted on the right hand wall within the mausoleum. In the public part of her will, Miss Dawson left large sums of money to many organisations of the Church of Scotland and to other charitable concerns. Ten of her Carron Company shares were transferred to John Little Mounsey, a partner of J.C. Brodie & Sons, the Company's law agents, who then became a partner; the remaining 124 shares became the holding of the Dawson Trust[2]. At the time, Carron Company was found to owe her estate the sum of £90,000, from loans advanced by her[3]. Powfoulis House, which had been extended by Miss Dawson at the turn of the century, was given to the Church of Scotland and in 1926 it became their first Eventide Home[4]; it was converted into a hotel in the early 1950s. As far as is known, the rest of her property became the holding of the Dawson Trust.

The first 'official' chairman of Carron Company in 1906 was James Joseph Maclaren (b.1842), a grandson of Joseph Stainton; he held 53 shares and had been a partner since 1879. At the same time, a grandson of Henry Stainton, Francis Lionel Burder, held 12 and was also a partner. Both men had been the Trustees of the late Henry Tibbats Stainton who had died in 1892; at the end of the first World War his former shares were then in the hands of various members of the Burder family and some with the children of Mrs Elizabeth Stainton Clarke, the eldest daughter of Henry Stainton, and with Alice Stainton Russell, a great-granddaughter of Henry Stainton[5]. Others of consequence, were held by the descendants or trustees of Henry Dawson, James Gibson Craig, and Charles Elphinstone Adam and surprisingly, there were 3 held by the trustees of the late Miss Margaret Minyer whose ancestor John Minyer had first acquired a half-share in Carron Company from Dr Roebuck in 1766[6]. Archibald George Brown, who had been assistant for many years to Sir T D Brodie at JC Brodie & Sons, succeeded Sir Thomas as Company Secretary, Voting Partner and member of the Standing Committee; these responsibilities he carried out successfully until his death in 1924. Charles Marshall Brown succeeded his father as Company Secretary. The majority of the shareholders were from a background in no way connected with engineering or iron, some have even referred to the Standing Committee as a 'gentleman's club'. In 1908, James Joseph Maclaren inherited the old Stainton estate of Biggarshiels from his mother Caroline[7] and he adopted the name of Stainton; from that time onwards, he was known as James Joseph Stainton Maclaren.

Always interested in the running of the works, Maclaren gave up a large conveyancing practice in England to devote his time to Carron Company. This long-bearded, venerable gentleman was also interested in the well being of its workforce and the locality in which they lived. In October 1899, for example, he was invited to lay the completion stone of the McLaren

The Engineering Department at Carron

Memorial Church (now Stenhouse and Carron Church) named in honour of
the Rev John McLaren of Larbert Parish Church. He also contributed in no
small way, to the foundation of the Carron and Carronshore Bowling Club
in 1902/1903, where he became the first Patron with Miss Dawson as first
Patroness. He was keen to encourage others, especially his employees, to
take an active interest in sport, to "refresh their bodies and minds after long
hours of toil" and he was Patron of the Stenhouse and Carron Curling Club,
an honorary member of the Stenhousemuir Bowling Club and the
Stenhousemuir Cricket Club and one time vice-president of the Larbert
Unionist Association. Maclaren also made financial contributions to the
many local miners' gala days, and, as was his way, he would often turn up
on the day to offer encouragement. He and his wife Mabel lived at Ratho
Park, Midlothian. When he died in 1927, his Carron Company shares were
transferred to F L Burder, his successor as chairman, who received 20, Robert
C L Clarke, another grandson of Henry Stainton, known as a musical
composer, who got 20 and Harold Edward White who received 138. H E
White was the son of the late Rev Charles White who had been a partner
and a descendant of many of that name who had worked for the Company
from at least 1800. He was no stranger to Carron where, in the years after
the First World War, he and his brother, P E White, were stalwarts of the
Carron Amateur Cricket Club. In 1932, White took up residence at
Biggarshiels House, which J J S Maclaren had used as a shooting lodge.
Children's playgrounds were provided at Stenhousemuir and Carron in 1928
and 1929 and given the name of Maclaren Memorial Parks, in his memory;
he is still commemorated locally by Maclaren Terrace at Carron. James J S
Maclaren and his wife are both interred in the churchyard of St. Mary's

Episcopal Church, Dalmahoy. These people were the main partners who decided policy for the first quarter of this century.

More expansion followed in 1900 with the construction of the Engineering or 'E' Department, completed in 1901 at a cost of £30,508. As had been the case with Mungal Foundry, a department (engineering) was moved there from the old works at Carron, the vacated space taken over there by the foundries department. Archibald McLellan was still manager, but Bamforth again oversaw the whole operation. That year, McLellan had to retire from the management due to a sudden illness and Thomas Bamforth became manager. As Carron Company's business had become so large and diverse, it was decided by the Standing Committee to institute the position of Assistant Manager; the first incumbent was George Pate. The following year, the Brass Foundry was built near to Mungal Foundry. Another important acquisition at the time was the purchase of the Phoenix Foundry in Sheffield which had a reputation for making fine goods.

From the beginning of Bamforth's management, a whole new range of goods was introduced. In 1903, the manufacture of heavy duty catering equipment commenced and almost at once, the products were being installed in the kitchens of leading hotels, ships and hospitals. In April of that year, certain changes were made to the 'constitution' and 'bye-laws' of the Company[9]. It was resolved that shareholders would then receive, at the terms of Whitsunday and Martinmas in each year, a copy of the Abstract of the Balance Sheet for the half-year ending 31st December or 30th June immediately preceding. A modification was also made to the Company crest or seal, giving prominence to the fact that the company had been incorporated by Royal Charter in 1773[10]. The Company's letterheads then displayed the new crest, and also "and Phoenix Foundry, Furnace Hill, Sheffield". The demand for cast-iron baths increased, due to the fact that the public water supply increasingly found its way into homes. In 1892, the Glasgow Enamel Company had been acquired and enamelling operations started the following year at Carron, with the surfaces of baths, sinks, basins, etc., being porcelain enamelled to a superior degree. By 1908, the output of baths from Carron Works had grown to 15,000 per year.[11]

Carron Park, built as a private residence for William Cadell junior in 1763, and in the possession of the Cadell family since, was bought by Carron Company in 1905 from Henry M Cadell of Grange and it was here in the attics of the old house, that the old correspondence between Roebuck, Garbett and the Cadells had been kept, since the early 1760s[12]. These had been made available in 1898 to the Rev A N Bogle by the Cadell family as source material for his book, *The Founding of Carron Company*. George Pate,

The bridge which carried the road across the river from 1775 until 1905.
Immediately to the left was the iron bridge which carried the tram or waggon
way from the works to the canal at Bainsford. It was fixed to the side of the stone
bridge. Note the remnants of the tram lines of the waggon way at the front left.

who was also a keen company historian, was allowed to record some of
them, the results being used by the Company in articles about the early
days. A portfolio of drawings of James Watt's steam engines and other
devices had also been kept at Carron Park, but was found to be missing
when the house was sold. Carron Park was demolished around 1910[13], as it
was said to be rat infested[14]. Larbert High School Annexe now stands on
the site.

With the coming of the Falkirk tramway, it was found that the old humped
road bridge over the river at the Works was unsuitable for the purpose. One
summer morning, at 3.00am on the 23rd June 1905, the arches of the old
bridge were blown out[15]. The new bridge was built using seven girders with
blue brick arches between them and it is possible that the two stone piers
from the old bridge were kept, as the Iron Bridge used many years before to
carry the tramway from the works, was fixed along them. This was used as
a temporary bridge while the new one, which was constructed in two parts,
(the eastern side was finished first), was being built. Two of the inscribed
stone blocks from the original bridge of 1775 were incorporated into the
side walls of the replacement.

The Carron electric cooker was introduced in 1910, augmenting the gas
variety first made in 1902. According to publicity, some of these early electric

cookers were still being used as late as 1959. In this age of electricity, the Company generated its own supply, from power stations at Carron Works and E Department. All of the products were being made to a high standard which led to the term "Carron finish" being used as a by-word for the peak of perfection. To enable competition to be met in the supply of pig iron, cheaper grades were offered for the first time, but it was felt that there would always be a market for superior quality iron.

Thomas Bamforth died at Carron Grange on the 2nd December 1912 aged 72 years. He had been the last manager to use as his official transport, a pony and trap; his chauffeur was Mr. Robert Kay of 17, East Carron. George Pate took over as manager, vacated his home at Blacktown House and became the fourth incumbent of Carron Grange, the manager's official residence. In 1913, the Company was appointed, by Royal Warrant, Ironfounders to His Majesty, King George V. The Company's last tangible link with Keswick ended with the death of Alex Mitchell Dawson, a voting partner and a grandson of Henry Dawson. He had lived in Keswick in a quaintly named house called "Shu-le-Crow", which once belonged to his grandfather[16].

Carron Company's activities then included collieries, coke ovens, ironstone mines, limestone mines, refractory brick works, foundries for every type of casting imaginable, blast furnaces, fitting shops, a plating shop; galvanising, porcelain, vitreous and stove enamelling shops and a non-ferrous foundry. There were also machine shops, forges, repair shops and locomotives complete with service departments. The company also had a large stock of housing, a fleet of ships, warehouses and showrooms in London, Liverpool, Bristol, Birmingham, Newcastle, Dublin, Glasgow and Edinburgh, with agents world-wide.

From 1899 until 1902, Carron Company had again manufactured armaments, this time for the Boer War, and with the outbreak of hostilities in 1914, Carron Works, Mungal Foundry and E Department were designated 'Government Controlled Establishments'.Plants were built for the manufacture of shells, aerial bombs, mortar bombs and grenades as the Company responded to demands of war in the same way as it had done throughout its 150 year history. Under the manager's personal supervision, women, girls and unskilled workers were trained to operate turning lathes, boring and drilling machines and they augmented the depleted workforce at Carron, replacing those who had gone off to war. All deliveries were met well within the specified periods laid down in the contracts. George Pate was often in attendance at the Ministry of Munitions where his advice was eagerly sought; at the end of the war, for his services, he received the OBE.

The Heavy Foundry around 1900

A section of one of the moulding shops around 1900

In 1922, an old and worthy name reappeared on the list of Company shareholders. Henry Moubray Cadell of Grange, a great great grandson of William Cadell junior, purchased one share of Carron Company stock from the Trustee of the late William Thornton, at a cost £1700[17]. The Company had always been a private concern and as such, under the provisions of its Charter, had no dealings on the Stock Exchange. It was a rare occurrence when a Carron share became available and it is apparent that some of the smaller shareholders knew little or nothing about who was behind the scenes at the Company: -

> The affairs of the company are ostensibly conducted by what are termed 'Voting Partners'. Who they are, or how many there are, I don't know, but I understand the qualification is a holding of 10 or more shares". [Thornton's Trustee.][18]

The person selling shares had to inform the Company Secretary that he wished to do so and to state the selling price. The Secretary then had to inform the voting partners, who had then to decide if the Company wished to purchase. The seller had to be notified within ten days of their decision, and if the Company did not wish to purchase, the seller could go ahead with the sale at the price already given to the Company. At no time was it necessary to disclose the buyer's identity.

A visit to the works by royalty was nothing new - the Archdukes of Austria had already made the Works part of their tour in 1815 and Prince Nicholas of Russia visited Carron in 1821, closely followed by Prince Leopold and Prince Maximilian of Austria in 1822[19]. In 1859, the centenary year of Carron Company, the young Prince of Wales, later Edward VII had visited accompanied by his tutor, Dr Lyon Playfair[20]. He arrived at Grahamston Station on the morning of Saturday 30th July and drove in a "carriage and four" to Carron. He spent two hours at the Works and, before departing for Stirling, giving the manager William Dawson the sum of five pounds, to be distributed by the Rev John McLaren among the poor of Larbert Parish.

Seventy years later, on the morning of 18th January 1932[21], the huge crowd lining the Stenhouse Road beside the main office building grew restless and all eyes were on the clock above them as the large hand moved nearer to 11.30 am, the appointed time of the visit. Most of the throng consisted of children and their teachers, from nearby Carron School. After two false alarms, which had them in fits of laughter, the Bentley carrying the Royal visitor drew up in front of the works. Prince George, later Duke of Kent, was greeted by manager George Pate, chairman Francis Lionel

Burder, secretary Charles Marshall Brown and two other partners, Henry Hilton Brown and Harold E. White. After the party had gone through the main gate, they were confronted by a display of Carron cannon and the famous carronades. The Prince was then shown a cast from the No 6 Blast Furnace before being taken by the works hoist to the top of that furnace where, for a few seconds only, the great bell was lowered to allow him to see the flames emerging. From the north side of the furnace platform, the party paused to look at the breathtaking view of the Carron Dams and company estates and in the distance the Ochil Hills, all bathed in sunshine.

The Prince was then taken round various departments where Mr Pate and Mr Burder explained the operations to him. As they moved from the dressing shop to the bath enamelling shop, they met Peter Rae who at 81 years of age, was one of the oldest men employed at the works. He told the Prince that he had worked there for 67 years and that he had been born at Forge Row. To the surprise of all present Mr Rae then presented Prince George with a picture of himself, which was duly accepted! The visit finished with a luncheon held in the boardroom, attended by the Provost of Falkirk, the Town Clerk and the Lord Lieutenant of the County of Stirling. By 2.15pm., the Royal visitor had left for Falkirk, where he officially opened the new Falkirk Royal Infirmary. Amongst the many photographers present that day at Carron, it was reported that there were "cinema-photographers", with "talking picture apparatus"!

Life at Carron Works in the 1930s was exquisitely 'pictured' in an article written by William Brown of the Publicity Department in 1978. The hours of work then were Monday to Friday 8.00am to 5.30pm and on Saturdays it was 8.00am till 12.00 noon. Staff then could be ordered to work overtime without payment and canteen facilities were non-existent, with those who lived some distance from the works having to bring with them, their ubiquitous 'piece'. Most of the employees had to travel to and from the works by bus or tram, with extra vehicles being brought in at starting and stopping times. The offices were equipped with long high wooden desks and the clerks sat at those on high stools, the rooms themselves were lit by gas jets, once very modern in the 1880s. One notable sight, which was a sign of the times, was the continuous long queue of men applying for vacancies. This line stretched along the front of the office block and it contained men from almost every conceivable background, including painters, carpenters and tailors! School leavers aged 14 years would have to apply for a job at the works, "in their own handwriting" and be prepared to sit a "test" where they might be required to write an essay on why they wanted to work there. (A similar type of entrance examination was still being given to apprentices in the early 1960s.) Relatives of those already employed there seemed to get preference, as they always had done. Whole families, and there could be several generations there at any one time, could trace their 'pedigree' back to people who had worked at Carron in the 19th and occasionally, the 18th century. In those days, an office boy would start on 9/- per week rising to 39/- per week when he reached the age of 21, after that it was up to the performance of the individual. Girls, on the other hand, started on 1/- per week less than that paid to the boys and apparently they never caught up on the scale. The decade of the 1930s was a time when promotion was unheard of before the age of forty, but after that age, anyone unlucky enough to lose their job had little prospect of ever being employed again.

According to manager George Pate, 1933 had opened with the very meagre promise of prosperity in any branch of industry in Carron Company's large and varied undertaking. In the spring of that year, the light castings branch experienced a welcome increase in demand for baths, ranges, mantel registers, rainwater and soil pipes. However, there was no similar improvement in the fortunes of the engineering and general castings divisions, but goods destined for the shipbuilding industries were on the increase. Carron Company according to Pate, was suffering, as were other firms, from the general political climate of uncertainty and suspicion. At the Annual Staff Dinner held in the Dobbie Hall Larbert on Saturday the 20th January 1934, Pate was honoured by the Voting Partners and staff on the occasion of his 40 years with the company, 21 of which he had served as manager.

Despite the grim conditions of the 1930s Carron Company's wide range of products and reputation for high quality enabled the firm to weather the storm. As well as continuing to supply armaments the Works produced castings of all kinds for heavy and light engineering, steam engines, rainwater goods, 'sad irons' of every description and size, golf club-heads, cemetery lair markers etc. 'Finer' goods included ornate fireplaces, hobs and ranges, and by the early years of the century, the cast iron bath was beginning to make its mark. It was these domestic products which captured the imagination of the general public and became synonymous with the name of Carron Company. The years between both the World Wars was the heyday of the Carron manufacture of mantels, firegrates, fireplace suites, and ranges though the huge number of products in this sphere would soon be rationalised[22]. Fireplace suites were available in various period styles, for example, Jacobean, Tudor and Georgian as well as in the famous Adam style using original designs. Hob, basket and dog grates were there in

numerous forms - the now famous Adam jewel dog grate was only one of many. They were faithfully reproduced, but some contained modern improvements such as removable ash pans, dampers and "Blacktoun patent hollow bars", named after the house at Carron, which improved combustion. A large range of accessories complemented these, such as: fire dogs, log boxes, coal boxes [known as Coal Vases], companion sets, coal scoops, kerbs and fenders, all beautifully designed and now highly collectable. The 'Modern Fireplace Suites' of the 1920s and 1930s were primarily for the general market and many are still familiar today, having been installed in pre-war housing and later removed in the 1960s, when fashion dictated a change. These are also much sought after. The basic design featured a small opening with a one-piece back, set in a tiled surround and encased in a wooden mantle. The grates and fronts were numerous including 'Gleneagles', 'Bervie', 'Nos 1 and 2 Segmental' and 'No 2 Carron Stool', to name but a few. There was also the 'Shire Series' of interior grates complete with damper which came with wonderfully designed cast iron surrounds. Some of the more 'classical' models incorporated panels cast from the Haworth patterns. Carron Company also possessed a great number of original Sussex Firebacks and these were used as patterns for the reproductions.

Surprisingly, the 'range', that combination of fireplace and cooker, was still being manufactured and the line included 'The Nairobi', 'The Beeton', 'The Cambrian', 'The Carron' and 'The Carronade'. These models were complimented by a portable type known as 'The Beetonette', "strongly made and well finished". This particular model had been manufactured since the 1880s.[23] Gas and electric cookers came in various sizes, governed by the number and, or size, of burners or hot plates. Carron gas cookers could be fitted with the 'Carrontrol' Patent Automatic Heat Controller, an oven thermostat! The 'Cathedral Series' was a range of portable electric fires: another, the 'Benbow', had a special feature, the realistic imitation of a live coal fire. Gas fires, "specially designed for Municipal Housing Schemes", were supplied mounted on an integral cast iron hearth and mantel register.

Baths came in a similar wide range of styles and colours: "all Carron Baths in addition to being supplied Porcelain Enamelled White or Greenstone, can now be had in the following colours: Blue, Pink, Cream and Yellow". The basic bath came as a 'parallel' or a 'taper', with sides tapering to follow body contours, the 'combination' meant that taps were fitted as standard. The parallel bath range included: 'Carron Grange', 'Letham', 'Carbrook' and 'Glenbervie', the latter being the top of the range which included a modern feature, panels. In addition, it was available with a spray and shower arrangement, with glass panels mounted on a tubular

The Company's showrooms in London's west end.

A 1930s Adam style fireplace suite

brass frame. At this time, the company had showrooms in the major cities:

Liverpool	22-30 Redcross Street.
Bristol	62 Prince Street.
Glasgow	123 Buchanan Street.
Edinburgh	114 George Street.
London (City)	15 Upper Thames Street.
London (West End)	50 Berners Street.

Until the second decade of this century, there had been others, in Manchester, Newcastle upon Tyne, Birmingham, Southampton and Dublin. 50 Berners Street, replaced earlier premises at 23 Princes Street, Cavendish Square and was unquestionably the most extensive and lavish showroom in the group. Its floors were divided into distinct sections, displaying fireplace suites etc. in the following period styles: Tudor, Elizabethan, Jacobean, Georgian, Adam, French, Louis X1V, XV, XV1 and Empire. In each section,

> authentic reproductions and genuine antiques are arranged, enabling clients to see at a glance, the effect of such combinations correctly assembled in suitable surroundings.

By the late 1930s however, the premises at Berners Street were no longer being used and the showroom at Upper Thames Street serving as the main outlet in the city for Carron wares. In the 1950s, the London and Liverpool showrooms underwent modernisation.

To mark the occasion of his ten years as chairman of Carron Company, Francis Lionel Burder of Deanston House near Doune, opened the Burder Park in front of the works in 1937; it replaced a landscaped area, which had existed there since the reconstruction of the works in the 1880s. On George Pate's recommendation, the Bannockburn Colliery and Carnock Coke Ovens and By-Product Plant were purchased from the Alloa Coal Company. In that same year, George Pate celebrated twenty-five years as manager [it was always referred to as manager 'for' Carron Company] and for his efforts he was presented with a framed illuminated scroll, testifying to his great achievements over that period[24]. It also included a photograph of himself and other aerial and panoramic views of the Works. The scroll had been signed by the chairman and partners, and by heads of departments. Some of these views of the Works would be used in future publications like the one which appeared the following year, to coincide with the Empire Exhibition being held at Bellahouston Park in Glasgow, at which the

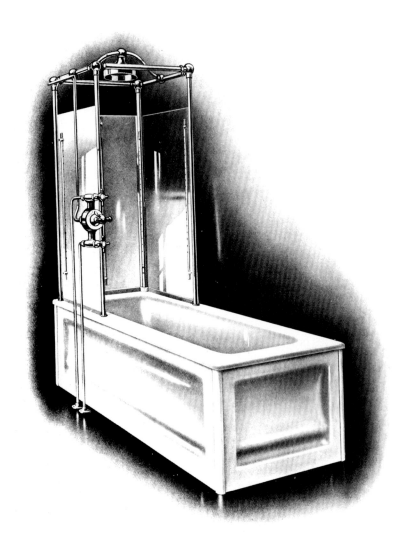

Carron's 1930s luxury 'Glenbervie' bath with 'spray and shower arrangement'.

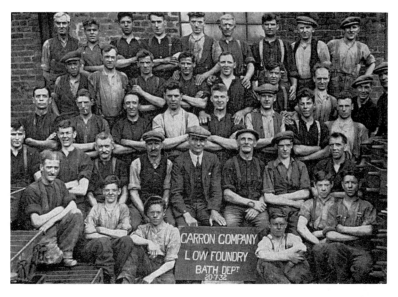

The bath department workforce in 1932

Company ably displayed its wares. It was entitled, *Carron Company, from the reign of George the Second to the reign of George the Sixth* and it gave a résumé of the Company's history and products. Also that year, the Ministry of Supply awakening to events taking place in Europe, placed an order with Carron Company for 25-pounder high explosive shells, for which a special factory was laid down. The following year, the country was again at war and, as previously, George Pate was asked to mobilise the facilities of Carron Company for the production of war materials.

In 1939, Carron Works, Mungal Foundry and E Department were deemed to be "protected places" under the Defence Regulations and each factory was placed on the Ministry of Supply list of vital factories[25]. On the 8th December of that year, the Duke of Kent, who had visited the works seven years previously, returned to Carron to see the first stages of war production.[26] A staggering 98% of production at Carron during the war years was for the Ministries of Supply, Admiralty, Aircraft Production, War Transport, Fuel, Power, etc. There were over 5,000 employees then, of whom, 1,600 were women. It was recorded that one woman, Mrs Margaret Gardner, regularly turned out 1,000 25-pounder shells per 8 hour shift, adding to the 6 million produced then. Almost one thousand employees joined the armed services and with so many away as in the previous war, help in production came

George Pate

from the many women recruited, who learned how to operate lathes and other machines, hitherto the preserve of male employees in peacetime. On a floor where electric cookers had been assembled before the war, a grenade factory was installed; however, it was not just weapons that were made - armies had to survive using other necessities such as stoves and cooking apparatus. A typical list was: 92,000 slow combustion stoves, 7,000 double oven 'Beeton' ranges, 21,000 portable boilers and 7,500 enamelled iron lavatory basins. In addition, 5,000 portable boilers were supplied for the use of the French Army during the retreat of 1940. The order for the boilers was received on a Saturday morning and 1,800 were loaded and dispatched over the weekend, the order being fully completed after one week, thanks to the assistance received from "ironfounding friends" in the Falkirk district. In that same year, the Company gifted an ambulance to the St Andrews Ambulance Association. Catering equipment was installed in canteens of military establishments all over the country by Carron workers, and this inevitably depleted the workforce at Carron. Carron products on ships that had been damaged at sea were repaired by fitters sent from Falkirk who had to work under the most hazardous conditions until these vessels were again sea worthy.

In 1941, F.L. Burder retired from the chairmanship and handed over to H.E. White. A small tree was later planted in the centre of the Burder Park, with a suitably engraved plaque, to honour his term in office. Mr. White "did his bit" to aid the war effort near to his home at Biggar, where he organised the local ARP wardens in true "Dad's Army" fashion[27].

Duplex electric furnaces, for the manufacture of tank tracks in manganese steel, were installed at Carron in 1942 - the Company had never made steel before, but the challenge was taken up and the plant operated by the staff of the Low Foundry with two and a half million of these track links being made for Churchill, Cromwell, Comet and Valentine tanks[28]. War had another effect on production; it brought the curtailment of the rich foreign ores, previously imported for use at the blast furnaces. Lower quality grades had to be substituted and obtained in England. For the aircraft industry, alloy steel and light alloy drop forgings for aero engines and aeroplanes, were supplied by the thousand for Bristol, Rolls-Royce and Armstrong Siddely engines. The following bombers and fighters were equipped with Carron parts[29]: Fairey Battle, Spitfire and Seafire, Fairey Bulmar, Hurricane and Tempest, Fairey Barracuda,Whitely and Wellington, Lancaster, Sunderland and Halifax.

From the Carnock coke-ovens near Airth, came an uninterrupted supply of coke for the blast furnace, sulphate of ammonia for agricultural purposes, benzol for fuel and toluene for the manufacture of TNT. War however did have its lighter side and in the canteens set up at Carron and Mungal for the use of the workforce on constant shifts round the clock, seven days a week, 'ENSA' and 'CEMA' concerts were held and employees were entertained by the BBC Scottish Orchestra and Miss Evelyn Laye among others[30]. Carron Company premises thankfully escaped most of the damage inflicted on similar concerns. The warehouses and offices at London were "scarred" but left intact, whilst the Liverpool Warehouse at Redcross Street, the old haunt of Henry Dawson in the previous century, was completely destroyed. At E Department, a watchtower was hastily erected, to warn of the approach of enemy aircraft. The three foundries, at Carron, Mungal and Mungalhead, were prime targets for German bombs but they were never hit, although a few near-misses occurred at close-by Carronside and Yonderhaugh farms and near to the 'Base' hospital at Bellsdyke Road. It was during the War, too, that the one and only strike by the staff who were particularly bitter over their low pay. After 3 days, George Pate had to agree to their demands.

In 1944 George Pate OBE. JP, retired after 32 years from the management at the age of 82! in 1944. Only Joseph Stainton had served for a longer period. He was as much a part of the fixtures at Carron, as the clock tower. Pate 'ruled' with a rod of iron, a manager of the old school. Early on in his career as manager, he had taken a direct personal interest in the collieries and mineral fields and was responsible for the development and working of those at Cadder, Nethercroy, Shieldhill, Carronhall, Letham, Craigend, Easter Jaw, Gardrum and Newbigging. He also instigated the use of coal-washing plants at the more important collieries. During his time, "almost every section at Carron Works, Mungal Foundry and E Department was modernised and extended, the latest plant and processes adopted". According to a tribute paid to him: "His capacity for work and his knowledge of all the complex dealings of the Company's business was astonishing; he was involved with many associations connected with coal mining, iron-smelting, ironfounding and the shipping industries". He was also, it would seem, a man of two sides being on the one hand a strict Company man, whilst on the other, and mostly hidden, he was fair and kind. Employees, warned of his approach from his home at Carron Grange, from where there was a path leading to the works, by the sight and sound of his two dogs running in front, would "keep their heads down", being seen to be busy. When it came to wage negotiations at Carron, he was loath to part with an extra penny, but when he acted as chairman at some wage tribunal at another works, the workers there knew they would get a fair hearing. He was particularly good to older employees at the Works - for the 'old men of Carron' there was a job for as long as they wanted. In 1902, he was the force behind the establishment of the Carron and Carronshore Bowling Club, arranging for large donations of money from some of the partners of Carron Company and procuring the ground for the new bowling green at the Carron Inns Park, on the same site as a previous bowling green built by William Dawson around 1869. His eldest son, George junior, who had served his apprenticeship at Carron, was managing director and later Chairman, of the Albion Motor Company of Scotstoun who supplied most of Carron Company's road transport fleet; his other son William, was works manager. As well as his obvious concern with all that happened at Carron, he was also interested in the Company's past being a keen historian. His notes and early plans of the works and surrounding area were kept in three leather bound volumes, now a part of the Carron Company Papers held by the Scottish Record Office[31]. He died at Carron Grange in 1945.

Pate's successor was Andrew C Bernard. He had been Works Manager at E Department from 1936, but had left the Company in 1939, returning to his previous employer, the Blochairn Steel Works of Glasgow, as General Manager. In 1942, he came back to Carron as Chief Works Manager. It was his responsibility after the War had ended, to oversee the smooth transition to peacetime production. Around 1945, Carron Company entered into an agreement with Scaw Metals Limited of Johannesburg; the plan was to erect a mechanised bath foundry and enamelling works there, but there were delays in implementing this project. During his period of management two major changes which were beyond his control came when the collieries were nationalised in 1947 and the shipping part of the business was merged with others one year earlier. It could have been even more traumatic! In 1948 the Company's name appeared on a Government list for possible nationalisation but in the end this came to nothing. In the same year, under Bernard's guidance, the mechanised bath foundry was opened at Carron. It had been anticipated that at the end of the war there would be a shortage of skilled moulders and that there would also be a huge re-building programme,

Another bath in process of enamelling in the new bath foundry

so it was decided to erect this plant for the automated production of bath castings. The foundry consisted of sand conditioning and handling equipment; three sand-slinger moulding machine units; cupolas, which resembled miniature blast furnaces; wheelabrator and dressing section. In August of that year, whilst on holiday in the north of Scotland, Mr Bernard died. His successor was Benjamin William Payne who had been Managing Director of Smith and Wellstood Limited in Bonnybridge. One of his first actions was to establish a Research and Development Department. By 1949, the mechanised bath foundry and enamelling works had been completed at Germiston near Johannesburg but serious difficulties were experienced with this operation culminating in a visit from a Carron deputation, which included manager Payne, the chairman, H E White, and the company secretary, James Little Mounsey. The outcome was that Carron Company was to take over the major part of the shareholding, re-organise the works and send out a Works Manager and Assistant Manager to take charge of production. It was 1952 before it could be reported that the general efficiency of the Germiston Works had risen. Carron Company (South Africa) as it became known, later amalgamated with City Engineering Works Limited of Pretoria, in 1958.

In 1950, a 'Senior Executive Staff' was appointed, consisting of M H Metcalfe (deputy manager), Mr Carbarns (book-keeper and senior financial adviser), E J Leaver (chartered accountant), Mr Patrick (manager, light castings foundry production), C. Thomson (manager, home sales) and W. Angus (manager export sales)[32.] At that time, a new range of electric cookers was introduced. This was the Carron 'H' series, "the results of the practical wants of many genuine users". The 'H2' had two hotplates and the 'H3' had three plus a modern glass oven door and included with every cooker was the *Carron Cookery Book* which included tips, methods and recipes which even today are appropriate.

From the time of the reconstruction, there had existed within the works, a narrow gauge rail network which linked most of the departments. Small bogies could then be pulled along this permanent way, by horse. Horses such as 'Major' and 'Jock' were still used then, but were being superseded by a small battery-operated vehicle called the 'electric eel'. It was at the suggestion of manager B. William Payne in January 1950, that the Company magazine known as *Carron Cupola* was introduced and its first editor was William Brown of the Publicity Department. Some of the young ladies, employed in different departments within the Works, were recruited as models and used to publicise the Company's products, often appearing in the magazine. Through the pages of the *Cupola*, now an important social document of the period, employees, friends and customers, were kept informed by photographs and articles, of the latest developments at Carron and of events from the past such as: "The Mechanised Bath Plant at Carron

Works" and periodically, "Cavalcade of Carron" which was a series of historical features. Mr. Brown was another employee who was interested in the history of the company and never failed to promote its past as a link to its current products. Obituaries and intimations were recorded, as well as presentations to those retiring after many years in the Company's service. Not surprisingly at the outset, most of the retirers were the 'EGCs' or 'elderly gentlemen of Carron' and no female employees were involved in the presentations which took place in the Boardroom. Some of these men had completed almost 70 years of service with the Company having started at Carron under David Cowan's management, long before the requisite retiral age was set at at 65 or even 60.

On the 30th April 1951, 199 employees, each with 50 years' service and over, were invited to a presentation dinner held in the Dobbie Hall, Larbert. Only 16 of these employees could not be present and those that were, received gifts, chosen by themselves. This presentation appears to have been unique, in that all subsequent events were as already mentioned, held in the Boardroom. Other regular items in the *Cupola* were a cookery page by Jeanette Heron, photographs of new employees, which initially only included apprentices, known as 'Garvies' but was later extended to female employees, and an "Our People" page.

"Our People No 18", gave an insight into life at the works in the earlier years of this century. William Inglis, assistant to the Low Foundry manager, remembered that the local bairns used to bring food to their fathers and relatives at work. Cans containing soup were slung on rods, and 'pieces' were carried in red handkerchiefs knotted to their arms. Unofficially they also assisted their fathers at work during school holidays and sometimes at weekends. When Mr Inglis was eight years old, he went with his father to the works at 4.00am on a Saturday morning. He would be lifted over the wall at Forge Row and from there, ran through the High Foundry to meet up with his father again at the Low Foundry. William would then assist by shovelling sand, always being careful to look out for the timekeeper! Little gems like that helped to preserve the memory of a by-gone era. M H Metcalfe, who had been chief assistant to the managers since 1925 and who was also a keen Company historian and author of many articles and historical pamphlets like *Famous Men* and *Carron Works*, decided to retire and his place was taken by Eric John Leaver who had been chief accountant.

At this period in time, the ownership of a car was still the privilege of a minority and, as in previous decades, employees had to travel to and from the works on foot, by bicycle or by public transport. At lunchtime, many thought nothing of walking to their homes at Bainsford or Stenhousemuir

FROM THE CARRON CUPOLA OF 1953

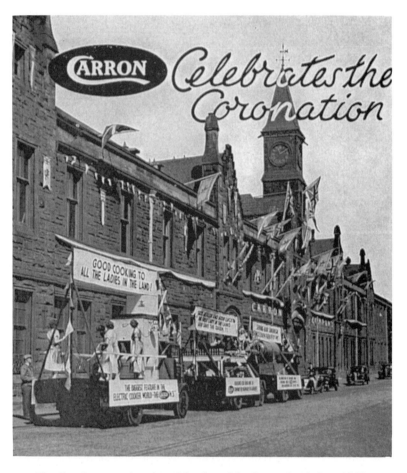

The Cupola reported on the celebration of the Coronation in June 1953 including photographs of the decorated Carron floats which won second and third prize in a local competition. It was won by D W Smith, Plumbers of Larbert. One of the Carron floats had a huge mock up of a cannon and the other carried a giant Carron electric cooker.

FROM THE CARRON CUPOLA OF 1956

Carron used members of staff as models in their advertising campaigns and in this 1956 picture a new coloured electric cooker is being demonstrated by Hannah Cowan of the Hollerith Department.

and then back again, all in the space of a one-hour break. When all three works, Mungal, E Department and Carron, concluded their day's business, the employees leaving resembled those spilling out of some great football stadium. A fully equipped works was opened in Glasgow in 1951 where sheet-metal work was undertaken and heavy-duty cooking equipment for ships, hospitals, hotels, schools and canteens was serviced. In 1952, Carron Company purchased a controlling interest in the patents and processes of Conrad Parlanti, and a new company was formed called "Carron Parlanti" which made "NIFORGE CASTINGS" in aluminium, iron and steel, by the Parlanti Mould Process. These products were used in radar, aircraft, high pressure and "super high quality" engineering work. As a result of this acquisition the business was transferred to Carron from Herne Bay.

In the same year, 1952, the Carron Works Recreation Club and sports grounds were opened in the Carron Inns Park and the clubrooms replaced an earlier one, which had started at Mungal Foundry in 1920. At the beginning, membership stood at 1,500. Various leisure time organisations existed at Carron Works over the years, such as the "Dandy Darkies" in the 1920s, a forerunner of the Black and White Minstrel type of entertainers, a male-voice choir, stamp and chess clubs. For the more energetic, there were football teams known as Carron Violet, Carron Primrose and Carron Villa and almost every department at Carron had their own team. Other games included cricket, table bowls, tennis and a women's netball team. Music had always played an important part in the lives of some of the employees; in the middle years of the previous century, West Carron village had its own band which could be heard at rehearsal if the weather was fine, on the summit of the cinder hill. Earlier in the century, the Company had its own orchestra, whilst Frank Macdonald led the Carron Works Brass Band resplendent in their "company uniforms" and they were always in demand for local functions. They rehearsed in the "practice hall" which stood on the "island", the strip of land opposite the works so called because it had the private canal on one side and the river Carron on the other. The Kinnaird Colliery also had a brass band at that time, but in more modern times the Carrona Band provided music in the Carron area. Each year, 'green fingered' employees took part in the Horticultural Exhibition which was held in the Recreation Club. For many years, Miss Roy organised the Carron Scottish Country Dance class; as a young girl, she had lived at Mount Carron when her father, R P Roy was the house factor and property agent for the Company.

Again in 1952, the automated bath process at Carron Works was augmented by another, this time at Mungal Foundry. A new building was erected on the north side of the foundry and a mechanised plant for casting

Fitter John Kennedy assembling pillar boxes in the Structural Department in 1958

Telephone kiosks during assembly in the Structural Department in 1959

rainwater and soil pipes was laid down[33], as envisaged by Mr Payne back in 1948. Due to the extensive building programme then, there was a heavy demand for these pipes and the foundry was designed to maintain a large output, but with a reduced labour force. It was here at Mungal in the Structural Department, that pillar-boxes, telephone kiosks, cabinets and repeater boxes were turned out by the thousand, for the Post Office. Carron Company had made pillar-boxes from at least 1860. Mungal Foundry also had its own pattern shop and cupola furnace and one sight familiar to those outside the works, was the large bay of moulding boxes stretching towards the fields of Mungal Mill Farm. For many years, dairy cattle occupied those fields, seemingly unaffected by the noise and smell of the neighbouring foundry.

Following the resignation of Mr. Payne, Mr Leaver became manager for Carron Company on the 15th May 1954. Eric John Leaver had joined the company in 1942 as Cost Accountant, becoming Chief Accountant in 1950. Under his guidance, the Company continued to prosper. Harold Edward White, Chairman of the Standing Committee since 1941, died in 1955, ending a connection with the firm dating back to the 18th Century. Charles Henry Burder, son of Francis Lionel Burder and a great grandson of Henry Stainton, became Chairman.

Eric J Leaver

On Thursday evening, 15th November 1956, BBC Television came to Carron Works for a live outside broadcast called appropriately, "Bathnight". Mr. Leaver and various employees were interviewed by Jamieson Clark and James Buchan and a summary of the history of the works was given including a demonstration of a carronade and the old musket, used at one time to defend Carron ships. The highlight of the evening, was the workforce of the bath plant demonstarting the 'art' of making a Carron bath. At around this time, some of the older buildings built in the previous century were demolished and new workshops erected. Eric Leaver instigated this second period of modernisation; the Fitting Shop then was described by him as the most modern in Scotland. Carron Company, seemingly then always at the forefront of some new project, put on a demonstration of a prototype electric tractor. This took place at Bensfield Farm, Larbert, on the 24th September 1958, before a large gathering of pressmen, photographers and BBC Television crew. The tractor was developed at E Department in collaboration with the Ministry of Power and the inventor, Major A McDowall of Castle Douglas. It was designed to be used should there ever be an oil crisis.

The bi-centenary year, 1959, was a most important one for Carron Company and full advantage was taken of this special occasion. All of the newspapers, local and national, contained features and the transport fleet was painted in 'bi-centenary green', replacing the more drab brown colour of the previous livery. On the 26th, 28th and 30th of May, banquets were held for employees and invited guests, the function suite for those evenings was part of a new building erected for the manufacture of cooking and heating units. Special invitation cards were issued to all, informing them of the date of 'their' banquet and the menu cards were illustrated with a scene showing the industry of Carron Company. Senator Roebuck, a great great grandson of Dr Roebuck, was a guest speaker and it had been hoped that Air Commodore Cadell and Captain Sir John Walsham, direct descendants of William Cadell and Samuel Garbett, would be there also, but both were abroad at the time. The Chairman's speech however, given the circumstances in which they were all gathered, was 'cautionary', warning against complacency and of relying too much upon tradition. After being 'wined and dined', the guests were treated to a grand cabaret featuring Alec Finlay, John Glen, Sheila Milne, Margaret McDermot, the Caledonia Choir, Jimmy Neil, Joan Rhodes, the strong woman, the May Moxon Young Ladies, the Falcons and the Chalmers Wood Orchestra. Later, for the benefit of employees in England, dinners were held in Liverpool and London, attended by Eric Leaver, Charles Henry Burder, Air Commodore Cadell and their wives. The children of employees were not forgotten; in November they were invited to Carron Grange where a spectacular fireworks display was held.

As part of the commemoration *The Story of Carron Company, 200 Years of Service*, was published, and for the first time a fuller account of the Company's story was given. This is thought to have been the work of Matthew Metcalfe, the former deputy manager. It was free to employees and to others it cost 6 shillings. Probably due to the success of this, a more detailed analysis of the economic and social history of the firm was completed in 1961. It was simply called, *Carron Company,* and was written by R H Campbell, then of Strathclyde University. This meticulous piece of work, which was published by Oliver and Boyd at a cost of 30 shillings, was the first major historical account of the Carron enterprise and is still a very valuable source of information on the Company's early history.

As the 1960s opened, times were indeed changing and nowhere was this more evident than within Carron Company. In October 1961, it was announced that the Company had won a £2 million contract to supply tunnel segment castings for the Jarrow-Howden Tunnel beneath the river Tyne. The three year contract was believed to have been the largest ever obtained by a Scottish ironfounder: "Our management feel that if the Channel Tunnel ever happens, we will be in a highly competitive position to win a major share of the work in lining it." Sixteen months previously, the Company had been awarded, against strong English competition, a similar contract for the Whiteinch tunnel beneath the River Clyde. A completely new foundry had to be built at Carron and there, every segment was cast. Every month, two or three of the segments were deliberately broken, to test for porosity. The tunnel segments were then transported to Engineering Department where they were 'milled' and finished. For the Clyde Tunnel, Carron Company supplied 1,302 complete rings, that is, 14,765 tons of iron. A complete ring consisted of 13 ordinary segments, two tops and a key and the internal diameter of the ring was 29 feet 6 inches. The first manufactured ring was laid out and underwent a 100% dimensional check; it was then stamped and remained in the factory. Periodically, a complete ring was built on top of this master ring, and then submitted to exhaustive checks for accuracy. Tunnel segment work augmented the production of haulage gear and winches, for which this division was particularly famous. At that time, brass 'ship's sidelights', which had been cast at the Brass Foundry, were also brought to E. Department for finishing. Flanges for pipe-work and door hinges for Volvo cars were stamped out by the steam-driven drop hammers of the forge and then turned or milled there. There must still be many older inhabitants of Bainsford who can remember the constant thud of these hammers, which seemed to continue around the clock, although no one complained. The Engineering Department also had its own Test Room, where Carron metal underwent the stretching and punching by machines, designed to test its breaking strain or hardness. Much of the work done here was for the Admiralty, a tradition carried on over many years. Another new product introduced at this time, and manufactured under a licence from a Canadian company, was the Carron side-loading transporter, a device that allowed vehicles to be loaded from the dockside onto a ship via a side entrance. One in particular was fitted to the S S Canberra. However, 'also in October of 1961, it was recorded that Mungal Foundry and E Department had each made losses of over £10,000 in the previous half-year[34]. Another change in the managerial structure of Carron Company was in the offing.

A Chief Executive, who was to be in effect a Technical Director, was to be appointed and Eric Leaver, who had apparently given notice of his retiral, was offered a three year contract to remain as manager, which he accepted[35]. Only one of the members of the Standing Committee had "strongly disapproved" of this proposition, known as 'Resolution 7900'. Henry Carlyle Wilson Bennetts, an industrial consultant, was appointed Chief Executive from the 1st February 1962[36]. However, on the 21st June 1962, Eric Leaver accepted the terms for his resignation[37] and handed over to "younger and no doubt, abler men". He wrote a final few words for the readers of the *Cupola*, remembering the time when he had assumed the post of manager in 1954. He had stated then, that his term in office would be judged on how much better or worse Carron Company would be at its conclusion. Now he could say "In all modesty, I feel that my bitterest and most ill-informed critics must grant that it is better". As had been the case in 1874, a different structure of management was put in place "to take care of the fortunes of our great Company in the years that lie ahead". Carron Company was to be administered by an Executive Committee composed of certain departmental managers under the chairmanship of Wilson Bennetts[38]. In 1962 the men entrusted with the task of assisting Bennets steer the Company through the

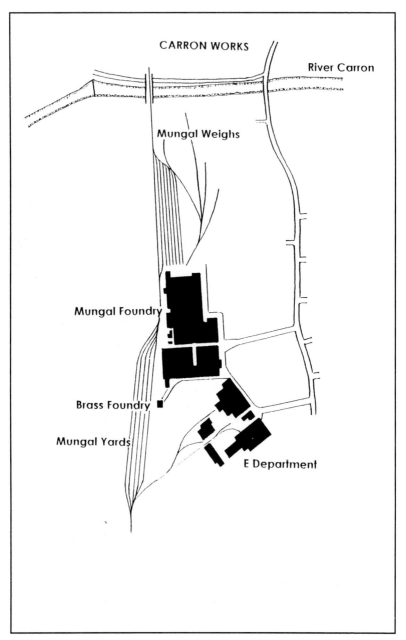

Plan of Mungal Foundry and the Engineering (or E) Department around 1960

The Standing Committee of partners in London in October 1962

difficult conditions which now prevailed were James Gardiner Keith (Manager, Bath and Blast Furnace Divisions); John Lambie (Manager, Foundries Division); A C Langmuir (Chief Accountant); D H Masey (Controller, Finance); J J Paton (General Sales Manager); and J E Yelton (Manager, Engineering Division). H Matheson was appointed Commercial Manager in 1963. They were to be responsible for carrying out the policies laid down by the Standing Committee of Partners[39], effectively the Board of Directors. On the 4th October 1962, this committee met at the Company's offices at Upper Thames Street London, the first monthly meeting of the Standing Committee to have been held in London since the 7th April 1774. The photograph above was taken on that occasion and shows, sitting, Ian Smith (Secretary), Charles H Burder (Chairman), Captain C K Adam and Dr A A Hilton Brown, and standing, C S R Stroyan, Air-Commodore C S Cadell and H C Wilson Bennets (Chief Executive). The Vice-Chairman, Dr H Hilton Brown was not present when this photograph was taken. Three of those members, were direct descendants of early partners and the Hilton Browns, father and son, were descended from A G. Brown, who became a partner before the turn of the century. Henry Hilton Brown had been a member of the deputation which had accompanied Prince George on his visit to the works in 1932.

In August 1962 the Company supplied all the heavy-duty kitchen equipment in the new £1million Falkirk Technical College as well as the catering equipment for use by the students.

A Supplementary Charter[40] was given Royal assent on the 16th January 1963, updating the Royal Charter of 1773 and allowing Carron Company to expand and progress in a more modern fashion. It also meant that the company's Capital could be increased and its low limit of borrowing removed; the term 'voting partner' was changed to 'director'. Many events of note occurred that year. In London, Carron Company's office at 15 Upper Thames Street was vacated and operations transferred to premises at Wellesley Road, Croydon. When the Prime Minister's official residence at 10 Downing Street had to undergo rebuilding, it was Carron Company who supplied replacement firegrates; 1963 also saw the introduction of another department, Carron CHATELAINE, a wholly owned subsidiary of Carron Company which manufactured solid fuel room heaters and commercial catering equipment. A range of stainless steel equipment, including trays, serving dishes and sink tops was produced resulting from a link with a Scandinavian company, Metalliteous Oy. Also available, was a new range of baths including the 'Swallow' and the extravagant 'Forum', designed for the company by David Ogle Associates. The 'Forum' was ahead of its time, with features such as remote control operation.

In July 1964, Wilson Bennetts announced the formation of a new Company for the production of stainless steel sinks to be known as 'Carron Stainless Products Limited'[41]. Carron Company had a 60% holding in this new venture, providing the finance and the manufacturing facilities. The 'know-how' came from its partner, a West German company established in 1924, called Gerdburder-Thielmann. They were to be the first to produce stainless steel sinks in Scotland. A new purpose-built factory was laid down at West Carron. By this time the Carron Group of Companies included Carron Company (Falkirk/London/Liverpool); Chatelaine Limited; Carron & Continental Wharves Limited; City Engineering & Carron Limited (South Africa); Carron Hume Limited; Bathgate Foundry Limited and The Lothians Metal Company Limited.

That same year, the Company's housing stock was offered for sale and an Estate Agent's office was established in vacated property at Dawson Terrace, for that purpose. Sitting tenants who were employees, were given a more favourable price for their homes, for example, houses at Carrona Terrace were sold for £1,200 to employees and at around £1,300 to others. Following on from this, in 1965, came the auction of 'The Carron Estates' held on Wednesday the 28th July at the Albert Halls, Stirling[42]. The property was divided into nine blocks, which totalled about 6,535 acres of ground. Some of this, including the Glenbervie Golf Course, was sold by previous arrangement and finalised on the following day, at the Powfoulis Hotel, once the home of the Dawsons. It may be of interest to note that nowhere in the sale catalogue is there a mention that it was Carron Company's property that was being sold. By this time the old blast furnaces were gone along with a number of familiar tall chimneys from the same period. The old railway system was uprooted with road haulage now the sole method of transportation. Other reminders of the past such as West Carron village where there had been dwelling houses since the earliest days of the Works, and East Carron were only fond memories. The Company had always been quick to exploit its history for publicity purposes but when it came to buildings of historical interest, the attitude was very different.

The use of plastic as a material for the construction of Carron baths was begun in 1965 when the Company acquired a long established firm called Lanarkite. The opening of Carron Plastics Limited sounded the death knell of the cast iron variety which had brought much work and income to Carron for over a century. In June 1966, the Company bought the Glasgow firm of Beckett and Anderson and their products were added to the Carron range of maine deck machinery. The Engineering Division became known as Becander Limited. September of the same year saw the demolition of the old blast furnaces and hot stoves; the outer cladding was cut away using propane blow pipes and the inner shells were then pulled apart. The recovered iron was melted in the new blast furnaces and used as pig iron.

The following decade brought further reorganisation with Carron Company just one part of 'Carron Company (Holdings) Limited' whose Board of Directors [the voting partners] were responsible for policy, finance and development. At Carron the Executive Committee continued to look after the day to day management; the Chief Exective, Wilson Bennetts, served for a time as chairman of the Company and, on his death in the late 1970s, John Lambie, the General Manager of the Foundries Division, became Managing Director. Within the group each product had a division, which was to be a separate profit centre, and each division had a general manager in charge of the operation, employment of labour and wage negotiations. There was a Hydraulics Division at the Michelson Industrial Estate, Kirkcaldy, a manhole cover department in South Wales and a radiator factory at Waterford, Eire. A warehouse also existed at Bow, London, for the distribution of products in the south of England[43].

As change swept through Carron Works, a decision was taken to empty one of the two surviving dams; the original furnace pool had gone in the last

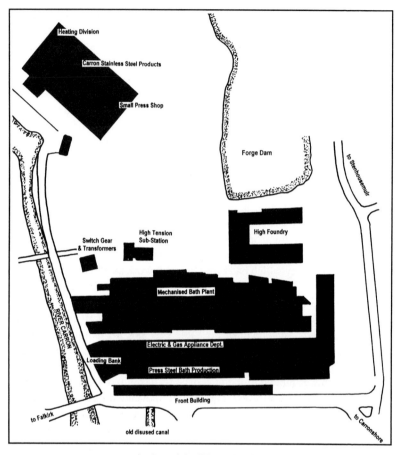

A plan of the Works in 1970

years of the previous century when more space had been required for railway sidings. The reason given for this latest proposal was that a consultant had found that the dam wall was unsafe and the Company did not want to have their employees or their property put at risk. This caused a public outcry. Permission was then requested to allow for the emptying of the dams in order that a new factory and warehouse which would provide jobs, could be built. Finally, after more representations from the public, the water supply to the lade was closed and the dams allowed to empty. The promised factory never appeared, supposedly because of the delay taken to grant permission for the building and some observers have said that this factory, if it had gone ahead, may have helped combat the problems that lay ahead. On the

The battery of reproduction Carronades at Elizabeth Castle in St Helier, Jersey

product list in the late 1960s were cast iron , pressed steel and plastic baths, stainless steel sinks, vanity basins, radiators, pipes and pipe fittings, telephone kiosks, pillar boxes, gas and electric cookers, hydraulic motors and winches, engineering castings, manhole covers and frames. The Company still had a nationwide sales force and a rapidly growing export trade. At a trade fair or exhibition of the time, a reproduction of one of their old products was put on display, to enhance the Carron stand with a little bit of history. The interest shown in this reproduction Carronade was amazing and William Brown of the Publicity Department soon managed to convince the management that there was indeed a market for this 'new' product[44] It was not long before enquiries were received from North America with Brown being offered window space in a New York store, though the proprietor wanted to see the product first and not a 'gimmicky photograph'. Thus, a new range of products was introduced, known as 'Living Traditions' which included reproductions of the Government Gun of 1796 and a Carronade based on the design of the gun on display at the Tower of London. A boatload of these reproduction Carronades was dispatched to Jersey to replace those removed by the Germans during the occupation of the island and others went to far off places such as Newfoundland. Nearer home, two guns were presented to and installed in the new shopping centre at Stenhousemuir. Although these guns are not entirely faithful to the originals, possibly due to cost and or production reasons, it was a great idea and, ironically, would probably have been even more successful today.

In August 1976, David Beveridge, who had started there as an apprentice 25 years previously, and who was by then the foundry manager, cast the last 'box' at Mungal Foundry. Paton Millar, the general manager of Carron Company's foundries division, blamed the closure of this plant on a continuing lack of orders and in particular, those from the nationalised industries. "The foundry was very old fashioned", he said, "and we had to rationalise our interests"[45]. Mungal Foundry had been on short-time working for many months and about 20 employees were made redundant with another

50 being absorbed within Carron Company. Production of pillar-boxes, telephone kiosks etc. was transferred to 'Old Carron' and located within the old moulding shops. E. Department had closed a few years before in 1969 and its buildings had long since been demolished; now that was to be the fate of its 'partner'. It was the intention of the Company to clear the site at Mungal for redevelopment, and by the following year, the land between Mungal Foundry and the River Carron became part of an extensive plan for a hypermarket/petrol station complex. However, that scheme did not comply with the then current policy of the local authority which limited such developments to the town centre. Some of the workshops at Mungal Foundry continued to be used by outside concerns.

Carron Company's last profitable year was 1979[46], just twenty years after the heady days of the bi-centenary, when the future had looked as promising as it ever had. Some of the products then included, the 'Capri Three' electric cooker, the 'Au Pair' and 'Culinaire' electric ovens, and the 'Cuisine' gas oven. In 1980, a new plant was installed, using an advanced vacuum moulding technology; two six-ton capacity electric melting units were built, supplying high-grade iron on a 24-hour basis. This process was "environmentally more acceptable" and the end product was a "clean, true-to-size casting." Despite such investment, between 1980 and 1981, losses amounted to almost £3 million and the workforce was cut dramatically[47]. Over 400 employees were made redundant, leaving a workforce of around 1300. Property at Mungal, Croy, the Chatelaine Works and a London Warehouse were sold, in an effort to raise funds. There was no improvement by the early months of 1982 and, in an attempt to further reduce debt which, by the end of 1981 had stood at £10 million, the Appliance Division, which manufactured cookers, was sold in May, in a deal worth almost £2 million, to Cannon Industries, a subsidiary of GEC. This division alone had made a loss in 1981 of £342,000 and its demise in July 1982 resulted in 215 redundancies. Objections were made by the local MP and by the Trade Unions, after the company waived the usual 90 days notice given to those made redundant[48]. Department of Employment officials had apparently advised Carron Company that the statutory 90 days notice could be waived because of special circumstances[49]. The workforce at Carron was then down to 800 with another 400 employees in England.

On Tuesday the 3rd August 1982 at 2.00pm, the receivers were called in and at 2.30pm, all Carron Company share dealings were suspended. Union representatives were given the details at 3.00pm, followed by the assembled workforce at 3.30pm, who found the news very hard to take it in! Carron Company was in debt to its two banks for a sum approaching £12 million and this, managing director, John Lambie, blamed on the recession in the building trade and on high interest rates. "It was a fatal combination", he said. Colin Stroyan, a partner of law firm Brodies, who was by then the chairman, believed that most of the business could survive. Not only was the workforce stunned by these events; the shareholders, many of whom had connections with the firm going back many years, were equally devastated. The major individual shareholder was still the Dawson Trust, holding almost 1/5th of the total, bequeathed in 1910 by Miss Dawson.

The Company still had assets in the form of land locally and in London and of course there were still departments that were profitable, which included the 'jewel in the crown', the Stainless Steel Sinks Division. Buyers were looked for, with Alexanders Coachbuilders of Falkirk showing an interest in this division, as did a consortium made up of ex-Carron Company directors[50]. Alexanders withdrew and the consortium was given until the 8th September to put together a package which would be acceptable to the receiver. This they did with the help of various agencies, and the Stainless Steel Sinks Division was purchased for £1.2 million, a considerable achievement in such a short period of time[51]. This division was renamed, 'Carron Stainless Steel Products Limited' and later became 'Carron Phoenix'. Other new companies arose, like the proverbial phoenix in the old Company crest, from the ashes of the old. They included, 'Carron Plastics (1982)' and 'Carron Steelyne' later taken over by the English company, Shires. The demolition men moved in and every part of Carron Works no longer required was systematically razed to the ground including, in 1983, Mungal Foundry.

By the 1990s, the land at Mungal and Mungalhead was redeveloped with shopping centres, housing and a new road which winds its way past the site of Joseph Stainton's old home, Mungal Cottage where all that remains is the orchard wall, the cottage having been demolished around the turn of the century. Ground opposite the works which had once been the Carron Inns Park, also went the way of the property developer with a new housing estate though this part of the Company's property had always been used for recreational purposes only. Perhaps the greatest change to the landscape at Carron, and one which caused the greatest indignation among the general public, was the demolition of the 'front building' at Carron Works. Despite a powerful campaign led by the redoubtable Findlay Russell the cause was lost. All that was left was the clock tower with its embrasure of Carron guns and the cast iron mementos of the past, such as the Watt cylinder of 1766 and the lintel of the first Blast Furnace of 1760, built into its walls. Whilst this was a very public blow to tradition, an even more important building had already been dismantled within the works, without even a whisper. It was the old No 8 Foundry, which had been incorporated into the High Foundry at the time of the re-organisation in the 1870s. Here was the last remnant of an even older Carron Works dating from about 1800 and originally used for the casting of the last Carronades and cannon. Having said that, it would be less than fair to suggest that business men carry the sole responsibility and expense of preserving our history. Others in the community have a part to play if our heritage is to be preserved and presented to future generations.

The three companies formed after the demise of Carron Company in 1982 went from strength to strength, but unfortunately in 1998, Shires which had taken over Carron Steelyne and successfully continued to produce pressed steel baths, decided to rationalise their operation and move to England. The remaining firms are world leaders in their particular fields, but still take a pride in the traditions of quality and design which were laid down by Carron Company for more than two hundred years.

Carron Bathrooms Limited produces one of the largest ranges of acrylic baths in the world in their 150,000 square foot factory, the products of modern technology and innovative design. The popularity of the acrylic bath accelerated after its introduction in the 1960s; today's products are stain resistant and of consistently good quality and colour. The materials used are 'PERSPEX SW' from ICI and the specially developed and patented 'CARRONITE', a "unique, specially reinforced acrylic with properties more associated with cast iron". This company were winners of the Queen's Award for Export Achievement in 1993 and 1995. It remains in the ownership of the original buy-out team.

Carron Phoenix Limited, formerly Carron Stainless Steel Products, is now recognised throughout Europe as a leader in the development and manufacture of high quality kitchen sinks, and for its success in the field of exports, was granted the Queens Award for Export Achievement in 1995. Described in 1982 as Carron Company's "jewel in the crown", it has more than fulfilled the expectations shown in the early days. Back in 1982 former Carron Company directors Roy Mitchell, Manolo Blazquez, John Macleod and Stephen Elster, with the help of the Bank of Scotland and other financial institutions, managed to raise £1.2 million within a period of twenty days, which enabled them to purchase the firm from the Carron Company receivers. When financial and marketing teams analysed the business plan, they concluded that the stainless division had been starved of investment for a number of years prior to the Carron collapse[52]. The first move by the company was to develop a new range of upmarket stainless steel sinks.

Major new customers were found, in DIY chains and in the large private builders such as Barratt and Wimpey. However, it was soon realised that with only one product, stainless steel sinks, the Company was in a vulnerable position. Around 1983, the demand for coloured sinks was growing, with the major supplier based in Germany. Under license to this German company, Schocke, machinery was put in place at Carron and the manufacture of sinks in a material based on a mixture of silicas and polymers, commenced. These 'Silquartz' sinks had a successful press launch in London in March 1985. The advent of this new line was fortuitous, for in the following year, the demand for the stainless steel sink decreased sharply. However, demand for the luxury stainless steel sink was on the increase.

At the end of 1989, in a move designed to capture a larger market share and increase customer choice, the Company began the manufacture of sinks in a new material called 'Granite', also licensed from Schocke. The modern-day 'Carron' sink is thus available in different colours and styles, made from a variety of materials which have specific qualities and characteristics. Having proved that 'Silquartz' and 'Granite' (the compounds are actually mixed on site) were better than any similar material on the market, the company, by then renamed 'Carron Phoenix', became "very attractive" to the Franke Group of Switzerland, the world's largest sink manufacturer[53]. In January 1990, the sale to the Swiss company was finalised.

By the mid 1990s, Carron Phoenix was the largest producer of 'granite' sinks in the world, but realised that the stainless steel plant had not kept pace with modern technology[54]. Under the supervision of managing director Roger Clark, this was rectified by building the most advanced computer-controlled production plant for stainless steel sinks in the world. The new facility is due to be opened by HRH The Princess Royal in October 1998. Carron Phoenix hold the ownership of the old Carron Company crest with the phoenix rising from its ashes, the crossed cannon and the motto: 'Esto Perpetua', devised by Charles Gascoigne. But now the risen phoenix looks in different direction from the bird of 1774. Now it looks forward, hopefully to a bright and prosperous future.

CARRON PHOENIX

Epilogue

As time passes, the memory of Carron Company, the great provider and the place of toil of so many, and of her achievements and contributions to society, will no doubt fade, hence the purpose of this story. The Works were the first of their kind in Scotland and showed the way for others to follow. Their foundation was due to the foresight of Dr John Roebuck, though shortly afterwards, other challenges took his attention. The early years were a constant struggle, fraught with all sorts of unexpected difficulty, while the founders, and in particular William Cadell junior and Samuel Garbett, came to terms with a project which had outgrown in scale even the the original grand plan. Charles Gascoigne then took on the task of reorganising the production methods, securing additional finance and reforming the corporate status of Carron Company. Much of his, and the Company's success at that time, was linked to the introduction of the Carronade gun, which restored Carron's credibility and ensured financial stability. Gascoigne's personal affairs have tended to obscure his great achievements at Carron and in Russia, where his pioneering work with Charles Baird in introducing new technology, has never been fully recognised in this country.

His successor at Carron, Joseph Stainton, with shrewd business acumen, consolidated the success of the enterprise and at the same time guaranteed its future, by leaving it in the capable hands of his descendants, a dynasty which lasted through the 19th century and into the next. It was a highly lucrative time for the Company, but even more so for some of the individuals at the helm whose accounting methods led to such legal and financial wrangling. In the aftermath of this infamy came a period of great expansion and modernisation and a host of philanthropic activities, in part perhaps to make amends for the failings of the previous period.

Wars and Carron Company seemed to go hand in hand and the Works was always there to help arm the nation in turbulent times; this in turn ensured continuity of production and employment in periods when there was a downturn in demand for goods in general. Carron Works became world famous and at one time was the largest of its kind in Europe with many of its products becoming 'household names'. The whole of the surrounding district was shaped by the influence of the ironworks, transforming from an agricultural economy to an industrial one, and one with a rapidly rising population.

Many of the people who came to the works brought with them skills which were of great benefit while others learned their trade at Carron. There weresome who took this knowledge to other places and even commenced similar undertakings to that at Carron, men such as Thomas Edington, John Baildon, Charles Baird, James Baird, George Sherriff, John Hardie and George Ure. Most of the iron foundries established in the Falkirk area and beyond in the last century, employed many who had previously plied their trade at Carron Works.

Despite the regularity of employment, life was never completely rosy at Carron - wages were far from extravagant, working conditions, especially until after the second World War, left much to be desired - but a great many people enjoyed the life there, a view confirmed by many old employees many years after leaving the Works for the last time under such unhappy conditions. Many, through their own efforts, acquired their own homes and most had reasonably comfortable lifestyles. Future historians will no doubt examine more closely the events of the final years, which, with the passing of time, may become clearer.

Most of the fabric of the Works is gone now along with the Roebucks, Garbetts, Cadells, Staintons, Dawsons, and Maclarens and individuals like Gascoigne, Gordon, Cowan, Bamforth, Pate, Leaver and countless others of lesser magnitude who nonetheless contributed in their own way to the history of this great venture where, for over two centuries, the iron ran like water.

Appendix 1

Ordnance Manufacture at Carron

The Carronade of 1778 referred to on page 47 was completely different from the final, fully developed gun, of the early 1800s[1]. Over the years many improvements had to be made. It started out resembling a mortar, with a large calibre but very short length, for example the 18-pounder was only 2ft 4ins[2]. This shortness led to a problem since the gun did not protrude far from the side of the ship, some of the burning wadding from the charge could blow back on board and ignite the rigging. This was one of the reasons why the gun was slow to be accepted by the Captains of the ships of the Navy. By 1793, the 18-pounder had been increased in length to 3ft. 4in[3]. The early versions of the gun had trunnions, two bars or axles on the side of the barrel, which allowed for mounting on a trunnion carriage. Sometime in the late 1780s, the trunnions were replaced by a Carronade 'loop', fitted to the underside of the gun. The gun was then fitted via a bolt arrangement to a slab of wood and known as a 'Joint Carronade'; this method also gave more clearance of the side of the ship.

Later, in the early 1790s, the Carronade was re-designed to incorporate a nozzle, which gave an extension to the muzzle to assist in carrying the blast away from the side of the ship. This nozzle is not counted as part of the firing length of the gun[4]; this was achieved by scooping out the inside of the nozzle back as far as the muzzle. At the same time, the 'dispart sight' on top of the muzzle was moved to the middle reinforce ring. Joseph Stainton quite rightly stated in 1795 that "the guns have been much changed since the last war."[5] Small carronade type guns were later made by others including the Falkirk Iron Company, for use on merchant ships, from about 1800. Some guns exist which have the nozzle, but are fitted with the earlier trunnions and not the 'Carronade Loop'. However, examples exist which were not manufactured by Carron Company. One such specimen, in the possession of the Western Australian Maritime Museum, bears the inscription: "James Carronade, Founder initial F, 1830." The well known illustration (see page 50) of the Joint Carronade from about 1790, often used by Carron Company in publications, is an example of the gun without the nozzle [the Carronade of six diameters] but with the loop or joint mounting and shown on a fixed slide bolted to a ship's side. This appears to have been the first version of the slide, able to be unhooked and wheeled to the required gun port. This arrangement, although it was not realised at the time, was a major step forward in the evolution of the concept of the fixed gun mount. They had taken the carriage which, in the normal fashion was mounted on four 'trucks' or wheels, and turned it into a fixed assembly with a built-in recoil unit. The next step involved the removal of the wheels from the carriage, which by this time served no useful purpose. Then, to give the assembly more manoeuvrability, a pin was fitted to the front edge of the slide and with wheels eventually being fitted at the rear, to allow it to swivel in a horizontal plane. This was the forerunner of the modern naval gun mount, without wheels and with recoil capability. Looking back on this feature now, it was probably just as revolutionary as the gun it was designed to support, but strangely enough, or perhaps typically, no one realised the implications of what they had developed:

> This was in effect the introduction of the front pintle gun mount to naval war-fare and its general adoption at that time, with modifications for long guns, would have greatly influenced naval gunnery which waited for another 60 years before the traditional trucked carriage finally became obsolete.[6]

Another novel version of the slide had wheels at each end and was pivoted in the centre, allowing the gun to be fired from either side of the ship. The final version of the slide, with the front pin or pivot and wheels at the rear, could be mounted either in the 'inside' or 'outside' positions. The outside version had the pivot fitted to a small ledge or plinth, which protruded from the gun port allowing for further clearance of the gun from the side of the ship. Another way of using the gun was known as the 'non-recoil method. It had been devised by Bentham, Inspector General of Naval Works in 1796 and other versions were used by one Captain Philip Broke[7]. The gun was fixed so it could not run back on the slide, or 'skead' in the case of the carriages mounted on wheels, so recoil was stopped, supposedly adding more energy to the shot. It was never used as standard practice.

Most of these improvements were introduced after Gascoigne's time, when the Works was under Joseph Stainton's management. He would personally supervise the loading of the guns at the Carron Wharf at Carronshore, the ships not being allowed to sail unless they were fully laden. In 1799, Carron Company was warned of the dangers of overloading after the sloop 'Carron' had to dispose of part of her cargo at sea, for safety reasons. By the early years of the 19th century, the Carronade was fully developed, well designed and well made.

The Carronade Mountings.

1. A wooden trolley (skid or skead) with four wheels (trucks)[8].

2. A wooden trolley with two wheels (the block trail)[9].

3. A wooden support with a pivot at one end and small wheels at the rear enabling the gun to be moved horizontally, or swivelled. It was a wooden carriage which could be fixed to the side of a ship. The top part holding the gun was slotted into a groove cut out of the bottom part and on recoil, this top section with the gun would slip back in the groove of its counterpart. It was then, by the use of a block and tackle, pulled back into firing position. It was known as a slide.

4. Trunnion Carriage. It was fitted to the same slide, but was designed to support the early guns fitted with trunnions[10].

5. Joint Carriage. As above, but for the Carronade with the loop or joint[11].

6. Iron Carriage. Similar to that used with the long guns, but with two wheels[12].

Testing the Guns
Orders for the Government were sent for proving to Woolwich Warren and the Company was required to follow detailed instructions like the following dated 20th July 1790 when only Carronades were being accepted:

> The proofs to commence within two months after the arrival of the guns and finish in one month. Any deviation from the directions or Drafts given more than Schedule A allows or if they shall not stand two rounds with charge mentioned in Schedule B with two high junk wads of shot of full weight of gauze or in case any hole shall be found 1/5 deep behind the first reinforce ring or 1/4 deep before it or if in case of proof by water to be carried on by forcing Engines any shall penetrate thro or in case of any honeycomb flaw or spots within which the officer may think of consequence. Then the said officer may reject such guns as they think proper.
>
> Schedule A (dimensions) i.e. bore, vent, trunnions, length etc.
> Schedule B Charges of Powder specified.[13]

Later it was said that the mixture of the ores and the composition of the metal were the only secret worth knowing[14]. The iron used was the 'cold blast' type [grey metal was always required] from the old open top furnaces and because of the need for this variety, not all of the blast furnaces in the 1830s were converted to the 'hot blast'. The guns were also said to have been cast in a vertical position [*History of Stirlingshire* 1880, and *Journal of Jacob Pattisson* c1780]; from about 1800 this took place in the No 8 Foundry. During casting, an extra two feet of metal was allowed at the muzzle end; this was later cut off and gave the muzzle a more accurate finish[15].

A book exists in the Company archives from the 1820s, which may be termed a moulders or caster's record book[16]. In it the results of the casting of ordnance were recorded and it is assumed that these refer to work done at the Gun Moulders Shop, later known as the No 8 Foundry. As an example, on Wednesday May 7th 1823, two guns were cast - known as the '1st cast' by Messrs. McOustra and Boyd and another two - known as the '2nd cast', by Messrs. Ure and McGiven. Gun No 84676 was an 18-pounder Carronade and was annotated "Woolwich pr.", which meant that it would be destined for Government service, to be sent for proving to Woolwich. (Guns intended for government service would also have the Royal Cipher mark.) The second gun, No 84677 was a 24-pounder Carronade, probably for private sale. "Trial bars" were used, indicating that the iron available had been graded. There follows a description of this iron; "pig too firm, white", but there is no indication as to whether this iron was eventually used. The outcome was that the "heads" were very good. We may assume that "heads" referred to the muzzle which was a critical part of the gun being cast and which, if not properly executed, tended to burst or upset. There is also a reference to "77 chips" which may allude to irregularities in the outer casing. The four moulders named above were frequently named in the book at this period.

It was noted previously that one of the main differences between the Carronade and the cannon was the 'windage' or space allowed between the shot and the wall of the gun. On the cannon it was 0.3 of an inch, but on the Carronade, it was 0.15 of an inch[17]. This tighter fit allowed for less waste of energy, so a smaller charge could be used. It was only possible because of the accuracy of the boring machine. With the cannon, where this windage was greater, the cannonball could theoretically bounce off the wall of the barrel and leave the mouth of the gun in a direction opposite to where it last touched the gun whereas the shot from the Carronade left the muzzle in almost a straight line. However, this finer fit also led to a problem. At the time, cannonballs were stored in the ship's hold and in those damp conditions, would rust. This coating of rust prevented the ball from being loaded into the Carronade, so thereafter, it is said that the cannonballs of the British Navy were painted to prevent corrosion[18]. Another first was the use of an elevating or tangent screw at the rear, which was used to adjust the angle of the gun; it replaced the wooden wedge or quoin, which always became dislodged on recoil. This method was found to be slower during engagements and so the quoin was re-adopted.

The Carronade in service.

The gun's first Naval success was at the Battle of the Saintes, off Dominica on the 12th April 1782, when Admiral George, Lord Rodney, encountered the French Admiral Comte de Grasse. Nelson afterwards called it "the greatest victory, if it had been followed up, that our country ever saw". Many more battles and encounters have been recorded praising the deadly abilities of the gun, but latterly, there was another side to the story. The success and popularity of the Carronades and of their devastating effect at a time when opposing ships engaged at close quarters, is not in doubt; but as that tactic changed, and enemy vessels learned to keep out of their range, the need for the Carronade diminished. Woe betide the ship solely fitted with Carronades finding the enemy able to keep out of their striking distance, but well able to strike themselves, using long guns. It was still kept as a special weapon such as on HMS 'Victory' where six 18-pounders and two 68-pounders, one of which fired the first shot at Trafalgar in 1805, augmented the cannon. At a range of about 6 yards, the Carronade fired a combination of one round shot and a cannister shot containing 300 musket balls, through the stern windows of the French ship, 'Bucentaures'. Carronades were also fitted to many ships of the United States Navy such as the USS Constitution 'Old Ironsides', built in 1797. Her long guns were complimented by 20 x 32-pounder Carronades. Another example is the US brig 'Niagara', armed almost exclusively with 18 x 32-pounder Carronades and used with deadly effect against the British Navy at the Battle of Lake Erie on the 10th September 1813, a pivotal event in the war of 1812. Incidentally the 68-pounder Carronades were the largest to be used successfully though the record shows that even larger versions were made. For example, experiments were carried out on the 14th September 1781 at the mouth of the River Carron and on the 1st October 1781 at the New Battery Leith, with a 100-pounder Carronade[19]. It proved a failure due to its size and weight of shot, being difficult to manoeuvre and load. On a list of the Company's products around 1815, there appears, a 132-pounder Carronade which had evidently been the idea of Patrick Miller!

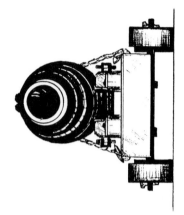

A 12-Pounder Carronade of 1803 on display at Carron Works

Summary of the Carronade.
The arrival of the lighter weight of gun was achieved because the accuracy of the new boring machine allowed for a reduced windage. A much smaller charge of powder was then required. As the quality of the powder improved, allowing an even smaller charge to be utilised, the amount of iron used in the construction of the gun was further reduced. Because of its lighter weight, the number of men required to operate it was also reduced. As well as the general principle of the gun with its large bore and short length, Carron Company came up with another notable achievement, the advanced recoil carriage, now almost forgotten..

The last order for Carronades was sent, ironically, to France in 1852 and the patterns for the guns were reputedly destroyed by Thomas Heggie in 1877 when the old Works were being dismantled to make way for re-construction. The guns eventually became obsolete because of their limited range, but they had served the purpose for which they had been designed, close combat at sea. On display at the works today, are two fine examples of 'lesser' Carronades, both 12-pounders, of the type fitted to all Carron Company owned ships at that time. They are 2 ft. 8 ins. in length and each weighs 6 hundredweight. Their serial numbers are 63991 and 75990, cast at Carron Works in 1803 and 1810 respectively, and they are the final fully developed version. Carron Company also appears to have had in its possession a Carronade mounted on a slide, as shown in a photograph taken during the Royal visit of 1932. It is not known what became of this gun and the photograph is the only record of its existence.

The other Carron Guns.
More than twenty years passed before Carron Company was once again asked to make long guns for the Board of Ordnance. According to Ruth Brown of the Royal Armouries, the Board of Ordnance was always suspicious of Carron guns, believing as late as 1791 that the Carron metal "would not answer". However, by 1795 the Board was forced, owing to a shortage of other suppliers, to reconsider Carron as a manufacturer of long guns[20]. Only Walkers of Rotherham [some of their guns can be seen at Stirling Castle, along with those made at Carron] could match the output from Carron. In 1796, other firms were given contracts to cast smaller 'carronades '[the British Government had always been concerned that Gascoigne would patent the Carronade, which it would appear he never did], freeing Carron Company to make the larger long guns and the larger of the Carronades[21].

Also to be seen on display at the Works, are two of the Company's cannon or 'long guns' which, it was claimed, saw service at Waterloo in

The Blomefield Gun c1796 (above) and the Congreve Gun c1815 (below)

1815, but this is not correct[22], as only brass field guns were used by the British Army at that battle. It has also been inferred that Carron guns were used by Wellington in his siege train at Badajos in Southern Spain on the night of the 5th April 1812. The famous correspondence from Wellington noting his preference for Carron guns and shot for use in sieges, was indeed written in 1812, before the Siege of Badajos:

[To] The Honourable Admiral Berkeley   Treveda

My Dear Sir,

I have received your letter of the 31st January. I have had enough of sieges with defective artillery, and I will never undertake another without the best. Therefore in all my letters I have desired to have either 29 prs. 9 feet long, Carron manufacture, or 29 prs. 8 feet long of the same manufacture, and Carron shot.

Ever, My Dear Sir,

Faithfully Yours,

WELLINGTON.

His letter is certainly confirmation that he had used and preferred Carron guns; however, the evidence suggests that whilst Wellington's request was genuine enough, he never received these Carron guns[23]. Carronades were used on land fortifications and in some siege conditions along with the larger cannon and these may also have been used by Wellington. Another letter from one of his officers states "We have received the wrong carriages for the Carronades." The two cannon on display at the works have the serial numbers 55231 and 55287, cast at Carron in 1797 and are both 9-pounders, 7 feet long with a 4.2 inch bore and weighing 24 hundredweight. They were manufactured under the direction of Colonel Thomas Blomefield, Inspector of Artillery, from 1796 after the prohibition banning Carron Company from making long guns for the Government, was lifted. They are known as the 'Standard Blomefield Pattern', or 'Government Guns' and were designed as naval guns[24]. They were made in 32, 24, 18, 12, 9 and 6-pounder versions, the 9-pounder offered in two different lengths and the 6-pounder in four. At the rear end, or cascable, there is a breech ring that owes its origin to the Carronade. The cannon at the Works are mounted on 'garrison carriages' of non-Carron manufacture which are not the proper size for these guns, being instead, for 24-pounders; this interchanging seems to have been quite a common occurrence. The iron carriages were only used to support the guns on land fortifications during peacetime, as they were easily shattered if hit

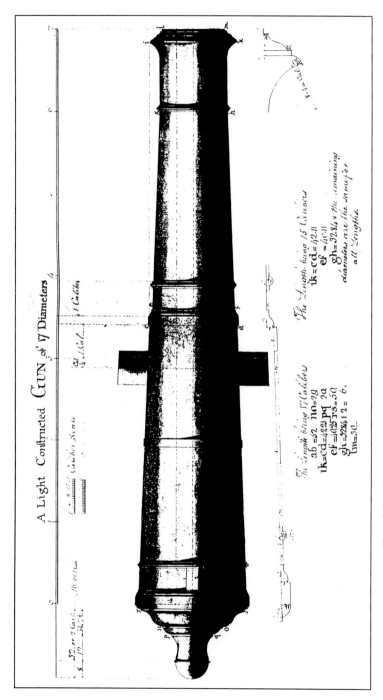

The original drawing for 'A Light Constructed Gun' of 1776. (SRO GD 58/8/87)

by shot; in wartime, they were replaced by wooden carriages. Sometimes the cannon are erroneously referred to as Carronades, for example, Gibson in *Lands and Lairds of Larbert and Dunipace*, described these as such. He also correctly states that they stood for many years at Carron Grange. The present Works display affords the observer the opportunity to compare the two types of gun.

By the early 1800s, the quality of Carron guns was excellent. From 1807, the Company were making mortars for the Government, and in 1813, an order was obtained to cast 300 'Congreve guns'. These were 24-pounder guns designed by William Congreve and were a cross between a Carronade and a long gun. It was Sir William Congreve who accompanied Prince Nicholas, later Czar Nicholas, of Russia on his visit to Falkirk and Carron Works in 1821. In 1900, a long gun made at Carron in 1792, was brought back from Bellary Fort in India by Henry M Cadell and was gifted to the town of Bo'ness in 1902[25]. However, during the second World War, it was removed from its site in the town's Victoria Park and taken for melting down[26]. It was not a Government Gun but one of Carron Company's own 'light new constructed guns' and had most likely belonged to the East India Company which before 1857, was the British presence in India. This company seemingly favoured Carron Company as their supplier of guns and the reason for this may well have been, as already noted, because of the connection with the Honourable William Elphinstone.

A long gun usually began its active life on a newly built or important ship and would, after service, be transferred to an older or less important one ending up as a garrison gun for the rest of its working life ...... or worse still, as a bollard[27]. When the Blomefield gun was designed, it had been intended to have a version for garrison use but without the breeching loop; this was abandoned as it was found that there were enough old guns available for the purpose, especially after the French wars.

The Scale of Dimensions of the Guns.

The scale of the Carron guns was based on the calibre or bore. The 'Light New Constructed Guns' were offered in two scales of 17 or 15 calibres in length, the length measured from the muzzle to the base ring[28]. Each gun, from 1-pounder to 32-pounders, was therefore available in two lengths, that is, 17 or 15 times the diameter of the bore. The positioning of the reinforce rings was determined by the calibre, and the diameter of the trunnions and the pommel were each one calibre. Even the thickness of the metal at various points was based on part divisions of the calibre. The diameter of the shot which was, of course, slightly less than that of the calibre, was used to determine the proportions of the mouldings. The Carronade, after it had evolved from its original design, was based on the same set of rules, but the word 'calibre' was replaced by 'diameter.[29] The gun was then offered in lengths of 6 diameters and finally, when it was fitted with the nozzle, in lengths of 7 diameters[30]. The 'Blomefield' or 'Government Gun, does not conform to the same law of proportions as the original Carron designs.

Shot.

Shot was offered in different types: Langridge, Shell, Grape, Bar, Star and Chain. An excellent description of Carron shot is given in the Journal of Jacob Pattisson. The 'Shrapnel Shell' was invented by Major-General Henry Shrapnel around 1800. He came to Carron and personally supervised the experiments, on land not far from the Works.

Identification marks on Carron guns.

All guns with trunnions, that is, cannon and Carronades. On the end of the left-hand trunnion, the serial number, makers mark - "Carron", and the date of casting. On the end of the right hand trunnion, the size of the gun e.g. 9p for 9-pounder.

Carronades with the loop or joint mounting. The details are on the flat piece (or coin patch) underneath at the rear of the gun. The size of the gun is also to be found on the top of the joint mounting bush, for example, 12 for 12-pounder.

Serial numbers were given to guns as they were cast, irrespective of their type or model[31].

Model Guns.

Over the years, models of Carron guns were manufactured for special occasions and for the souvenir market. Two adorned the fireplace in the Boardroom and in 1932, two model Carronades made from 'Carronium', were presented to Prince George during his visit to Carron. In the early 1960s, model Carronades were constructed in a variety of materials including brass and aluminium; they were boxed complete with a certificate showing a drawing and a history of the gun. Some were mounted on a wooden base, others on an integral aluminium base. The latter used a design shown in publications from the early part of this century. An exquisite "professionally-made" model, of the "Carronade at the Tower of London", was made when the Company decided to introduce the Living Traditions range.

Carron Ordnance 1765 - 1847 [32]

Year	Serial No	Year	Serial No	Year	Serial No
1765	1-	1807	71820	1828	85420
1771	02000	1808	73950	1829	85860
1778	24000	1809	75630	1830	
1789	47880	1810	76890	1831	86150
1790	48120	1811	77750	1832	86345
1791		1812	80230	1833	86445
1792		1813	81930	1834	86560
1793	51120	1814	83680	1835	86680
1794		1815	84025	1836	
1795		1816	84120	1837	
1796		1817	84275	1838	
1797	56450	1818	84340	1839	86695
1798	59530	1819	84390	1840	86710
1799		1820	84460	1841	86726
1800		1821	84515	1842	86747
1801	62460	1822	84560	1843	
1802	63320	1823	84694	1844	
1803	64570	1824	84708	1845	86810
1804	67150	1825	85140	1846	86820
1805	69450	1826	85285	1847	86827
1806	70630	1827	85390		

Guns advertised in Company's Goods List, thought to be c1800.

Cohorns, proved	3,4,6,9,12 pounders.
Carronade Swivels, proved.	2,3,4,6 pounders
Carronades, viewed & proved	3,4,6,9,12,18,24,32,42, 68,100,132 pounders.
Guns of Light New Construction, viewed & proved.	Swivels ½ pounders. Guns 1,2,3,4,6,9,12,18, 24 pounders
Guns of Government Pattern	¼, ½,1,2,4,6,9,12,18,24, 32,42 pounders

Appendix 2

Carron Company's Shipping Interests

The very first vessel built by the Company in 1760, was the 'flatt' which was a barge or lighter.[1] It was used for moving goods to and from larger ships anchored in the deeper waters of the River Carron at the Greenbrae Reach. Two of these early lighters were in service from 1760 and were used on the river as far upstream as the Stenhouse Damhead[2]. After the new boring mill was constructed in 1771, they were able to reach the interior of the Works using the waters of the mill race which connected with the Stenhouse Mill Lade. The Mill Race became the basis of the private canal, in 1782.

After 1763, Samuel Garbett and Company began to handle the shipping business of Carron Company and in particular operating a service between Carronshore and London. The Garbett ships were; the 'Glasgow' (1763), 'Paisley' (1764), 'Stirling' (1767), 'Forth' (1768) and latterly 'Kingston'. Another ship, the 'Carron' belonging to the Company, was used by Garbett and Company from 1765; her master was Captain Porteous. Due to the increase in business, these ships were augmented by chartered sloops. These ships never operated under sail whilst in the river, but had to be pulled or tracked by men, sometimes numbering 12 to 20, from the banks. Garbett & Company also owned 60 lighters and a brig called the 'Earl of Denbigh'[3]. At the Carronshore harbour at this time, it was the practice for the ships to berth on the mudflats and tie up to "polls" [poles], with the banks reached by planks. Charles Gascoigne himself, took over the lease of the port of Carronshore from Carron Company in 1765 and made many changes there, including the building of a new stone wharf complete with a crane. It was constructed further downstream, on the loop of the river away from the existing wharf and opposite Carron House; this became the base for the Garbett ships. Apart from small leases still held by Carron Company and by Alex Fiddes the former harbourmaster, Gascoigne had complete say in the operation of the port and immediately increased the harbour dues and tried to ride roughshod over all and sundry. He also promoted the Carron Wharf at the expense of the harbour. Fiddes leased the granary at the harbour and Gascoigne then set about blocking his access to the shore. It was alleged that Gascoigne and his men actually physically assaulted Mr Fiddes on one occasion, and at other times they simply confiscated his goods, obstructing

---

At CARRON—For LONDON,

To fail March 5, 1779.

THE GLASGOW, Robert Paterfon mafter, mounting fourteen twelve pounders, and men anfwerable. For freight or paffage, apply to Mr. G. Hamilton, Glafgow, Meff. James Anderfon & Co. Leith, or the Carron Shipping Company at Carron Wharf.

N. B. The Carron veffels are fitted out in the moft complete manner for defence, at a very confiderable expence, and are well provided with fmall arms. All mariners, recruiting parties, foldiers upon furlow, and all other fteerage paffengers who have been accuftomed to the ufe of fire arms, and who will engage to affift in defending themfelves, will be accommodated with their paffage to or from London, upon fatisfying the matters for their provifions, which in no inftance fhall exceed 10s. 6d, fterling.

The Carron veffels fail regularly as ufual, without waiting for the convoy.

A sailing bill from 1792 for the Carron Shipping Company vessel 'Glasgow'

his trade[4]. When the local people saw what was happening they feared for their own livelihood and so rose up against Gascoigne forcing him to compromise[5]. After the collapse of Garbett & Company in 1772, the shipping part of the business was carried on by Trustees until 1778.

It was then that four of the ships were put up for sale and were purchased by a firm, confusingly named, "The Carron Shipping Company", whose premises were on the south bank of the river Carron, on land later occupied by the Grangemouth Dockyard Company [Midland Dockyard Company]. The owner of this concern was Gascoigne's cousin, the Honourable William Elphinstone. These four vessels, the 'Glasgow', 'Paisley', 'Stirling' and 'Forth' along with two others, the 'Carron' and the 'Lady Charlotte', were, in that same year, fitted out with the prototype Carronades. Carron Company also began to use their own ships at this time, between Carronshore and the larger port of Leith; they were the 'Roebuck', 'Falkirk', 'Furnace', 'Eagle' and the 'Robert and Mary'. A ship re-named 'The King of Spain' had been bought in 1777 for the purpose of delivering guns to Spain and was later, in 1782, re-named again, 'The Earl of Dunmore'; possibly in recognition of the part played by the Earl of Dunmore in persuading the King to order trials of the Carronade gun at Woolwich.

The Carron Shipping Company continued to operate the Garbett ships from the Carron Wharf and used shipping agents such as Carron Company's Gilbert Hamilton at Glasgow. William Elphinstone relinquished his share in the Carron Shipping Company in 1782, and it continued to trade under two men who had become his partners, D. and A. Gordon[6]. It has often been asserted that Elphinstone then took up privateering, but this is not quite true; he was employed by the East India Company and eventually became a director and later chairman of that Company. The Carron Shipping Company was only ever a 'sideline'. The reference to "privateering" had some substance, but should not be attributed directly to Elphinstone himself, but to the way in which he operated: -

To George Auld jnr., Aberdeen.   6th January 1781

The Honourable Captain Elphinstone, to whom the whole property of the Carron Shipping Company belongs, has sent out two Privateers within these last six days, armed with gun Carronades. The plan he observes with respect to manning his vessel is as follows:- He gives the men their usual wages per month, and one-third of the prizes they may take, devisable according to the note annexed: the adventures in privateering from the Clyde give their crew only one-fourth of the prizes, devisable in the same manner.

Carron Company[7]

Carron Company then utilised the former Garbett ships, putting them on the London run, delivering ordnance to Woolwich. They were heavily armed with 12-pounder Carronades - the 'Glasgow' had 14 of these - and did not require the services of a convoy for protection. The 'Falkirk' and the 'Forth' were both wrecked in 1782 and the 'Glasgow' in 1786, the year that the Gordon brothers opened the Carron Wharf at Grangemouth[8]. In 1785 Carron Company bought a ship of 170 tons which they appropriately re-named 'The Empress of all the Russias', to be used in their trade with Russia. This ship was later sold, following the episode with Captain Strathearn and his clandestine attempt to take Carron workmen to Russia. Various sloops [single masters] were then acquired for use on the new Forth and Clyde Canal including, the 'Carron', 'Glasgow', 'Leith', 'Banton', 'Falkirk' and the 'Prince of Wales'.

The Carron Shipping Company which, from 1792 had been in the ownership of one Captain Hamilton, an ex-Carron shipmaster, was still used by Carron Company, until its demise in 1805. By the end of the eighteenth century, Carron Company ships included, the 'Bellona' (69 tons), 'Pallas', 'Apollo' (56 tons) and the new 'Banton Packet' (61 tons). They had also

purchased the 'Jamie and Jenny' (37 tons),
for use on the River Forth, it had previously
been owned by a consortium headed by
William Benson, the Carron clerk
associated with the reply to Burns. The
'Stirling' which belonged to the Carron
Shipping Company, was used to transport
Carron guns to London and one of the long
guns on display at the Works today was
dispatched on that same ship, in 1797.

In the early years of the 19th century,
the Company's ships included the 'Doris'
with John Smith as master in 1805[9],
'Despatch', 'St. Patrick' (56 tons), 'Thetis',
'Panope' (138 tons), 'Galatea' and
'Melampus' (86 tons), and these sailed from
the Carron Wharf at Grangemouth, by then
owned by Carron Company. These may
have been the first Carron ships to have a
'cannonball in the mast', the symbol of the
Company's ownership; this is reputed to
have acted as a sign of recognition of a
Carron ship, as opposed to a privateer. The

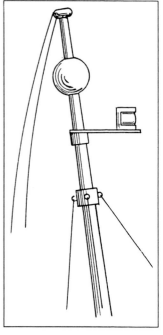

A cannonball at the masthead;
the symbol of Carron Company

Shipmasters of the Carron vessels had to adhere to a strict code of operation[10].
On arrival at their destination, whether it was the River Carron, Woolwich
or the wharf at London, the Master had to make sure that no one left the
ship, with the exception of a boy who would be sent with the Ship's Papers
to the wharfinger or someone in charge.

During and after the Napoleonic Wars, a fleet of schooners was built up,
the 'Minerva' (188 tons) in 1808, 'Penelope' (153 tons) in 1811, 'Juno'
(190 tons) in 1812 and 'Proserpine' (156 tons) in 1813. They were followed
by 'Dynamene' (167 tons) in 1818, 'Abeona' (174 tons) in 1825, and
'Vulcan' in 1840. The names of these ships can be seen on an old sailing
bill of around 1850, advertising weekly sailings from the Carron Wharf at
East Smithfield in London, to the River Carron. From that same source
comes the names of the masters of these vessels at that time: 'Juno' (Thomas
McAlley), 'Abeona' (Andrew Walker), 'Vulcan' (Andrew Graham),
'Minerva' (Alexander Watt), 'Penelope' (John Nicol), 'Dynamene' (Richard
Webster), 'Proserpine' (Walter Bain). Between 1802 and 1810, Walter Bain
sailed in the Carron ships 'Apollo' and 'Melampus', engaged in trading

CARRON WHARF,
No. 47, LOWER EAST SMITHFIELD.

GLASGOW.

ONE OF THE CARRON COMPANY'S UNDER-MENTIONED FAST-SAILING SCHOONERS,

Sails regularly every SATURDAY NIGHT, for

THE RIVER CARRON,

WITH GOODS AND PASSENGERS FOR THE FOLLOWING PLACES, VIZ.

GRANGEMOUTH	GLASGOW	GREENOCK	PAISLEY	PORT GLASGOW
Borrowstowness	Renfrew	Saltcoats	Wigton	Linlithgow
Dunfermline	Dunblane	Maybole	Stranraer	Bathgate
Clackmannan	Kilsyth	Dumbarton	Campbeltown	Rutherglen
Kincardine	Ayr	Stirling	Hamilton	Kirkcudbright
Kirkintilloch	Beith	Alloa	Dumfries	Kilmarnock
Lanark	Irvine	Falkirk	Inverary	And all places adjacent

between Grangemouth and Liverpool; in 1810 he was press-ganged into the Navy, serving on HMS 'Duncan' for four years[11]. In 1816 he joined the Carron ship 'Proserpine' trading to London; for 36 years he served in that vessel, 23 years as mate and 13 years as master[12]. The 'wharfinger', or person in charge of the wharf at East Smithfield, was Henry White, an ancestor of H E White, chairman of Carron Company from 1941 until 1955.

Another line of ships, 'Argo' (71 tons), 'Melampus' (86 tons), 'Latona' (86 tons), 'Milo' (83 tons), 'Luna' (90 tons) and 'Nestor' (89 tons), were used between Grangemouth and Liverpool. One of these vessels, the 'Latona', was involved quite innocently in a curious event which took place at George's Dock, Liverpool on Monday the 9th October 1826[13]. Three casks had been taken down to the quay to be shipped on the 'Latona', they were addressed to, "Mr G. Ironson, Edinburgh" and were marked, "Bitter Salts." These casks remained on the quay overnight, but on the following day as they were about to be loaded on to the ship, it was noticed that a horrible smell was emanating from them. Thomas Crosthwaite, the Carron Company agent, immediately contacted the Police who opened the casks. It was found that they did not contain Bitter Salts but instead held eleven dead bodies, "salted and pickled." The carter who had delivered them, led the Police to a cellar in Hope Street, situated below the schoolroom of one Dr McGowan, a teacher of languages where a further 22 bodies were found. It transpired that McGowan's premises had been let to a man called Henderson from Greenock, who was supposed to be in the oil trade. He had fled, never to be called to account for his deeds. An accomplice called James Donaldson, was caught, fined £50 and jailed for twelve months. The contents of the casks were presumed to have been destined for the anatomy classes of the University of Edinburgh!

Other vessels owned by Carron Company around 1836 were the 'Rebecca' (153 tons) and the 'Eliza' (27 tons)[14]. These and other Carron Company vessels were gradually superseded by a fleet of steam-assisted ships, all with the exception of two, named after rivers. The first steamship owned by Carron Company, and named 'Carron', was built in 1851 by Smith and Rogers[15]. The second steamship to bear that name, was built by Barclay, Curle & Company in 1860. She ran her first trip between Grangemouth and London in 38½ hours under Master Andrew Graham, former master of the sloop 'Vulcan'[16]. The fleet of 1877 is recorded here, along with the names of the masters: SS 'Derwent' (389 tons, built 1874, Peter McKay), SS.'Greta' (John Hardie), SS.'Avon (554 tons, built 1865, James Charles), SS 'Clutha' (533 tons, built 1864, Thomas Millar), SS 'Forth' (498 tons, built 1862, Robert Andersen), SS 'Carron' (447 tons, built 1860, James G. Bain) and the SS 'Tay' (Charles Thomson)[17]. The SS 'Thames' (454 tons), was built in 1860. The two exceptions were, the 'Margaret' (250 tons, built 1878) and the 'Caroline' (646 tons, built 1878), thought to have been named after William Dawson's wife Margaret and Joseph Stainton's daughter Caroline. At about 1.30am on the morning of the 16th July 1874, the SS 'Avon' struck the Bass Rock; she underwent repairs to her helm at Granton. In July 1880, the 'Caroline' went ashore on Fidra Island, laden with a cargo of castings and whisky; after a tricky operation to refloat her, she was taken to Leith for repairs. Her salvage engineer Thomas Napier Armit, who had previously been involved in the recovery of the collapsed Tay Bridge, took an action against Carron Company in the Court of Session, demanding proper recompense for salving the ship. He won his case and was awarded £400 plus expenses. Carron Company were among the first traders on the Forth and Clyde Canal to convert to steam; their fleet of lighters operated between Grangemouth and Port Dundas. Instead of being given names, these vessels all had numbers, for example No 9 and No 12.

The last Carron steamship, the 'Forth' built in 1927

The London and Continental Wharf at St. Katharine's Way London was built in 1881 on the site of Downe's Wharf and, along with neighbouring Carron Wharf at Upper Thames Street, handled the Company's goods along with a new trade, the warehousing of tea, wines and spirits. These items were kept in bonded warehouses and vaults, under the control of the Customs and Excise. The shipping company handled all types of goods, not only its own products, but even those of its competitors such as the Falkirk Iron Company.

The 'Forth', 'Carron' and 'Clutha' were replaced in the 1880s and two new 'screw-driven' steamships named 'Forth' (869 tons) and 'Thames' (869 tons), were built in 1887 by Messrs A & J Inglis of Pointhouse at the instigation of manager David Cowan; these were designed to carry passengers as well as goods. Both vessels were of identical dimensions, 230 feet long, 31.2 feet broad and 14.35 feet depth of hold. Their engines were 2300HP and during trials on the Clyde, both ships exceeded their guaranteed speed of 14 knots. Thomas Dawson Brodie, along with invited guests such as the managing director of Falkirk Iron Company and the owner of the shipyard, were wined and dined onboard the 'Thames' as she completed her sea trials off the Kyles of Bute. Both vessels sailed between Grangemouth and London, three times per week, on alternate days. A 'goods only service operated from Bo'ness every Monday, returning from London on Thursdays and another 'goods only' service went between Grangemouth and Hull. A new vessel, 'Grange' (1518 tons) followed in 1892, and 'Avon' (1722 tons) in 1897.

In 1907, the Carron Dock at Grangemouth was brought into service and in that same year, the 'Forth' and 'Thames' were modified on the recommendation of George Pate, after consultation with naval architects. The ships were lengthened by 40 feet and 50 feet respectively. The 'Carron' was replaced by another 'Carron', the fourth of that name, in 1909, and during the first World War, the 'Avon', 'Forth','Thames' and 'Caroline' were lost in the North Sea.

In the period before and after the first World War, the Company offered a series of seasonal tours to London and published an illustrated tourist guide. During these voyages, a 'contract ticket' could be purchased for 10 shillings which covered the cost of all meals served during the trip, which could last for a minimum of thirty hours. At Grangemouth, passenger trains ran to the quayside, providing an easy connection. However, passenger services were abandoned in 1920 due to the high cost of providing replacement ships. The last Carron Company ship to be built was the SS.'Forth' in 1927. She was built by the Clyde Shipbuilding and Engineering Company at Port Glasgow, with many of her fittings made at Carron; Captain R S Little was master from 1933 until 1947[18]. This ship gave the Company sterling service, averaging 50 round trips to London per year. In 1930, the SS 'Carron' was reconditioned and re-boilered; by this time, the 'regular sailings' of the Carron Line, between Grangemouth and London, were only twice-weekly. The SS 'Carron' was requisitioned by the Government in 1940, taken to Rosyth Dockyard where, after a modification, she was filled with stones and cement. She was then taken to Scapa Flow and scuttled in sixteen feet of water, to block one of the entrances to that anchorage, guarding against the intrusion of more enemy submarines. The SS 'Forth', frequently commodore ship in the convoys, was attacked by the German Luftwaffe in the Thames estuary and survived, though severely damaged.

The Carron Line, "the oldest established shipping business in the world"[19], amalgamated in 1946 with the Clyde Shipping Company Limited, the General Steam Navigation Company Limited and the London & Edinburgh Shipping Company Limited, to form London Scottish Lines; but Carron Company still held an interest. After this merger, a new company, Carron and Continental Wharves Limited, was formed. The SS 'Forth' was sold to Indian buyers in February 1947 and was re-named, 'Bharat Balla'[20].

Appendix 3

Carron Company - Miscellaneous Topics

Many interesting subjects connected with Carron Company touched on in the main text deserve closer attention and have been included here in alphabetical order.

The Adam family, Carron Company's longest serving partners.
In the early 1760s, John Adam, one of the famous family of architects and designers, became a Carron Company partner. For the Company this was indeed a fortuitous appointment; not only was Adam held in high esteem but he, and his family had many important connections. He was, for example, the Board of Ordnance's contractor in Scotland. Adam who is reputed to have brought Haworth to Carron to execute in wood the designs provided by his brothers. The most enduring of these are the dog grates and exquisite mantels, some of which contain instantly recognisable Adam features such as fluted strips, and were available in wood and marble. This style is still copied by today's manufacturers. William, youngest of the brothers, was a partner in the firm of Adam and Wiggin, set up in London to specifically handle the business of Carron Company. There also existed a connection between the Adam family and the Elphinstone family, which meant an association with Charles Gascoigne.

Eleonora, a sister of Lord John, William and George Elphinstone, and a cousin of Charles Gascoigne, was married on the 7th May 1777 to William, only surviving son of John Adam of Maryburgh, mentioned above[1]. William Adam became the Rt Hon William Adam of Blair-Adam and a Carron partner; his second son, Admiral Sir Charles Adam, succeeded him at Blair-Adam. Sir Charles' son, the Rt Hon William Patrick Adam was, from 1853 to 1858, private secretary to the Governor of Bombay, who just happened to be the 13th Lord Elphinstone! He assisted his Lordship during the mutiny of 1857, and in 1880 he himself became Governor of Madras. He was also a partner and is thought to have been the chairman of the Standing Committee formed in 1888. His son, Sir Charles Elphinstone Adam, MP for Kinross, also became a partner. Around 1920, the Trustees of the Sir Charles held 16 shares of Carron Company stock[2]; he was succeeded by his nephew Captain Charles Keith Adam, who became a member of the Standing Committee of partners, upholding the Adam connection within Carron Company.

Arthur's O'on or Oven.

This "famouse piece of Antiquity", was an igloo shaped building which stood in the Stenhouse Estate near to the road from the Stenhouse Ford. It was built of dressed freestone, was over 20 feet in diameter at its base and rose to a height of 22 feet. Entrance to the O'on was by means of a doorway of about 9 ft. high, over which there was an even smaller window[3]. Part of the domed roof was open to the heavens. The whole structure is thought to have been mounted on a stone base. Its origin is uncertain, but antiquarians over the years have proclaimed that it was Roman and probably a temple or triumphal monument connected with the Antonine Wall, which is only two miles away. It has been ascribed: "Templi or Templum Termini". The structure was dismantled in 1743 on the instructions of Sir Michael Bruce of Stenhouse, the stones being used to either build or repair the Stenhouse Mill Damhead on the River Carron. This action brought the protests of antiquarians far and wide.

Arthur's O'on also came under the scrutiny of William Jack[4]. He stated that when he was a boy around1830, he had seen one of the stones from the O'on. It lay under a hedgerow near to the "green" opposite Forge Row. Workmen had apparently discovered it when a well had been sunk. The stone was approximately 5 ft. in length and 16 ins. in breadth and depth; there was a hole at each end. This "green", near to the site of Arthur's O'on, was the drying green associated with the Forge Row, and had been walled in, the stone possibly being used as a part of the foundation. He was also convinced that the old damhead constructed from the O'on stones still existed, underneath the works: "where it has remained after the river course had been diverted". However as yet, no concrete evidence has been found to suggest that the river was indeed diverted. He was also aware of Stukely and Gordon's writings on the subject. Drawings of the O'on exist, made by Adair around 1700, Stukely in 1720, and Gordon in 1726. Another lesser known illustration was executed by the Rev William Nimmo[5] before the building was dismantled; it may well have been his painting that was shown in the *Carron Cupola* in the 1950s, at that time it was in the possession of a Mr McGregor[6]. William Haworth of Carron Company, who was a painter as well as a carver, later copied Nimmo's work[7]. From time to time, fanciful theories emerge which connect the O'on to the legend of King Arthur, suggesting for example, that it may have been the "Round Table", a corruption of "Rotunda" referring to round house.

Bazaars and Philanthropists.

It has often been said that the old Victorian 'captains of industry' were sparing with their money when it came to paying wages and Carron was probably no different. However, those in power at the Company, especially from the last quarter of the 19th century, could never be accused of being backward when it came to aiding a good cause in their locality. Thomas Dawson Brodie was one of the first, with gifts to the Bainsford Poors Fund, providing a complete set of instruments for the Carron Works Brass Band, giving money to the Grangemouth Victoria Library and assisting with the establishment of Bainsford Church. His wife and her sister followed his example. At the turn of the century, it was the fashion to hold a bazaar, as a means of raising money for the more ambitious schemes in the neighbourhood and James Joseph Maclaren acted as chairman at many of these functions. In 1902, he lent his support to the bazaar held in Falkirk Town Hall to raise money for the McLaren Memorial Church; he had been an old friend of Dr McLaren, to whose memory the church was dedicated. In 1903, he supported two bazaars, both at the Dobbie Hall Larbert. The first was in aid of the building fund for Lodge 139 at Stenhousemuir and the second was to boost the funds of the newly opened Carron and Carronshore Bowling Club. Some of his friends and colleagues, and also some of the hierarchy of Carron Company, were often cajoled into assisting. At Carron and Carronshore Bowling Club, from its inception in 1902, it was always normal procedure to invite the manager and some of the directors of Carron Company to become honorary members, thus ensuring a yearly "donation" to their funds!

The Blackmill.

In the days when this mill was used by the tenants of Skaithmuir as a meal mill, it was known as the Nether or Lower Skaithmuir Mill. In an agreement made by Thomas Dundas and Carron Company dated 13th June 1761[8], permission was given for the Company to convey water from the pumping engine at Quarrole Pit to the Lower Mill and to make a dam above this mill, for "preserving the water". It is evident now that Carron Company was using this mill at that early date, to grind charcoal, or 'blacking', for use in casting. On a plan of 1797[9], it can be seen that a brewery existed, at the rear of what is now the Blackmill Inn. The first Ordnance Survey Map, and the Ordnance Survey Name Book of 1860, do not show the Inn, only the blacking mill with a few dwelling houses attached. A Directory of 1898 mentions the Inn and its proprietor Mrs Margaret R Waugh, but by the beginning of the 20th century, the Inn was owned by James Williamson.

Blacktown.

Blacktown House stood on high ground at the rear of where the Carron Church stood. There was a farmstead there known as Mill Quarter at the time of the beginning of the Works in 1759 and as with all of the land in this area then, it belonged to Sir Michael Bruce of Stenhouse. Some of the land of Mill Quarter was 'exchanged' under a contract of 'excambion', by the Company in 1782[10]. A plan of 1797[11] notes that it was "Mill Quarter or Blacktown", and was then in the possession of farmer John Hardie who farmed the land between the Stenhouse Mill Lade and Potter's Farm (Old Roughlands). "John Melvins House" stood beside it, probably referring to the son of the original farmer/miller who had held the ground where the works had been built, and who also held the ground on the 'island' known as "Melvin's Green". The tenant of Mill Quarter (or Blacktown) later complained to Bruce of Stenhouse about the pollution from the Works which caused his land to be not fit to grow even thistles, so Carron Company promptly took over the lease. This property was made over to Joseph Dawson for Carron Company in 1841, the year in which his brother William got married. All that is shown on the feuing plan[12] is one building [John Melvin's house] and a barnyard; the farm road was to be diverted from the front of this site beside the old mill lade, to the rear of it. William Dawson then leased this land and on it he built Blacktown House which was William's home until his death there in 1874. Blacktown House was probably then sold to Carron Company, for use as accommodation for those in 'higher' positions at the works. In the late 1870s, James Clelland the manager of the mines lived there, and in 1881 it was home to two families, that of William Jardine, company shipping agent, and Robert Baillie, a commercial clerk who was also President of the Carron Works Brass Band. George Pate is known to have lived at Blacktown in 1902 and was there until 1912 when he moved to Carron Grange. Thereafter it was inhabited by various heads of departments at Carron Works including for many years this century, by Mr Peebles of the mining department. The house was eventually demolished in the late 1960s.

The Carron Friendly Society.

On the evening of Friday the 28th December 1888, a soiree and ball was held in the Drill Hall, Stenhousemuir, "which had been decorated for the occasion by Mr. Temple, Mr. Brodie's gardener at Carron House"[13]. The reason for the gathering was to stimulate interest in the Carron Friendly Society, which had been dormant for 20 or 30 years. On the platform were Thomas Dawson Brodie, Miss Dawson, and David Cowan along with local ministers and representatives of other iron foundries. Mr Brodie explained that the Society was to be opened to all and not just, as in the past, to those employed at Carron. It had never been open to the Company's miners so other friendly societies such as The Carronhall and Kinnaird, The Kinnaird Colliery and The Carronhall Row Friendly Societies had served their needs. The terms, he said, were as good as any comparable organisation.

The Society had been first established on the 6th November 1762, for the benefit of members in distress and,

> for their families at death, also to promote friendship and charity upon all just occasions, to assist and support each other". Another feature was that, "Every member at his marriage was to have one pound paid to him out of the box, and that there was to be a feast at Christmas, which was to be met by a levy on the members, all that was not spent was to go to the box.

The original rules and regulations were revised, amended and enlarged in June 1795 in the terms of two Acts of Parliament, under a committee consisting of Joseph Stainton, manager for Carron Company, James Fenwick, clerk at Carron, George Espie, Malcolm Clark, William McLaughlan, John Pollock, Alexander Munro, John Binnie and William Harley, moulders; James Millar and John Barbour, smiths; Andrew and John Miller, loam moulders; John Masterton, patternmaker; James Dunlop, dresser; Andrew Fyfe, magazine-keeper and Joseph Jerome, file cutter. Three new members admitted in 1795 were the young clerks, Henry Stainton, Thomas Crosthwaite and Edward Banks, all natives of Keswick, and there was also Alexander Benson and John Hardie, whose descendant founded the Falkirk Iron Company.

The Society continued until 1912 and the advent of National Insurance which removed the reason for its existence. Its two shares of Carron Company stock from which it received income, were sold back to the Company. It is thought that Elizabeth Stainton Clarke, eldest daughter of Henry Stainton, had gifted these shares[14].

Another identical organisation, "The Carron Park Friendly Society", was instituted on the 2nd of March 1772 and revised under the same two Acts of Parliament, in 1797. It probably came under the auspices of William Cadell of Carron Park. However it is known that William Cadell & Sons had also supported the Carron Friendly Society through its early years.

Carron House.

This property has, through its long life, had many connections with people associated with Carron Company. Although it was built initially for Charles Gascoigne from stone from the quarry at Kinnaird, it did not remain in his possession for long since his estate was sequestered in 1779. The original building was built to his specifications, around a courtyard; the southern river facing frontage, which survives today, has the remains of a granary at its western corner. Between that and the eastern portion there is a loggia giving a cloistered effect. It also contained offices and a counting house and was probably, in part, the headquarters of Garbett & Company. It was also Gascoigne's private residence, having no less than thirteen "Fire Rooms" or rooms with fire-places, on one floor alone![15]

The next owner John Ogilvie, probably the factor or coal agent on the Dunmore Estate, bought it at a cheap price from Gascoigne's creditors and lived there for many years. Ogilvie was succeeded by John Walker Ogilvie, who was in possession of the Lands of Gairdoch until about 1838. The house is reputed to have caught fire at some point in its early existence and, while the date of that occurrence is not known, alterations were carried out by Ogilvie around 1789[16] and this may have been the reason. Around 1829, the estate of Abbotshaugh was apparently divided into lots[17] and in 1838, it came into the possession of Henry Stainton, within the "Lands of Gairdoch". During Henry's time, the house probably lay empty and is believed to have been looked after by someone who lived nearby, although the land attached to the house was farmed in the 1850s and 1860s by a Thomas Wood who is shown in the Census of 1851 as being at Carron House. In 1858 it was reported that someone had stolen the lead from the roof, which would support the notion that it was uninhabited. By 1859 it had come into the ownership of William Dawson of Powfoulis. The present Carron House, built within the remains of the older house, was probably constructed in the late 19th century, at the time of the Dawson Brodies. Various plans exist from 1884[18], detailing the "house within a house", and it was then the property of Thomas Dawson Brodie though inhabited by the head gardener Mungo Temple and his family and George Collier, garden labourer, and his family. Three "gardener domestic servants", Robert Hardie, James Nisbet and Charlie Millar lived at the "Gardeners Bothy" and another gardener and two apprentice gardeners were accommodated nearby. The sole purpose of this workforce was to maintain the gardens and hothouses so beloved of the Dawson sisters. These gardens are said to have been constructed from 1876, the year in which Anne Dawson married Thomas Brodie. The gardens were maintained until 1910, when Dinah Margaret died.

Carron Lodge Inn.

This inn stood on the west side of the Falkirk road opposite the Carronbridge Inn and quite near to the Mulloch farm. An old plan of the building drawn in 1883[19] shows that it was owned by Carron Company who were proposing to have it converted into dwelling houses for their employees; this must have gone ahead as there were Carron workers living there by at least 1891. It was a two-storey building with bedrooms and dining room on the first floor and extra bedding space on the attic floor. On the ground floor were the kitchen, rooms and a bar. Various outbuildings housed the stables, harness room, beer cellar and cellars. On the drawing of the front elevation of the Inn, there are two lines shown, one approximately two feet from the ground level and the other at about five feet. The top line is annotated, "Flood Level of August 1877" and the bottom, "Flood Level of February 1882". The Carron Lodge Inn was in the possession of Mrs Jenny Stein from about 1804 until her death in 1854, when the remainder of the lease which had 5 years to run, was offered for sale. The next proprietor was a Thomas McEwan who probably sold the property to Carron Company. The old inn still appeared on the Ordinance Survey map of 1921.

Carron Oil.

This was a mixture of linseed oil and limewater, used as a treatment for burns and scalds. Bottles of this strange concoction were still available from a chemist in Falkirk as late as the 1950s, according to an article in the *Carron Cupola.* On 30th July 1889, one Patrick Tully, a moulder with a burn on his foot, was the first patient in Falkirk's new cottage hospital in Thornhill Road, opened three days earlier by Sir Thomas Dawson Brodie. Patrick's treatment was a dressing of Carron Oil. Interestingly the terms 'Carron Oil' and 'Carronade' became part of the English language and are found in some dictionaries!

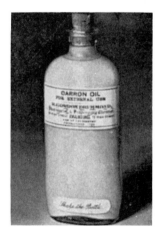

The Carron Schools.

An early school existed at West Carron village and was probably the one referred to as the "Ironworks School" when, in 1791, the schoolmaster was Ebenezer Picken[20]. The teacher's salary came from the pupil's fees and as

such was known as a private venture school, catering for up to 75. Another
school stood near to the works, to the north of Stenhouse Mill and is shown
as such on the Ordnance Survey map of 1860. It had room for 85 pupils and
was funded in the same fashion as its counterpart at West Carron. Both
establishments were the property of Carron Company. This second school
may well be the one known as the "Clubroom School" and which was in
existence in the Clubroom, belonging to the Carron Club, as early as 1786.
It is said to have had a dual-purpose, as a school and as a meeting place. The
head teacher in the 1830s and 1840s was Robert Smith known as "Dominie
Smith", who had previously been employed at the works. After an accident
there, he took up teaching, developing a style said to have been revolutionary
for the time; his assistant was a Mrs Williamson. He was one of the many
enterprising characters who seem to have flourished in the shadow of the
Works, being also involved with a "druggist shop"and the Carron Inn. Robert
died in 1843, aged 43 years and his friends and pupils erected a gravestone
in Larbert Churchyard.

By the time of the 1861 Census, the Clubroom was home to many of the
Company's employees. The Rev Park, Minister of Airth, opened the 'new'
school, nowadays remembered as the 'old school', on the 2nd May 1868.
He made his opening speech, from the "school pulpit"! This fine building
was provided through the generosity of William Dawson and the Company.
It was superseded when schooling became the responsibility of the School
Boards and then served a variety of purposes, being used for evening classes,
as a church before the advent of Carron UP Church, a chapel, and a venue
for late-night dances. Carron Public School was built in 1899, on the site of
the Nailer Row. This old row of two storeys had consisted of 41 houses and
was in two parts; the lower, near to the railway, was called the "Laigh Row".

The Carron Victualling Society.
This was an early co-operative society, one of the first, organised by the
workers and dating from before 1832[22]. It was only open to married people
who were householders and in the employment of Carron Company. Each
person wishing to become a member had to lodge £5-10/- with the treasurer;
£5 being the capital or share held by each member[23]. It has been said that
the high cost of a share put membership outside the reach of the ordinary
worker; but some made the effort, due to clever household management.
The organising Committee held four meetings each year, on the first Monday
of February, May, August and November, at which the books held by the
Treasurer were compared with the accounts paid by the shopman. An
inventory of the Society's effects was also taken then. Dividends in the

form of goods were paid to members after the General Meetings, which were held in June and December. In 1840, the members of the committee were James Mitchell (Presses), John Carmichael (Treasurer), John Dawson (clerk), William Braidwood, Thomas Anderson, Alexander Hunter, David Hotchkis, James Begg, John Andrew, James Bacon, William Clark and James Forrest. John Dawson was of course the brother of William and Joseph. Most of the meetings were held in the Clubroom, Carron, which was also the school, but this one in particular was held in the Barber's Shop Carron:

BS. Carron 25th May 1847

At a Committee Meeting held here this evening a state of the Society's Affairs was read over on which there appeared a gain of £153-18-11 Stl. for the Quarter ending the 3rd May. In terms of Art[icle] 10, the following members will lose one half of their respective profits for this Quarter i.e. Mr. Philip, Ploughman. In terms of the said Art[icle], the following members will lose the whole of their respective shares of the profits for this Quarter i.e. Mrs Jas. Burden, David Connochie, Mrs Higgie, Jas. McKenzie, Alex. McKenzie, L. McLaren, Wm. Smith, Andrew Young, James Henderson S Keeper [the shopkeeper?] and Arch. Waugh, Collier. In terms of Art[icle] 8, P. Allan's (moulder) Share having been taken out in the Goods of the Society, his heirs have no further claim on the society.

Henry Donaldson Presses

On Monday the 10th July 1854, a committee appointed by the shareholders of the Victualling Society, presented John Dawson, James Mitchell and Henry Donaldson each with a pair of valuable gold spectacles in "richly mounted tortoise-shell cases" "to mark the high respect and esteem with which they were regarded as men, and for the strict integrity and business habits by which they were distinguished, as shown during the long period they had conducted the business of the society as clerk, treasurer and president".

The Rules and Regulations of the Society were amended in 1832, 1839 and 1857, during which time John Dawson was clerk. It has been said that before he took over that position, shareholders had been given a poor return on their investment. The Society had its shop at the Carron Bridge across from the Works. The name was eventually changed to the Carron Co-operative Society. This may have been the successor of the older Victualling Society. In the early months of 1766, the clerks at the Works were permitted to operate a 'shop', but Garbett had forbidden them to give credit, which could result in wages being stopped to pay debts[24].

The Carronshore Road.

The old road from the Stenhouse Ford to Airth via Stenhouse [the Crosshillmuirhead road] has been mentioned previously so it may be of further interest to note that the other branch of this highway, which began opposite the Works, to Carronshore, was constructed in 1755[25]. At that time, three bridges had to be built, one over the Stenhouse Mill Lade, near to present day Park Crescent, a second over the burn which was the march or boundary between Stenhouse and Skaithmuir lands, at the foot of present day Alloa Road and a third over the Chapel Burn at Blackmill. Part of its original route was still visible in 1998 in the form of the old wall to the east of Burder Park. This section was abandoned when the Works were being rebuilt, around 1876.

The Collieries.

Houses were built for the miners and included the Red Row at the village of Carronhall and nearer to Kinnaird on the "Longdyke", there was the "Red Houses" and the "Square of Houses". As late as 1871, there was the village of "Old Engine", on the north side of the Bellsdyke Road close to the eastern entrance to Kinnaird Estate. This was the site of the "Engine Pit", used for many years to pump water from the Kinnaird coalfield. Some of the miners lived at Back O' Dykes and at Bensfield, the latter at that time was a small "steading" to the east of the present day farmhouse of that name [which today stands opposite the site of Back O' Dykes]. Another village complete with a school was established near to Cuttyfield Farm and given the name "Kinnaird"; it was built by James Bruce. In Carronshore itself, the Bothy Row was home to many miners. Both villages at Carronhall and Kinnaird had their own friendly societies, early forms of insurance schemes. These operated independently from the main "Carron Founders Friendly Society" at the Works, as Carron Company had refused the miners entry to it, believing that it would encourage absenteeism at the pits.

As the coal became exhausted at the early pits, the workings were moved nearer to the harbour with the Carronhall Colliery Pit No 6, at the far end of Carronshore, the Carronhall Colliery Pit No 5, and the Blackmill Pit. In the 1860s, the Carronhall Colliery "William Pit" was opened, with housing provided for the miners. This was the largest of the Company's mining operations and remembered for its pit bing which was known locally as "Garabaldi". To the south of Falkirk, Carron Company had for many years obtained coal from a multitude of small pits including those at Blackbraes, the Parkhall Estate, Croftandie, Shieldhill, whose first manager was James Fish, formerly of Quarrole and Kinnaird, and Lochelridge and the coal was transported by a train of seemingly endless carts, down through the narrow streets of Falkirk, churning up the roads on their way to the Works. In the 20th century, Shieldhill, Jaw, Gardrum and Craigend were the main suppliers; Shieldhill, the largest, was equipped with its own coke-ovens and serviced by a railway link. In the west, early supplies of coal and ironstone were brought from the Banton estate of William Cadell and then from Nethercroy and Cadder, the latter, the scene of a mining disaster in 1912 following an underground fire. Of the 26 miners who were on that afternoon shift, only four survived. A memorial stone was erected in memory of those who perished.

A pit at Letham was opened in 1913 and, like the others at Carronshore, was served by the Carron Branch Railway. Many houses were built for the miners there, who numbered 400 in 1927, which would suggest that this operation was intended to have a long life. With the exception of Kinnaird, Quarrole and Blackmill, all of the previously mentioned pits were still in service at the beginning of the first World War, the total yearly output being approximately 700,000 tons[26]. At the beginning of the second World War, the only pit being worked near to Carron, was the Carronhall "William" Pit. It had always been the most profitable of the Carron Company mining operations, with its annual output at the turn of the Century being between 100,000 and 150,000 tons, with equal amounts of its coal going to the blast furnaces and to the Carron ships. Coke-ovens at Carnock estate, near Airth belonging to the Alloa Coal Company had long supplied the needs of Carron Company. When the owners wanted to modernise this operation, they were obliged to take note of the needs of their major customer, the ironworks, which in turn decided to purchase the concern.

The last collieries to be operated by Carron Company, Bridgeness [bought from the family of the late HM. Cadell of Grange around 1936], Carronhall, Pirnhall and Bannockburn were nationalised in 1948. In 1949, the area around the Carronhall pit, and the village of Skinflats was immortalised in the murder mystery novel by John Drummond called, *Behind Dark Shutters*. It was set in the period around 1890.

Curling at Carron Dams.

A curling pond once existed on land at the foot of Carronhill near Goshen, at the northwest corner of the dams. Activities started with the Stenhouse Curling Club who had their first meeting on the 24th October 1870. The first President of this club was John Campbell, head clerk at the Works who was also involved with the Carron Burns Club. At that time, the patrons were Sir William and Lady Cunningham Bruce of Stenhouse and their

Annual Meetings took place at the Carron Inn. By 1900, the club was known as the Stenhouse and Carron Curling Club and its members were competing for the "Brodie Medal" and the "patron's prizes" which were presented by James Joseph Maclaren of Carron Company. It was reported then that they had played a match, "on the Carron Dam". Maclaren was patron and Lady Brodie and Miss Dawson, the patronesses. The club had apparently ceased to exist by the early 1920s.

Elphinstone Tower.

The remains of Elphinstone Tower are situated close to the village of Airth. The house and lands were sold on the 7th January 1754 to the Earl of Dunmore for £16,000, £10,000 went to pay debts and the balance to the Trustees on Lord Elphinstone's death[27]. The Elphinstones then took up residence at Cumbernauld House, which had been the property of the Earl of Wigton, whose heiress, Lady Clementina Fleming, had married Charles the 10th Lord Elphinstone[28]. In 1771, under a financial arrangement, John and William Elphinstone, in the company of their cousin Charles Gascoigne manager of Carron Company, became Trustees of the property belonging to Lord Charles and Lady Clementina[29].

After the Earl of Dunmore acquired the property, coal from the estate was purchased by the fledgling Carron Company, but the contract was cancelled in the 1780's due to poor delivery times. The Earl and Carron Company appear to have been on friendly terms with each other; it was the Earl who persuaded the King to order trials of the Carronade and possibly as a gesture of thanks, the Company named a ship the 'The Earl of Dunmore'. The Carronade which stood at the Tower of London, is emblazoned with the coat of arms of the Earl of Dunmore. With the building of Dunmore House, Elphinstone Tower became ruinous, being used as the burial vault of the Murray family of Dunmore.

Firegrates and Stoves.

The Company's manufacture of firegrates began with the hob grate and dog grate, made famous by the extravagant Adam designed 'Jewel Dog Grate'. Other grates of a more utilitarian design were commonly made of wrought iron and accessories such as 'fire-dogs' usually accompanied these. These were set within the chimneypiece against ornately carved firebacks, based on 'Sussex Patterns'. Carron Company also made wood and coal burning stoves such as 'Cabbin stoves', many of which were exported to the far-flung corners of the Empire like Canada's Hudson's Bay Company, in 'kit form' and were re-assembled at their destination. Other stoves were designed

The 1930s Carron range

for more elegant surroundings and were suitably disguised as large Grecian urns etc. They were followed by the ubiquitous 'range', which served a multitude of purposes, that is, heating the room, heating water and cooking, via an integral oven. A fine example of a Carron range can be found in the kitchen of Brodick Castle on Arran. Another development in the late Victorian period was the 'register grate', the forerunner of the modern fireplace. The fireback was made of cast iron and the heat and smoke could then be controlled by a baffle. Whether it was a stove, fireback or cast iron fireplace, it would be decorated in varying degrees, sometimes from the original carvings of the Haworths. These stood the test of time since Haworth decorated fireplaces were still being offered for sale in the 1930s. In the 1950s, the 'Esto B' was a very successful 'all night', coal burning fire whilst the 'Carron Caskette' was a solid-fuel stove. Small portable electric fires called 'The Curtsey'and convector heaters, were also turned out by the thousand with even the heating elements made at the Works. One of the designs was a circular fire with a vertical element called the 'Firebird', which claimed to give "all round heat"

Forge Row.

Forge Row stood within the Works boundary wall [after the reconstruction of 1876] near to the Stenhouse Road and the site of Arthur's O'on and was a long row of two storeys with white-washed walls and a red pantile roof which overlooked the Forge Dam. This early example of company housing appears to have been built during the early years of the Company's existence, as it was the residence of Henry Haworth who worked at Carron from 1779 until his death in 1781. It provided housing for key workers such as the head clerks, the cashier and others, until the advent of the villas at Roebuck Park and Dawson Terrace, which were built for that purpose. In its original state, it faced the old road to Stenhousemuir, which once traversed the works site; when the works were extended, it then became enclosed by the new wall. A drying green, for the benefit of the occupants, once existed at the rear of the row on the opposite side of the road, on the Stenhouse estate below the site of Arthur's O'on. When old Peter Rae was presented to Prince George during the Royal visit to the Works in 1932, he informed the Prince that he had been born within the Works wall, at Forge Row. An old watercolour painting exists in the Carron Company archives and has been identified by the author as being Forge Row, in the latter years of the nineteenth century[30].

Hungry Hill.

This was a small farmstead situated on Carronhill, above Mount Carron. It was in existence before the advent of the ironworks and gave its name to the area, before the change to Carronhill[31]. However, the name of the steading, Hungry Hill, survived and in the mid-19th century, it was home to Carron workers such as David Forrester a gun borer and William Mathieson a labourer. In the middle years of the 20th century, it was inhabited by the manager's chauffeur, Mr Wright. All that remains today, is part of a wall and some scattered red bricks.

William Jack.

It is appropriate to acknowledge the work of this writer who has enriched our knowledge of Carron Works and the surrounding locality. He was brought as an infant to the Carron area in 1825 "either on the day of Joseph Stainton's death, or on the day of his funeral". His father was the gamekeeper on the Carronhall estate, at that time in the possession of Lady Eleanor Dundas. An article, in four parts, appeared in the *Falkirk Herald* in 1861 entitled *Memorabilia of a Carron Worthy*, based on the reminiscences of an old Carron Company employee called Lawrence McLaren, or 'old Lawrie' who had died that same year. The name of the author was not given, but it was almost certainly William Jack, who was a nephew of old Lawrie's wife. Lawrie had been born in Carronshore in 1776, and had related to his nephew many stories of his past life, including eyewitness accounts of the activities of James Bruce of Kinnaird, Thomas Dundas of Quarrole, William Symington, Joseph Stainton and many others. Lawrie at one time had actually carried out repairs on the 'Charlotte Dundas' when it lay at the Bainsford basin and recalled later that someone had come to see this boat and then went to America where he built his own. This may have been Robert Fulton. He also described life then around the port of Carronshore and the tales of the old smugglers and the press gangs, which were all ably retold by Jack. In 1885, another series appeared in that same newspaper, this time under the banner of *Reminiscences of Carron, 50 years ago*, by "Carronade". Again, the true name of the author was withheld.

This time, the articles consisted of anecdotes from the Works, featuring characters who had worked there around the years 1835 to 1840 and also some of the operations in the foundries then. In one of these, the author let it be known that some of his information had come from his old uncle, Lawrence McLaren. His vision of the future Carron district came with this uncanny prediction:

> In future years it is yet to become a great place and a modern town, wherein its streets, its squares, its avenues, its places and all such, shall be laid out in becoming beauty.................The old stone brig will be dynamited and a braw level crossing thrown across the Carron. Electric driven tramcars will run between Falkirk and Carronshore. What is known as the island will be utilised for grand suburban villas, the water sides being dressed and laid out with beautiful walks, all shaded with trees of large leaf, also flower plots, here and there.

He was also controversial in his theories on the diversion of the river at the works, on the inventor of the hot blast for the furnaces and on the origin of Arthur's O'on. In the week when his last article was published, the author died and his identity was revealed to the public at last. He had started his career at Carron Works and later became a ship's engineer, in which capacity he travelled extensively. His series had been so popular with readers at the time, that it was decided to reprint it in 1896. Recent researches have verified most of the characters and places mentioned in *Reminiscences* and to a certain extent in *Memorabilia*.

Kinnaird.

James Bruce, the celebrated 'Abyssinian Traveller' succeeded his father to the estate of Kinnaird in 1758. He leased his coalfields to the new ironworks at Carron while he went off on his travels. Samuel Garbett, his family and son-in-law Charles Gascoigne, were allowed to live at Kinnaird when they first came to this district. James Bruce rebuilt the house, in the 1770s. The Kinnaird coalfields were leased to Carron Company until 1781 when Bruce again took control. He had a new pumping engine erected on his estate around 1791, built at Carron works to a design of William Symington. This engine complemented, rather than replaced, the existing one erected by Carron Company. One day, Bruce, who had been conversing with manager Joseph Stainton inside the works, caught sight of Symington, put spurs to his horse and galloped towards him calling in a loud voice "Mr Symington, Mr Symington, you are forgetting me altogether". Symington replied: "No fears of that Mr Bruce, you must have patience and we will get you made allright by and by".[37]

Soon afterwards, Symington erected a winding engine, called 'Susanna', at the Cuttyfield Pit[38]. After Bruce's death in 1795, Symington was given the task of managing the Kinnaird Colliery and occupied a house on the estate[39]. In 1797, he built another winding engine, this time for the No 7 pit at Kinnaird[40]. He left there in 1802.

It would appear that James Bruce and Carron Company were nearly always at loggerheads, but ironically, his grave in Larbert Churchyard was marked by a huge monument of cast iron, made at Carron Works. In the early 1800s, one Robert Moffat of Carronshore was an apprentice gardener at Kinnaird; he later achieved fame in his career as a missionary in Africa and his daughter married David Livingstone. The house and estate of Kinnaird were purchased from the Free Church of Scotland in 1895, by one Robert Orr, who built the present Kinnaird House; when the old house was being demolished in 1897, the foundations of a keep were discovered.

Mount Carron.

Mount Carron was situated at the foot of Carronhill overlooking the lade. It was reached, either by the road from Goshen to Carron Grange and Hungry Hill, or by a private footbridge which spanned the lade in front of the house. It was of two-storeys, built of brick and finished with plaster, which was then whitewashed; the roof was slated. On the Company feuing plan of c1761, it is marked on its site in name only, as is Carron Park which was built in 1763. According to a letter addressed to William Cadell at Carron Park and dated January 1776[41], Mount Carron was inhabited then by William

Lowes and his wife. Lowes at that time was a Carron Company partner. However, in the following year of 1777, when Lowes was sent to London to take over the agency there from John Wiggin, the tenancy of the house was given up. It was then that the owner wrote to William Cadell junior at Carron Park for his advice on what to do with the house and lands. The owner was none other than Thomas Roebuck, one of the original founding partners and brother of 'the Doctor', so the house was probably built at the same time as Carron Park. Thomas had become bankrupt in 1772 and by then had left the partnership of Carron Company. Cadell later informed Roebuck that William Benson had offered to lease the house at £10 per year, which he believed "is as much as you can at present get for it, possibly a more proper tenant, may afterwards cast upon us". He also described the house, offices and garden, as being "altogether neat and genteel"[42]. Mrs Lowes had suggested to Cadell that the house and land be dealt with separately, with the ground between the 'lead' and the river Carron being offered to the workmen at a public roup; this suggestion was duly passed to Thomas Roebuck. Just before Mrs Lowes departed, Charles Gascoigne called on her at Mount Carron and asked her to send the key to him, "as he had written to Mr Roebuck concerning the house and lands". According to the Carron Company Minute Book of 1775-1805, Mrs Roebuck was to be given £40 per year in return for the house, but Mr Roebuck was to make sure that the property was free from legal claims.

From the same source, there is a reference to a Henry Gallaway of Mount Carron in 1786, who worked at Carron as General Superintendent of the Counting House. In 1787, it was home for a very short time to James Baird before he hurriedly left Carron to join his brother Charles, who had gone to Russia with Gascoigne the previous year. There is a possibility that the enterprising William Benson next occupied Mount Carron, until his death in 1816. It is known that he farmed in the West Carron area, having feued ten acres of ground from Thomas Roebuck in 1770 and, as noted previously, he had made an offer of rent for the house in 1777. The house appears on a feuing plan of Stenhouse of 1826 and at about that time it was inhabited by John Stainton, who was a farmer. By 1861, John Dawson was the occupant and here he kept a huge collection of various species of moths, suitably arranged in display cases. He died there in 1879 and within two years Mount Carron was the home of one Henry Boss [or Ross], a manager at the works. At the end of the 19th century, it was home for many years to R P Roy, the company housing factor and property agent. Thereafter, various employees made it their home. Mount Carron was demolished in the 1960s.

Quarrole (Quarrel, Quarrol or Quariol).

Thomas Dundas, son of Thomas Dundas of Fingask who owned the nearby estates of Letham and Powfoulis, purchased the lands of Quarrole in 1749. With this estate came the coal pits, the miners and their families; coal had been extracted there since the 16th century and exported from the harbour at Quarrolshoar, which also belonged to the estate. Dundas also owned the upper and nether Skaithmuir Mills and in 1751 purchased the estate of Torwood. In 1759, Carron Company agreed to buy coal from Dundas and the following year they leased his pits and worked the coal for themselves. In the late 1760s Thomas changed the name of his house and estate to Carronhall. The Company's coal lease there was surrendered in 1781 but a new contract was negotiated by Lady Eleanor Dundas, a cousin of Charles Gascoigne, wife of Major-General Thomas Dundas, 2nd of Carronhall, in the 1790s[43]. After her husband's death in 1794, she signed a long lease for the coal on her property to Carron Company, and then left Carronhall.

The house of Carronhall

Colonel Thomas Dundas succeeded his father and he in turn was succeeded by his son Joseph who married Margaret Isabella Moir, granddaughter of Sir William Bruce of Stenhouse. Their son, Thomas George Dundas, was the last Laird of Carronhall; he died in Canada in 1929. In the early years of the 20th century, the house became the property of Robert Dundas Orr, of the Philpstoun Shale Oil Company and James Ross Chemicals; he was the son of Robert Orr of nearby Kinnaird. After his death in 1914, Carron Company purchased the estate and the house was demolished in 1916.

The Railways of Carron Company.

After 1855, when it was decided to build a modern railway system to link into the main line, the biggest obstacle must have been the entry into the Works from the riverside. At a point only a few yards upstream from where the old Stenhouse Mill Damhead had been, a high level viaduct was built. On one of the arch supports on the West Carron Road there can clearly be seen inscribed, the date 1860. This has been accepted as the date on which the modern railway had commenced, but it was a year before the first locomotive was delivered from Hawthorns of Leith. It was known as the Carron No 1 and was followed by the Carron No.2 of similar design and from the same company, in 1862. These early locomotives, like the wagons of the time, had wooden buffers known as 'dumb buffers'. The stretch of track from Burnhouse to the Works was known as the southern railway and the section of this Carron Branch Railway, before it entered the Works, was later called the 'Mulloch Weighs' after the weighbridge there. The Carron 'pugs' were not allowed to go south beyond what became known as "the Mungal Yards" [a network of sidings behind Mungal Foundry]. Only the locomotives from the main line could come in to this point, to either pick up the wagons left by the Carron Branch, or to deposit wagon loads of limestone, iron ore, etc. The wagons with their load of minerals would then pass over the weighbridge, the weight of each consignment being noted by a keen-eyed clerk, before crossing the high level bridge into the works. At first, the railway only left the northern boundary of the works for a short distance, where it terminated alongside the coalfield tramway. With the reconstruction of the works in the 1870s, the number of sidings inside the works was increased, space being obtained by the demolition of old buildings and with the partial filling-in of the furnace pool and forge dam[44].

Gradually, the old tramway to the north was replaced by the railway, which by this time served the collieries at Carronshore. More locomotives were added to the Carron Branch Railway; in 1866, from Barclays of Kilmarnock, in 1874 and 1878, from a company called Allan Andrews of Kilmarnock and in 1889 and 1890 from the Manning Wardle Company. Two of these engines were still in service at Carron as late as 1958! The railway by this time played a large part in the operations at the blast furnaces, where slag ladles filled with the waste product from the production of pig iron were hauled out of the works via a single track between two of the reservoirs. The locomotives were augmented in 1892 by an engine from Dubs & Company of Glasgow and in 1895 and 1897 by engines from Neilsons. As an example of how things were done, the engine from Dubs & Co. was ordered by manager David Cowan in 1891; it had a 15½" cylinder

A Carron locomotive discharges another blazing load on the top of the Cinder Hill.

and three wheels on each side, of 3 ft 7" diameter. Because it was to be used at the Cadder No 15 Pit which had gradients, Cowan wrote to Dougald Drummond of the Glasgow Railway Engineering Works asking if this new locomotive would require special springing. He was told that this would not be required, but suggested certain alterations to the pitch of the flanges of the wheels. Whilst the boiler was being assembled, the Dubs' Works was visited at intervals by an inspector from the "Scottish Boiler Insurance and Engine Inspection Company Limited", who monitored its progress. A few months later, the locomotive was delivered and put together on the railway at Cadder, a process that took only eight days. There was a subsequent problem with this locomotive, with some wear on the tyres and a lack of pulling power. Dubs blamed this on the railway line at Cadder, which they said was 4ft. 8¼" wide instead of 4ft. 8½". They also stated that because of the number of curves in the railway at the pit, the engine suffered more wear in six months than a comparable engine on the main line did in two years! Carron Company, of course, denied this.[45]

All the Company locomotives with the exception of three, were 0-4-0, that is, four driving wheels. Of the three with six driving wheels (0-6-0), Dubs & Company supplied the one mentioned above, and the Andrew Barclay Company of Kilmarnock supplied another in 1911 which was used at Craigend and transferred to Bannockburn Coke Ovens in 1947. The third also came from Andrew Barclay in 1915, and went to Bannockburn Colliery in 1937. Locomotives with this type of 6-wheel arrangement could not be used at Carron Works. Andrew Barclay also supplied two more in 1913, one in 1922 and another in 1923. With the need for more fine quality sand for moulding, sandpits were opened on the old estate of Crownest and the network was extended there from the west of the Works past the slag hill. This line continued over the lade, where it could fork left for the sand pits of Crownest, later to become the'Lido' or to the right, to Goshen, where there was a coal depot.

Manufacturer's serial numbers exist for all of the locomotives and of course they all had works numbers ranging from 1 to 16. To complicate matters, some of these numbers were interchanged, for example, the No 3 was formerly No 3a, the No 5 was No 5a, the No 7 was No 6 and the No 12 was No.7a. Some were superseded by new models, which retained the old number. The first of the early ones to be scrapped was an Allan Andrews from the 1870s; this was in 1910. With the exception of the original Hawthorns scrapped in 1930 and 1936, the rest saw service until the 1950s and 1960s. In a Company publication of 1938, it was stated that they had at that time: 16 locomotives and 400 wagons for internal use at Carron and

Two Carron locomotives outside the High Foundry

400 wagons at their colliery at Bannockburn. They also had over 40 miles of track. During the second World War, the last steam locomotive was purchased from Bagnal of Stafford, but it is not recorded in the list of Company locomotives of 1948.

The year 1952 saw the arrival of the first Carron Company diesel locomotive and it was called appropriately, the No 1; it was in a green and red livery and was manufactured by John Fowler of Leeds. This engine was operated by manual gears and from all accounts was not the easiest of locomotives to work with. The diesel-electric from Ruston and Hornsey of Lincoln, bought in 1956, was a different machine altogether with its automatic gearing; it was also more powerful. Both of these were only used within the Works at Carron, Mungal and E Department and they were disposed of or scrapped with the last of the steam locomotives, on the demise of the Carron Branch Railway in the late 1960s. This branch had been a complete 'railway company' in miniature, with its own locomotive sheds where repairs and maintenance work was carried out. People were employed to construct and repair track, and to constantly lubricate the many points. At the top end of West Carron, where the line left the Works for the slag hill, there was what can only be described, as the Company's only semi-automated level crossing, operated by a hand-wheel in a control cabin. There was a signal box, although it was more of a lookout-tower, situated near to the

North Gate and used to watch for approaching traffic from Stenhousemuir or Falkirk. When an engine with its train of wagons destined for the collieries was about to appear, the gates of the level crossing would be closed to road users and two guards armed with red flags would warn the approaching vehicles. At Carronshore, travelling towards the pits, the railway came to a fork where it could bear left around the Gairdoch Park to the Carronhall Colliery No 5 and then on to the Carronhall Colliery 'William Pit'. Back at the fork or junction at Carronshore, this track once ran parallel to Main Street before turning right, into the Carron Colliery Pit No 6, situated at the rear of the village. The track to Letham Pit was the last extension of this railway, constructed after the pit opened in 1913. On its return from the pits, the fully laden train would have to be assisted with a second engine, and there was always someone ahead to see to the opening of the various level crossings such as at Ladies Gate, Alloa Road and finally the North Gate.

Stenhouse.

In 1759, 14 acres of the estate of Stenhouse was feued to Carron Company by Sir Michael Bruce and latterly, most of the ground around the Work's site and beyond, which had been part of the estate, came into the ownership of the Company. Sir Michael had been a benevolent Laird to the local parishioners and, along with the four other Heritors, provided them with cheap grain in "the year of the dear meal". After his death in 1795, the estate and title passed to his son Sir William who was in turn succeeded by his son Sir Michael, the 8th Baronet. From the Census of 1841, Sir Michael, who became a Carron Company shareholder in 1853, and Lady Bruce had a small band of servants to look after their needs and they included a butler, a footman, a lady's maid, a housekeeper, two housemaids, a laundry maid and a kitchen maid. The last of the Bruce family to occupy the house was Sir Michael's nephew, Sir William Cunningham Bruce, 9th Baronet, who 'broke the entail' and sold the house and estate to John Bell Sheriff of Carronvale in 1888.

It was acquired by Carron Company before 1920 and converted into flats for the use of the workmen. In 1954, the then Sir Michael Bruce mentioned in his autobiography *Tramp Royal*, that his dearest wish was to regain possession of the house. Two years later, when visiting Stenhouse for the first time, he received a promise from the Company that if the house was ever knocked down he could have the coat of arms which adorned the building. He died in 1957 and after the house was demolished in the 1960s to make way for a housing estate, the coat of arms went to Falkirk Museum.

Stenhouse Mill.

The existence of this mill may have been one of the reasons why Samuel Garbett chose the site for the new Works. The mill itself had existed for many years before the arrival of the ironworks, being used as the communal meal mill for the tenants of the Stenhouse Estate. It stood in an area which is now the northern end of the Burder Park and in 1759 was in the possession of John Liddell who was the miller. Not long after Carron Company was established, this mill along with many others in the vicinity, was taken over for industrial use, such were the demands for existing sources of waterpower. This one was transformed into a forge, and later became known as "old John Smith's forge". The wheel pit was widened and a centre parapet built, allowing two water wheels to operate. The wheel on the south side worked the forge and the other, a turning mill. John Glegg 'served his time' at the turning mill in the late 1820s and was still employed in that trade in 1881, but by then, all iron-turning was done within the confines of the new Works. Near to the Stenhouse Mill there was a clay mill - the last part of the Works to have had a connection with John Smeaton - and a grinding mill, driven by the same waters. In the 1840s, the claymill was the responsibility of John Reid, whilst the grinding mill came under the supervision of Bill Murray.

The Thief's Hole.

This intriguingly named area was situated inside the Works and just outside the western confines of the 'Low Foundry'; it is still shown as such on a plan drawn this century. It is difficult to determine where the name came from though many suggestions have been made. One claim is that the Company at one time employed ex-criminals, who worked there, kept apart from the main workforce. Considering the age of this building, it is little wonder that legends became attached to it. It was latterly used as a moulding and core shop and had been one of only three or four buildings to survive, when the old Works were demolished in the 1870s. It may in fact have been the oldest building left at the Works. It stood in line with the original blast furnace complex of pre-1870 and, in 1873, it was a moulding shop. What appears to be the same building, is shown as a warehouse on a plan of 1773. There was also an opening here called "the long drop", which connected with one of the culverts, many many feet below the building. A cast iron staircase ascended from here to the old Furnace Bank.

The Triangle, Carron Works.

It stood almost at the centre of the old Works, until the reorganisation. The Triangle consisted of three cast iron legs, assembled from various lengths of pipes bolted together. It was used mainly as a hoist and having a bell fixed to its apex, was also used to inform the workforce of starting and stopping times. When the bell was rung at 9.30am, it was known rather curiously as the "half-ten bell"[46]. The area in which it was situated was known as the "square", which was entered from the "square mouth" beside the Smithy Row and the Main Gate. The photograph above dates from the middle of the 19th century. Another photograph of the Works taken in 1912, also shows a 'Triangle' to the west of the blast furnaces.

West Carron.

On the feuing plan for the works drawn in 1761, a detail shows two rows of houses and the name "Carron". These two rows were to be recessed at their centres to form a square, obviously an English idea. In the end only one of them was built and then just half of what it should have been; it was of two storeys; a school also existed there from an early time. As the original course of the lade passed through this area until late 1761, the village could only have been built after that date. The only other housing there, from the end of the 18th century, was the two-storey row that was part of the western boundary of the works and it faced into the village; it was still in existence until the 1960s, but had undergone some form of conversion into units associated with the Works. It faced another small row, and the track between them was the road into West Carron. There was also another long row of houses, which stretched from the Stenhouse Road towards the village, but these were replaced by moulding shops in the early 19th century. Access to the village was probably just a track, somewhat to the north of the present West Carron road. When winters were severe enough to cause the Furnace Pool, known then as the "running dam", to freeze over, the inhabitants could skate into the Works, with at least one fatality recorded. The road as it is today with its walls, was constructed in 1830 and at the end at the entrance to the village, was the cinder hill, a huge smouldering mass every bit of which had been brought out of the Works! The approach to the original village, at the top of the West Carron road, was to the right over the cart road and later railway to the cinder hill, past the rows previously mentioned and then to the left. This is how it was at West Carron until the 1890s after the Works had been re-constructed. Some of the 'blocks' of recent memory were completed in 1894 at a cost of over £5000[47], and in July 1896, the sum of £650 was authorised for the removal of part of the Slag Hill [the old Cinder Hill], for "a site for workmen's houses"[48], the blocks nearest to the river. By April 1897, manager John Frew reported that the first block of 12 houses was built and the foundations, for the second block of 20 houses and a third of 12 houses, were being dug out. The old row of West Carron which some knew as Wester Carron was still standing in the middle of what became known as the square, even by the time Miss Dawson's Mission Hall had been built in 1902. It was still shown on the ordnance Survey map of 1921. Until the turn of the century, there had been an unrestricted view from the village over the "Dams", but when the furnace pool had been completely filled in, to allow for another expansion of the railway sidings. A corrugated iron fence was erected around the perimeter and up to the engine gates, where the lade turned into the dams.

A favourite walk on a summers day, was the footpath next to the lade, past the footbridge from Mount Carron which nestled in a array of azaleas and rhododendrons. The railway line to the slag hill ran close by and if the engine with its train of slag ladles passed, the traveller would feel the tremendous heat, and experience the smell and noise of the 'Manning Wardle', labouring along on its journey. The walk continued past the lands of Crownest, which had caused no end of bother to young William Cadell in 1760 with the tenant farmers demanding more money, when the lade was being built. This stroll was a favourite one of William Jack in the 1840s and of Dr John Roebuck years before, in the 1760s, shortly after he set the whole Carron project in motion and changed the life of this community for ever.

NOTES

Chapter 1. The Early Days and the building of the Works.

1 Jardine, 1796.
2 Roebuck,
3 Singer, Holmyard et al, 1958.
4 ibid.
5 Roebuck, 1961.
6 ibid
7 McVeigh, 1979.
8 Jardine, op cit.
9 Norris, 1958
10 Bogle, 1898.
11 ACC. 5381 Box 28.
12 OSA
13 ACC. 5381, op cit.
14 Campbell, 1961.
15 ACC 5381, op cit.
16 ibid
17 Glasgow Journal, 21st June 1762.
18 Norris, 1958, op cit.
19 ibid.

20 ACC. 5381, op cit.
21 ibid.
22 ibid.
23 GD 58/6/1/1.
24 ibid.
25 GD 58/1/3.
26 RHP 44368.
27 Nimmo,1880.
28 GD 65.
29 ibid.
30 GD 58/1/3.
31 ACC. 5381, op cit.
32 ibid.
33 GD 58/1/3, op cit.
34 Cadell, 1973.
35 ACC. 5381, op cit.
36 Bogle, 1898, op cit.
37 ACC. 5381, op cit.
38 ibid.

Chapter 2. The Troublesome First Decade

1 GD58/1/3.
2 ACC.5381.Box 28.
3 Bogle, 1898.
4 Raistrick, 1953.
5 GD 58/6/1/1.
6 ibid.
7 ACC. 5381 op cit.
8 ibid.
9 GD 58/6/1/1.
10 ibid.
11 Raistrick, 1953, op cit.
12 GD 58/6/1/1.
13 ibid.
14 RHPs 1497 and 1552.
15 RHP 44351.
16 Raistrick, 1953 op cit.
17 GD 58/6/1/1.
18 ibid.
19 ACC. 5381, op cit.
20 ibid.

21 GD 58/6/1/1.
22 bid.
23 Dundas, 1891.
24 RHP 1543.
25 ACC 5381, op cit.
26 Campbell, 1961.
27 ACC. 5381, op cit.
28 RHP 1552.
29 Science Museum, London.
30 ACC. 5381, op cit.
31 ibid.
32 GD 65 (courtesy GB Bailey.)
33 GD 58/8/6.
34 Campbell, 1961, op cit.
35 Carron Cupola, 1962.
36 ACC. 5381, op cit.
37 ibid.
38 ibid.
39 ibid.
40 ibid.

41 ibid. (Cadell, 21st May 1766).
42 ibid.
43 Cadell H M, 1912.
44 ACC. 5381 (Garbett, Sept 1766).
45 ibid.
46 ibid. (Cadell jnr, 19th June 1767).
47 ibid. (Cadell, 8th May 1767.
48 Love, 1928.
49 Lodge Carron, 1903.
50 Jack, 1885.
51 ACC. 5381 (Garbett, May 1767).
52 ACC. 5381, op cit.
53 Campbell, 1961.
54 Brown, 1995.
55 ibid.
56 Campbell, 1961, op cit.
57 Brown, 1995, op cit.
58 ibid.
59 ibid.
60 ACC.5381(Cadell 5th Nov 1766).

61 ibid. (Garbett 8th May 1766).
62 ibid. (Garbett 8th August 1767).
63 ibid. (Cadell 5th November 1766).
64 ibid.
65 ibid.
66 Garbett, S *Answers*, 1779.
67 Salmon, 1913.
68 ibid.
69 Mantoux, 1928.
70 GD 58/8/2.
71 ibid.
72 Garbett, 1779,op cit.
73 ibid.
74 ibid.
75 Salmon, 1913, op cit.
76 Metcalfe, 1949.
77 GD 58/2/1/2.
78 ACC. 5381, Cadell, H to Pate G.
79 ibid.
80 ibid.

Chapter 3. From Carron to Russia, the Gascoigne Years

1 Fraser, 1897.
2 The name appears in a variety
  of forms and spellings.
3 Colman, 1908.
4 IGI.
5 GD 58/4/24/1.
6 ibid.
7 ibid.
8 GD 58/8/9.
9 Garbett, 1779.
10 GD 58/8/11.
11 GD 65.
12 ACC.5381 (Garbett, March 1766).
13 ibid.
14 Garbett , 1779.
15 Campbell, 1961.
16 Garbett 1779, op cit.
17 ibid.
18 Cadell H M, 1912.
19 GD 58/4/1/1.
20 ACC. 5381 (Cadell jnr August 1770)

21 Garbett, 1779, op cit.
22 ibid.
23 ibid.
24 Campbell, 1961, op cit.
25 GD 58/1/6.
26 GD 58/8/91.
27 Cadell P, 1973.
28 Garbett, 1779, op cit.
29 ibid.
30 GD 58/2/3/1.
31 CS 96/3725.
32 ACC. 5381, op cit.
33 GD 58/6/1/12.
34 GD 58/6/4/2.
35 GD 58/1/9.
36 GD 58/2/1/1 1774
37 ACC. 5381 (Cadell jnr, June 1773).
38 ibid. (Cadell jnr, July 1780).
39 ibid. (*Bond of Relief etc.* Nov 1773).
40 Brown, 1995.
41 Butler, 1981.

42 Brown, op cit.
43 ACC. 5381, Garbett F, August 1765.
44 Love, 1928.
45 GD 58/6/1/12.
46 *Information for Carron Company. against James Goold,* April 1781.
47 Metcalfe, 1949.
48 *New Monthly etc....Register,* 1818.
49 GD 58/8/87.
50 Brown, op cit.
51 GD 58/2/3/1, 1768-1785.
52 Resolution 612.
53 Resolution 613.
54 Padfield, 1973.
55 GD 58/6/1/12.
56 ibid.
57 ACC 5381. Box 28 September 1770.
58 Campbell, op cit.
59 Bara, 1985.
60 GD 58/6/1/12.
61 GD 58/2/1/1. Res. No. 319.
62 Skempton, 1992, op cit.
63 GD 58/6/1/12.
64 Campbell, 1961, op cit.
65 ACC. 5381, (Garbett May 1767).
66 *Scots Magazine,* November 1768.
67 ibid.
68 RHP 700.
69 RHP 44494.
70 GD 58/1/12.
71 GD 58/2/1/2.
72 Campbell, 1961, op cit.
73 GD 58/2/1/2.
74 ibid.
75 ibid.
76 ibid, Resolution 749.
77 Campbell, 1961, op cit.
78 ACC. 5381, op cit.
79 Campbell, op cit.
80 ibid.
81 Metcalfe, unpublished MS, 1948
82 ibid.
83 Carron Company, 1959.
84 Metcalfe, 1948, op cit.
85 GD 58/22/3/7.
86 GD 58/8/44.
87 GD 58/2/1/2.
88 Dundas, 1891.
89 GD 58/18/56.
90 Bara, 1985, op cit.
91 ibid.
92 Fraser, 1889, op cit.
93 GD 58/2/1/2.
94 Resolution 1020.
95 GD 58/2/1/2.
96 Steuart, 1913.
97 Love, op cit.
98 ibid.
99 GD 58/2/1/2.
100 ibid.
101 Letter, Braid to Bartlett, 1985.
102 ibid.
103 Bartlett, 1981.
104 Brown, op cit.
105 Baird to Rennie, May 1790.
106 GD 58/8/33.
107 RG Thorne.
108 GD 58/3/1/1.
109 Steuart, 1913, op cit.
110 Bartlett, 1981, op cit.
111 Bara, 1985, op cit.
112 Smeaton, Reports 1812.
113 RHP 44494.
114 Love, 1928, op cit.
115 RHP 44494.
116 RHP 44353.
117 GD 58/8/2.
118 Campbell, 1961, op cit.
119 Mantoux, 1928, op cit.
120 OSA, Larbert Parish, 1791
121 Campbell, 1961, op cit.
122 Skempton, 1981, op cit.
123 ibid.
124 ibid.
125 ibid.
126 MS 6322.

Chapter 4. The Carron Family

1 GD 58/2/1/2.
2 Archive of Fifeshire Journal.
3 Love, 1928,
4 Lamont Brown, 1973.
5 Love, 1928, op cit.
6 Lamont Brown, 1973, op cit.
7 Harvey, 1899.
8 ibid.
9 Campbell, 1961.
10 ibid.
11 *Glasgow Mercury*, 20th Feb 1788.
12 Jack, 1861.
13 GD 58/8/40.
14 GD 58/8/31.
15 Campbell, 1961.
16 Bowman 1981.
17 Harvey and Downs-Rose, 1980.
18 Bowman, 1981, op cit.
19 Carron Company,1909.
20 The farm lay west of Kinnaird House.
21 Joseph Stainton was apparently known to many as "Stenton".
22 *The Croft House Andersons*.
23 GD 58/11/2.
24 ACC. 5381, Contract, 1800.
25 ibid. April 1801.
26 Campbell, 1961, op cit.
27 GD 58/6/3/1.
28 TD 850.
29 *Memorabilia etc*, 1861.
30 ibid.
31 Love, 1928, op cit; Reid, 1992.
32 Jack, 1885.
33 Metcalfe, unpublished MS, 1948.
34 ibid.
35 ibid.
36 ibid.
37 GD 58/2/1/3. Minute Book.
38 Campbell,1961, op cit.
39 Records of Larbert Parish.
40 ibid.
41 Nasmyth, *Autobiography*.
42 Carron Company, 1959.
43 GD 58/2/1/3. Resolution 2234.
44 ibid. Resolution 2258.
45 Campbell, 1961, op cit.
46 Records of St Benet, Guildhall.
47 West, 1983
48 Campbell, 1961, op cit.
49 ibid.
50 ibid.
51 John Kay, *Original Portraits*.
52 Jack, 1885, op cit.
53 ibid.
54 ibid.
55 ibid.
56 GD 58/8/31.
57 GD 58/5/8/3.
58 RHP 44360.
59 *Falkirk Herald*, 1858.
60 GD 58/8/91, Vol 1.
61 West, 1983, op cit.
62 Lewisham Library.
63 ACC. 5381Cadell , unpublished MS.
64 ibid.
65 ibid.
66 *Falkirk Herald* 1864.
67 GD 58/8/68.
68 GD 58/8/72.
69 ACC. 5381 HM Cadell, op cit.
70 *Falkirk Herald,* 1864, op cit.
71 ibid.
72 Campbell, 1961, op cit.
73 ibid.
74 GD 58/8/75.
75 Campbell, 1961, op cit.
76 ACC. 5381, H M Cadell, op cit.
77 ibid.
78 ibid.
79 ibid.
80 Bailey, unpublished notes.
81 GD 58/7/11.
82 Bremner, 1869
83 Bailey. op cit.

Chapter 5. The End of a Regime

1 Carr & Taplin.
2 ibid.
3 ibid.
4 Maver, 1874
5 ibid.
6 GD 58/8/77.
7 Maver, 1874, op cit.
8 ibid.
9 ibid.
10 Campbell, 1961
11 Carron Co, 1959
12 Campbell, 1961, op cit.
13 *Falkirk Herald* May 1879.
14 ibid.
15 ibid.
16 ibid.

17 ibid.
18 GD 58/2/1/1. Resolution 53.
19 GD 58/2/1/1. April 1773.
20 Aerial photographs of the works
21 Jack, 1885.
22 Feu Plan of Stenhouse.
23 Jack,1885, op cit.
24 ibid; Gibson, 1907
25 Cowan, 1886/7
26 Jack, 1885, op cit.
27 ibid.
28 ibid.
29 Campbell, 1961, op cit.
30 Metcalfe, unpublished MS, 1948.
31 GD58/2/4/2.

Chapter 6. Carron Company in the 20th Century.

1 Scott, 1989
2 GD 58/3/1/1.
3 Campbell, 1961
4 Scott and Ferguson, 1993
5 GD 58/3/1/1.
6 ibid.
7 TD 850.
8 GD 58/3/1/1.
9 ACC. 5381, Box 30, HM Cadell.
10 Campbell, 1961, op cit.
11 Carron Cupola,
12 ACC. 5381, op cit.
13 Love, 1928
14 ACC. 5381, op cit.
15 Love, 1928 op cit.
16 GD 58/3/1/1.
17 ACC. 5381, Box 30, op cit.
18 ibid.
19 Carron Company, 1959.
20 Bremner 1869
21 GD 58/20/1/39.

22 Carron Company, c1930.
23 *Catalogue* of Glasgow
   Exhibition, 1888.
24 GD 58/9/25.
25 GD 58/22/3/5.
26 Metcalfe, unpublished MS, 1948
27 Biggar Museum Trust.
28 GD 58/22/3/5.
29 ibid.
30 ibid.
31 GD 58/8/91-93.
32 *Carron Cupola*, 1950
33 Ibid. vol. 3, No. 4. October 1952.
34 GD 58/2/1/18.
35 ibid.
36 ibid.
37 ibid.
38 *Carron Cupola*, October 1962.
39 ibid.
40 GD 58/1/16.
41 *Falkirk Herald*.

42 Catalogue of Sale, 1965
43 Company Rule Book, 1974.
44 GD 58/22/3/30.
45 *Falkirk Herald.*
46 ibid, 6th August 1982.
47 ibid.
48 ibid. 12th May 1982.

49 ibid.
50 *Glasgow Herald*, August 1982.
51 ibid. 29th August 1982.
52 Carron Phoenix, 1987.
53 Carron Phoenix. 1998.
54 ibid.

Appendix 1: Ordnance at Carron

1 Lavery,1987.
2 ibid.
3 ibid.
4 ibid.
5 Campbell, 1961
6 Gibbs, 1982.
7 Padfield, 1973.
8 GD 58/18/56.
9 Gibbs,
10 GD 58/18/56.
11 ibid.
12 Gibbs, op cit.
13 GD 58/11/2.
14 NSA, Larbert Parish, 1845.
15 Bremner, 1869.
16 GD 58/14/51.

17 Padfield, 1982.
18 ibid.
19 GD 58/8/25
20 Brown.
21 ibid.
22 Royal Artillery Historical Trust.
23 ibid.
24 GD 58/11/2.
25 Cadell, 1912.
26 Information from. Russell Queenan,
.27 Brown, op cit.
28 GD 58/8/87.
29 GD 58/18/56; GD 58/11/2.
30 ibid.
31 GD 58/11/3.
32 Bailey, unpublished.

Appendix 2: Carron Company and its Shipping Interests.

1 GD 58/6/1/1.
2 GD 65/261.
3 CS 96.
4 GD 65/214.
5 ibid.
6 Bowman, 1978.
7 ACC. 5381, Box 29, (Pate to Cadell).
8 Bowman, 1978, op cit.
9 Shipmasters Instructions.
10 ibid.

11 Metcalfe, Unpublished MS. 1948.
12 ibid.
13 *Liverpool Mercury*, 13th Oct 1826.
14 *Falkirk Almanac*, 1836.
15 Metcalfe, 1948, op cit.
16 ibid.
17 GD 58/9/39.
18 *Carron Cupola*, October 1962.
19 ibid.
20 Metcalfe, 1948, op cit.

1 Fraser, 1897.
2 GD 58/3/1/1.
3 RCAHMS Stirlingshire, 1963.
4 Jack, 1885.
5 ibid.
6 *Carron Cupola*, April 1955.
7 Jack, op cit.
8 RHP 44351.
9 RHP 242.
10 RHP 44357.
11 RHP 242.
12 RHP 44360.
13 *Falkirk Herald.*
14 GD 58/3/1/1.
15 Carron Co. v John Ogilvie, 1802.
16 RHP 1503.
17 RHP 1486/1.
18 RHPs 44529 - 44533.
19 RHP 44528.
20 Love, 1928, op cit.
21 O.S. Name Book, Larbert, 1860.
22 GD 58/9/49.
23 GD 58/16/29. Company Rule Book.
24 ACC. 5381, Box 29, 2nd Jan 1766.

25 GD 65/238/5.
26 Campbell, 1961
27 Fraser, op cit,
28 ibid.
29 ibid.
30 GD 58/21.
31 RHP 1552.
32 Gibson, 1907.
33 ibid.
34 ibid.
35 Fleming, 1902.
36 Gibson, op cit.
37 *Memorabillia* etc, 1861
38 Harvey and Downs Rose, 1980.
39 ibid.
40 ibid.
41 ACC. 5381.
42 ibid. (Cadell jnr, February 1777).
43 Dundas, 1891.
44 Cowan, Plan of Carron Works. 1883.
45 GD 58/5/4/20.
46 Jack, 1885, op cit.
47 GD 58/2/1/6.
48 GD 58/2/4/2.

MANUSCRIPT SOURCES

ACC. 5381, Cadell of Grange Papers, National Library of Scotland.
CS 96 Court of Session. Scottish Record Office, Edinburgh
GD 58, Carron Company Papers, Scottish Record Office Edinburgh.
GD 65, Dundas of Fingask Papers, Scottish Record Office Edinburgh.
Register House Plans [RHPs] from GD 58 and GD 247 (Brodie, Cuthbertson and Watson Papers). Scottish Record Office, Edinburgh.
TD 850, Deeds to the Lands of Biggarshiels, Mitchell Library. Glasgow.

CORRESPONDENCE

Ruth Brown of the Royal Armouries - (Carron ordnance).
Michael Wright- Science Museum, London (Early Boring Machinery).
Anna Rundle-Science Museum, London (Late 18th C Iron Founding)
Dr Roger Bartlett, School of Slavonic and Eastern European Studies, London University. (Gascoigne and Carron's links with Russia)

GENERAL BIBLIOGRAPHY

Bailey, G.B. 'Along and across the River Carron', Calatria 2, (1992) 49-84.

Bara, J.L. Russian Artillery. Arms Collecting, vol. 23 No.2 May 1985.

Bartlett, R. P. Charles Gascoigne in Russia: Proceedings of 2nd International Conference on 18th Century Russia (1981)

Bogle, Rev. A. N. Founding of Carron Ironworks. (1898).

Bott, G. Keswick (1994).

Bowman, I. Symington and the Charlotte Dundas (1981)

Bowman, I. The Carron Line (1978) in Transport History, Volume 10.

Bremner, D. Industries of Scotland (1869).

Brown, R.L. Robert Burns' Tours of highlands and Stirlingshire (1973).

Bruce, Sir M. Tramp Royal (1954).

Burke. Landed Gentry.

Butler, R.D. 'The Fullers and Carron', Wealdon Iron Research Group (1981)

Cadell, HM. The Story of the Forth. (1912).

Cadell, P. The Ironmills at Cramond. (1973).

Campbell, R.H. Carron Company. (1961).

Carr, JC and Taplin, W. History of the British Steel Industry .

Carron Company. Story of Industrial Enterprise (1900); A Century and a Half (1909); Carron in Wartime (1945); Architects' Catalogue (c1930); From the Reign of King George the 2nd to the Reign of King George the 6th (1938); 200 Years of Service (1959); Carron Cupola.

Colman, F. S. A History of the Parish of Barwick-in-Elmet, in the County of York. (1908).

Cowan, D. Carron Ironworks of Scotland, Minutes of Proceedings of the Institution of Civil Engineers 1886/1887, Vol. 87.

Dott, G. Early Scottish Colliery Wagonways (1947).

Dundas, Isabella. Dundas of Fingask. (1891).

Fleming, J. S. Ancient Castles and Mansions of the Stirling Nobility (1902).

Fraser, Sir W. The Earls of Haddington. (1889).

Fraser, Sir W. The Elphinstones of Elphinstone. (1897).

Gregory, E. Metallurgy (1945).

Gibbs, K. Guns, Weapons and Militaria. Vol 1, No. 5 March 1982.

Gibson, J. Lands and Lairds of Dunipace and Larbert (1907).

Gillespie, R History of Stirlingshire (1868)

Hamilton, H. The Founding of Carron Ironworks, Scot. Hist. Rev. 25 (1927).

Harvey, W. Robert Burns in Stirlingshire (1899).

Harvey, WS and Downs-Rose, G. William Symington (1980).

Jack, W. 'Memorabilia of a Carron Worthy'. Falkirk Herald (1861);

Jack, W. 'Reminiscences of Carron, 50 years ago'. Falkirk Herald. (1885).
Jardine, A. Account of the life of Dr John Roebuck. (1796).
Lavery, B. The arming and fitting of English ships of war (1987).
Lodge Carron. Book of the Bazaar (1903).
Love, J. Antiquarian Notes and Queries. (1928).
Mantoux, P. The Industrial Revolution in the 18th Century. (1928).
Maver, J. Carron Ironworks, "Glasgow News" and "Falkirk Herald" 1874.
McVeigh, P. Scottish East Coast Potteries. (1979).
Metcalfe, M.H. 'Notes on the history of Carron Company, Falkirk' in the Transactions of the Falkirk Archaeological and Nat. History Society, (1949).
Nasmyth, J. Autobiography.
New Statistical Account of Scotland (NSA):Larbert, Rev J Bonar (1842)
Nimmo, W. The History of Stirlingshire. 3rd edition. 2 vols. (1880).
Norris, J.M. The Struggle for Carron, The Scot. Hist. Rev 37 (1958).
Padfield, P. Guns at Sea (1973).
Raistrick, A. Dynasty of Ironfounders. (1953).
Reid, J 'Local roads in the Eighteenth Century' in Calatria, 2 (1992)
RCAHMS Stirlingshire:Inventory of Ancient Monuments (1963)
Roebuck, AW. The Roebuck Story. (1961).
Salmon, TJ. History of Bo'ness. (1913).
Scott, I. Touch ane Touch a': Falkirk Infirmary 1889-1989 (1989)
Scott, I. and Ferguson, J. Larbert Old Parish Church (1993).
Singer, Holmyard et al (eds), A History of Technology. 1958.
Skempton, A.W. John Smeaton FRS. (1981).
Smiles, S. Industrial Biography (1863)
Statistical Account of Scotland (OSA); Larbert, Rev G Harvie (1791)
Steuart, AF. Scottish Influences in Russian History (1913).
Tripp, B.H. Grand Alliance (1951).
Thorne, R.G. History of Parliament 1790-1820.
West, J. Profile of Henry Tibbats Stainton (1983).

OTHER SOURCES.

Calatria, Journal of Falkirk Local History Society, Vols 1-12 (1992 on)
Falkirk Reference Library: Local History File, Census Returns, Falkirk Herald Archives, Old Parish Records of Larbert etc.
Stenhousemuir Library.
Jenny Smith of Stenhousemuir (Genealogical Research)

INDEX